GEEK ELDERS SPEAK

In Our Own Voices

This anthology explores
the undeniable history of women creators
in Science Fiction/Fantasy & Media fandom
during the mid- to late-20th century.

These women were Writers. Artists.
Librarians. Costumers. Editors. Gamers.
Scientists. Housewives.

Despite the odds, they claimed their own
voices and creative power, through the
years and in their own terms.

Each woman's experience is personal and
evocative, told in their own voices and each
with their own story.

GEEK ELDERS SPEAK

In Our Own Voices

EDITORS:
Jenni Hennig
Maggie Nowakowska

INTERVIEWS:
Tish Wells
Jenni Hennig

FOREST PATH BOOKS

Copyright Notice

For all the elder fannish sisters,
who found their own, truest voices
in the unlikeliest of places.

Table of Contents

Foreword

A long time ago, in a bookstore that no longer exists, I took my first step into the larger world of "Fandom" by picking up a copy of a fanzine called *Blue Harvest*.

The early 1990s were dark times for isolated *Star Wars* fans like myself. There were no prequels, sequels, or animated shows yet. The first of a slew of new *Star Wars* novels wouldn't drop until a few years later. Getting my hands on anything *Star Wars*-related required a bounty hunter's skills of tracking it down in local specialty book and comic shops. So after I found this little piece of *Blue Harvest* treasure (oh how I wish I still had that zine), I flipped through it, excited to read anything new about one of my favorite topics. And not only did I find juicy information within its pages, I also found my first uber geeky *Star Wars* friend.

You see, in the back of this fanzine there was a little column, where a woman by the name of Maggie Nowakowska was calling on any and all *Star Wars* fans to write to her—and yes, I'm talking letters inside envelopes delivered to people through snail mail—with their story of how they became a fan of the original *Star Wars* trilogy. I can't tell you how excited I was to find someone else to talk to. I had recently rented and watched VHS copies of *Star Wars*, *The Empire Strikes Back*, and *Return of the Jedi*, and binged them alone one rainy Seattle afternoon. It reawakened my obsession with the stories.

As I'm writing this, Maggie and I have been friends for over 25 years.

I'll never forget visiting her to talk about Our Favorite Subject, and being introduced to the early days of "Fandom on the Internet." It was still the early days of online forums, list servers, and chats (dial-up modems anyone?), and connecting with complete strangers to talk about science fiction and fantasy books, TV shows, comics, and movies. Maggie and her wife Susan introduced me to the comparative religion and mythology work of Joseph Campbell, the monomyth and *The Hero's Journey*, and helped me understand how Campbell's ideas were the foundation of the *Star Wars* mythos that George Lucas had created—which later helped me recognize how and why those patterns of myth and hero archetypes in *Star Wars* resonated for me so profoundly.

Maggie also introduced me to science fiction conventions and fannish gatherings, held frequently at her house. And let me tell you, those fannish gatherings were quite something. People came, sat, ate, and talked. And talked. And TALKED!

Eventually, this wonderful friendship inspired me to submit a panel idea to a relatively new convention I had attended several times in Seattle. GeekGirlCon is a fun fan convention with a mission of being "...an organization that works to empower women and girls to pursue their passions—whether they love science and technology, comics, literature, gaming, or anything else! Everybody is a geek at heart, in one way or another. Our mission is to ensure all these geeks are supported, welcomed, and encouraged to pursue what they love."

I named the panel: "Geek Elders Speak: How Media Fandom Empowered Women in the 60s, 70s, & 80s." Here's the description:

> *A long time ago in a galaxy far, far away, before fans were connecting in droves on the internet, there was snail mail, fanzines, and just plain getting together. In the 60s, 70s, and 80s, Star Trek and Star Wars (and insert other fandoms here) became a catalyst for fanzine fandoms that gave girl and women nerds ways of creating community with others like themselves, and helped them break out of their mid-century cocoons. Fandom gave them the boost and confidence they needed—to take a chance and become authors, merchandising pros, independent sculptors, and self-respecting women instead of just protected daughters and wives.*

The hour-long panel attracted a decent crowd, and quickly became a surprising and powerful slice of oral history that many young people in the audience had never heard before. It turned out to be a critically important way to reach back and center the efforts of fannish women who had blazed trails and created nerdy spaces in the years before GeekGirlCon was possible. My goal was to impress upon a young geek audience that hearing history from the mouths of the people who lived it can be a valuable resource, and a learning tool for the present and future.

To elaborate that particular point, I introduced the panel to the audience with an opening statement that included a quote from author Michael Meade's book *Fate and Destiny: The Two Agreements of the Soul (pg. 86):*

"In old traditions, those who acted as elders were considered to have one foot in the daily life, and the other foot in the Otherworld. Elders acted as a bridge between the visible world, and the unseen realms of spirit, and soul. A person in touch with the otherworld stands out because something normally invisible can be seen through them. The old word for having a foot in each world, is weird. The original sense of weird involved both fate and destiny. Becoming weird enough to be wise requires that a person learn to accommodate the strange way they are shaped within, and aimed at the world.

"...Elders are supposed to be weird, not simply 'weirdos', but strange and unusual in meaningful ways. Elders are supposed to be more in touch with the otherworld, but not out of touch with the struggles in this world. Elders have one foot firmly in the ground of survival, and another in the realm of great imagination. This double-minded stance serves to help the living community and even helps the species survive."

I have learned many things from Maggie and her partner Susan: from having respect for ideas from unfamiliar cultures, to having a generosity of spirit with the people around you at any given moment. As time passed, I realized that somehow along the way I had gained somewhat of an education on why fandom was so integral to helping women fans of science fiction become more literate in writing, publishing, photography, art, costuming, finance, and so many other areas.

This book of essays and knowledge is dedicated to Maggie, Susan, Jenni and all the amazing women who inspired me, supported me, and taught me that living my life to the fullest meant being authentic and following my bliss. May their experiences and understanding of the early days of geek culture educate and inspire you!

© *Jamala Henderson*
(Future Geek Elder)

In Memoriam

Denetia Arellanes — A. C. Crispin — Sara Campbell
Johanna Cantor — Bev Clark — Connie Crouch
Patricia D'Orazio — Gerry Downes — Barbara Drake
Sharon Emily — Syn Ferguson — Z. P. Florian
Susan M. Garrett — Barbara P. Gordon — Regina Gottesman
Bev Grant — Pat Grant — Robin Hill — Kathy Hintze
Jean Holmes — Ann Hupe — Carol Jones — Vel Jaeger
JEM — Kielle — Linda Knights — KOZ — Cynthia Levine
Mary N. Lonergan — Shirley Maiewski — Melissa Mastoris
Marion McChesney — Pat Nussman — Amanda Palumbo
Paulie — Linda Pfonner — Joanna Russ — Vonnie Shepard
Dawna Snyder — Cherry Steffey — Linda Stoops
Gennie Summers — Carol Walske — Ming Wathne
Cathie Whitehead — Sheila Willis — Joan Winston
Frances Zawacky — Anne Elizabeth Zeek — Beverly Zuk

Rest well, fannish sisters. You are Star People truly, now.

Kindly inform us if we have inadvertently left someone off this list.

*There will be a memorial to our fannish sisters kept
on the Forest Path Books website.*

GEEK ELDERS SPEAK

In Our Own Voices

Of course, women built fandom.
We know, because we were *there*.

PAULA SMITH
Fandom is a Way of Life

"At some point you may hear mundanes sneer, 'Ah, get a life!' But what kind of a life, a truly human life, can it be without using one's mind, heart, skills, time, and devotion to the betterment of what you love to do and people you are glad to be with, and in so doing, making reality itself better and more interesting?"
—Paula Smith

I am a fan today because my father joined the Science Fiction Book Club about the time I was born in 1951. Because there were those hardbound copies of Isaac Asimov, Arthur C. Clarke, and Wilson Tucker novels on the shelf in the rec room, along with plenty of paperback collections, I had great science fiction to read growing up. Because I read science fiction, I watched TV science fiction: *Twilight Zone*, *Outer Limits*, and (of course) *Star Trek*. Because I loved science fiction, in college I joined the Flying Saucer, Bug-Eyed Monster, Little Green Men, Science Fiction, Fantasy, Chowder, and Marching Society that met Thursday nights in the biology professor's living room. Because of the Society, I went to my first sf convention, the Detroit Triple Fan Fair in 1972, and discovered zines specializing in *Star Trek* stories, as well as met sf fans interested in *Star Trek*: Margaret and Laura Basta, Carol Lynn, and, through mutual friends, Sharon Ferraro. Because Sharon and I both lived in the same town, we started writing and publishing our own *Star Trek* zines, then driving hundreds of miles to sell them at cons (New York! Toronto! Champaign-Urbana!). Because we went to so many conventions, we decided to hold our own: KWest*Con in 1974 (Harlan Ellison as Guest of Honor), ReKWest*Con in 1975 (Gordon Dickson as GoH), SeKWester*Con in 1976 (the first no-GoH *Star Trek* con). Because of SeKWester*Con, Lori Chapek-Carleton started her series of *Star Trek*-cum-*Star Wars*-cum-whattayagot "media" conventions culminating in MediaWest*Con. Because of MediaWest, I published a lot of zines with Sharon, with Carol Lynn, with Cindy Walker and Nan Mack, and joined in chat rooms and list serves and Yahoo groups on the early Web. Because of the Internet... well, anything's possible.

The details change, but that is the story of a million fans over the last hundred years: from readers of Hugo Gernsback's *Amazing Stories* "scientifiction" magazine and the Baker Street Irregulars with the *Sherlock Holmes* canon, through post-World War II fanboys and their zines and Amateur Press Alliances, Boomer girls and their media fanfic, and Gen-Alphabetters who colonized the Internet, to post-Millennials now raising their heads and saying, "Now what shall I make?" And that's just in the English language. What about fans of manga and anime, zukumft Romanen, Bollywood movies?

Inspired by an idea, an image, a personality, a story narrative—a world previously unknown—we are driven to re-enter that world, enlarge it, embody it, and then (this is the important part) share it with others of like conviction. If you hear or see or read or are told a story about interesting people having interesting adventures, and after musing on these characters and plots you create in your mind further adventures or introduce new personalities to join in the adventures, then you're a~~geek~~ a very imaginative person who might be a writer someday. (While it is a proud and lonely thing to be a geek, the agony of being a misfit of whatever kind is that you bang up against the walls of your own soul, eventually. Though you are large and encompass worlds, you still need spiritual nourishment to develop and flourish. Whatever it is that you are geeked about, that is a clew, a lifeline to other oases of joy and delight in the human deserts of high school or suburbia.)

So you find others somehow, via lettercol or duckduckgo; perhaps you pass along your black notebook or thumbdrive or URL of stories that you've written down or video-cut and song-taped. And they *like* it, they're *geeked* to see your work! or maybe they're not, but you sure like their work and either way that inspires you to make *more*, or at least it has given you more of that world to enjoy. Suddenly that fictional world and the people who express it with you become brighter and more real than the everyday mundanity you chug through on your own. You plan your day around your netsurfing, your week around your TV program, your month around your letterzine, your year around your conventions. And that means, honey, you are a fan and you are in a fandom.

At some point you may hear mundanes sneer, "Ah, get a life!" But what kind of a life, a truly human life, can it be without using one's mind, heart, skills, time, and devotion to the betterment of what you love to do and people you are glad to be with, and in so doing, making reality itself better and more interesting. Moreover, by doing fandom together, we form communities. I have traveled over continents, hopping from one fan's spare room to another, people whose generous hospitality I can never repay directly, but which I do repay by bunking and feeding other fans. We make friendships, even marriages, that are lifelong. We pass on our work and our love to the next generations of fans, and watch, and listen with delight to the new stories they create and share. Some go pro, and create new worlds to inspire new fandoms.

Our lives and our creations change reality.

Incidentally, fandoms do not have to be about space travel—though the novels of Asimov, Clarke and even Tucker helped urge us along to the Moon—or "slash" pairings—though those stories had a hand in changing attitudes toward gay marriage and LGBTQ folks in general. The fannish impulse exists for politics, for religion, for any activity in which people visualize a world of better and more interesting personalities in better and more interesting circumstances, and then come together to share this vision and by working together to bring it closer to reality.

Fandom is a way of life. It has to do with poking our heads up above the weeds of daily life and looking farther off. It's about loving more than the material world. It is about groups of people meeting on more than just the physical plane. It is the most human thing about us all.

essay © 2020 Paula Smith

ROSALIE BLAZEJ
Explorations and Questions

"I wanted to be a scientist. I had read science fiction books since I first learned to read. I haunted my public library and tore through Heinlein's juvenile series and Arthur C. Clarke. Then I made my way to the hard stuff" —Rosalie Blazej

I wanted to be a scientist, but that was not possible. Girls in the '50s were not encouraged to become scientists or doctors. An office worker or a telephone operator if you finished high school, or, if you came from a comfortable middle-class family that could afford college, perhaps a nurse or teacher—those were the career paths open to you. I did not come from a comfortable middle-class family. But I could draw, so I got labeled an artist. I went to a vocational high school to learn to become a commercial artist. Then I continued, on scholarship, to get a BFA. I became a graphic designer.

I wanted to be a scientist.

I had read science fiction books since I first learned to read. I haunted my public library and tore through Heinlein's juvenile series and Arthur C. Clarke. Then I made my way to the hard stuff. I craved science fiction that was based on science and asked complex social questions—"hard" science fiction. No fantasy for me; no space operas. And only good writing. I was very particular.

Then came 1966 and *Star Trek*. Amazing. Here was a universe inhabited by interesting characters, who explored interesting ideas using interesting scientific principles. It wasn't perfect. The doctor, naturally, was a man and his nurse, naturally, was a woman. And all the women wore cute little miniskirts, while the men wore far more practical pants. But still. A half-alien science officer who was more distinguished by the way he acted than by the way he looked? An integrated crew that never drew attention to the fact they were integrated? A ship that traveled by means of bending the fabric of space rather than by rockets? I was hooked.

With video recording devices not widely available, I had to make sure I was in a position to watch each episode of *Star Trek* as it aired. Sometimes, that meant being home in time to watch it. Sometimes it

4

meant getting friends to turn it on for me when I visited. When *Star Trek* went off the air, I watched reruns. Over and over again.

Sometime in the late '70s, I read about a *Star Trek* convention nearby. The newspaper article mentioned "fanzines." I had never heard the term before. Fans writing their own new *Star Trek* adventures sounded like a wonderful idea. But the article didn't mention how to get a fanzine, and by that time, the convention was over.

I finally tracked down my first fanzine. Again, I was hooked. Even better, I started submitting stories and having them accepted. I carried hand-written drafts of stories I was writing with me wherever I went—on hikes to distant waterfalls, to meetings in case I had to wait, to visits to the dentist. I even carried a copy with me as I raced out the door on the way to the emergency room with my 11-year-old son and wrote by his bedside as he awoke from an appendectomy.

The *Star Trek* universe allowed me to ask questions and explore ideas. If a dream is so real it seems real, is it? Who are we? Are we the person we say we are, or the person other people see and claim to know?

I had help. Editors were all wonderful in critiquing my manuscripts, but perhaps, more importantly, they encouraged me and held my hand and told me I could do this. Once, at a *Star Trek*/science fiction convention in Santa Rosa, the science fiction writer Poul Anderson worked with me for over an hour, helping me with the astrophysics of a world I created for "Kin of the Same Womb Born".

A few years ago, I got a phone call asking permission to scan "Kin of the Same Womb Born" and add it to a collection of fanlit at Texas A&M. I agreed, and there it now sits—my bid for immortality. Again, amazing.

I no longer write fanlit, but I have continued to write science fiction stories and, though I never did become a scientist, I did eventually take some college-level science classes. (I lied about having the prerequisite coursework and got As in my classes.) In my career as a graphic designer, my clients have skewed heavily towards medical organizations, patient advocacy groups, and public utilities, where I am often called on to write articles that distill dense medical and technical jargon into understandable English. I don't think any of this would have been possible had it not been for a chance discovery of *Star Trek* fanzines.

I never became a scientist, but my son did, the same son beside whose hospital bed I wrote "Kin". As an undergraduate, he worked on the Human Genome Project, then went on to earn a PhD in bioengineering from UC Berkeley. A friend and fellow scientist of his is involved in a project that is dedicated to preserving the knowledge and biology of our planet. And I am going to be part of that endeavor. In the fall of 2021, my DNA will join DNA from other humans and other species to form the genetic blueprint of Earth. That blueprint will then travel to the moon on a NASA ULA Vulcan Centaur rocket launched from Cape Canaveral. There it will stay, preserved for the future.

I am going to the moon.

Amazing.

essay © Rosalie Blazej

CYNTHIA DRAKE
Letting the Freak Flag Proudly Fly

"The anti-slash contingent in Star Trek and science fiction fandom was actually bigger than the slashers, but our hearts were, if not precisely pure, stalwart. Once freed, we were not shutting up again—even though I am sure many wished we would. "
—Cynthia Drake

I wrote my first fan fiction when I was eleven years old, back during *The Man from U. N. C. L. E.*'s first season. I didn't call it fan fiction then, of course, and neither did anybody else. It was called a free choice homework writing assignment. We could write about whatever we liked. I liked *The Man from U. N. C. L. E.* (henceforth *MFU*).

"Liked" is an understatement. I was passionately, desperately, obsessively, in love with the show; with Illya Kuryakin specifically, and with Napoleon and Illya together. I loved their banter, their repartee, their ease with one another. I loved that they would reliably come to one another's rescue, even if with a barbed comment on their lips. I loved the way Robert Vaughn as Napoleon Solo, and David McCallum as Illya Kuryakin, looked together, and what they stood for. I loved that they were the good guys, that they worked for the good guys, and that even a Russian-Commie-better-Red-than-dead-Soviet could be a good guy.

So when the assignment was given, I leapt right to it.

I kept strictly to canon; not that I had that word, either. I wrote it out just as if it were the show, although in narrative form, not like a screenplay, which I am quite sure I would never have seen. I began with an Introduction, like the little teaser on the show, played before the credits would start. Then there were four Acts, like chapters, like the show. Get it? Just like the show. I tried to follow what I knew to be the formula, which called for rising tension over the first three acts, albeit with some humorous relief, and for things to look as bleak as possible as we enter Act 4. And at the very end of my story, Illya is tied up at the bottom of a well, water rising, facing certain death. But Napoleon comes back after completing the mission and rescues him. Illya says, "Why did you come back for me?" And Napoleon looks at him very seriously and says, "Because I like you so much."

Oh. My. Word. I anguished over those final lines. It seemed so self-revealing for homework. Why put that in? Why not a barbed comment? Illya could say, "Well it took you long enough," and Napoleon would say something about doing all the work as usual, which would have been far closer to canon. But I had always known that underneath the sarcasm was a very real, deep affection, and I had always wished they would voice it, at least once in a while. So if it was my story, and my dialog, by gum, they were going to say it. So they/I said it, and I turned it in.

My teacher read it aloud in class. I would have run away first, except that she was clearly very impressed with it. My first reader! I couldn't resist it. So I sat still for it, although when she announced to the class that I had written it, she added, "of course it's about that TV show", and everybody laughed. But she added that it was written "just like a real book, with chapters." I could tell that that was part of what impressed her.

Everybody was attentive, but all the while my stomach clenched and roiled because she would get to those two last lines and my strangeness, my... already I sensed it was a kind of sickness... would be exposed to all. She got there, and those lines came out just like all the other lines, and then she read "The End" and everybody burst into applause. I was stunned. For a few minutes I wasn't the class geek and target of bullies. I was ... I was a writer.

My teacher told me I had a gift and should pursue it, and later I learned that she had called my mother and told her the same thing—after, I am sure, a little mutual laughter over the fact that it was 'that TV show'. Because who else's child did that? Nobody's.

But nobody seemed to even notice those last two lines, which to me had dominated the whole thing. Nobody thought anything of them, or of the characters for saying them, or of me for writing them. Nobody at all. To me that was the strangest thing of all, far stranger than my temporary popularity, or even my newfound discovery of the power of words. It was so important, and noticeable, and powerful to me, and nobody else cared. Obviously I was the strange one, the weird one, the wrong one. The sick one.

Then came The Game. That's what I always called it to myself, with capital letters. The Game. It was *MFU*, of course, but by my early teens I had spun way off into AU (Alternate Universe) land. I had created an entire back story for Illya, which involved czars and concentration camps (demonstrating my vague grasp of Russian or even European history) and a fearsome amount of abuse. And I had a cohort.

Nicky. My best very best, ultra best friend. She loved *MFU*, too. She loved Illya and Napoleon too. She and I played endless scenarios, most of which I created and dictated. "Now Napoleon comes in and says..." "Now the Thrush scientist comes in with the electric shock device..." "Now Waverly tells them..." Nicky played Napoleon, and Waverly, and everybody else. I was Illya. I know. I know how that sounds. I'm sorry, Nicky. I think she did periodically ask to be Illya, and sometimes, probably if she threatened to go home, I would allow it, but it wasn't the same, it wasn't as much fun, and we always went back to the original casting.

We played it obsessively, every moment we could, every chance we got, every time we were alone. Solitude was necessary because by then there was some serious bondage and hurt/comfort going on. The bondage, let me say in our defense, came right from the show itself— canon, as it were. On a regular basis, Illya and/or Napoleon were tied up in assorted bizarre and elaborate ways. Nicky and I couldn't actually tie one another up with our assorted scarves, belts, and necklaces, because everything had to be able to be whisked away at the sound of a parental foot on the stairs, so we sort of draped the items suggestively. As to the hurt/comfort—oh, how we loved it. We didn't have that vernacular then, either, but one or the other (usually Illya because, let's face it, I was a story bully) was hurt or sick or tortured, and the other had to first rescue, then comfort and care for him. Neither one of us could have said why that had to be such a deep, dark secret from our parents, but both of us knew it did. They would never have let us be alone together again if they knew that instead of whatever they thought we were playing at for hours at a time in one or the other of our rooms, we were playing torture and rescue and comfort, over and over and over again.

Ironically, it was one of our more canon adventures that brought it to a close. Nicky was showing a dismaying inclination to marry Illya off to one of the guest star girls from the show—specifically Marian Raven, who was a love interest of his in two episodes and was also played by David McCallum's real-life wife. This actually was causing conflict between us. I didn't want Illya to marry Marian. I wanted Illya to stay best friends with Napoleon. Period. But I knew that wasn't right, that it was Nicky who was right and I who was... again, the wrong one, the sick one, the crazy one. So, reluctantly, I rewrote the script so Marian and Illya could have a brief pretend wedding. And at "you may kiss the bride", I pecked Nicky's lips with no enthusiasm on either side, and my mother saw us.

Our Game world ended at that moment. Nicky was sent home, and I was banished to my room. We were forbidden to ever see one another again.

We did, of course. I told my mother I was going to the library, and Nicky told hers that she was going to talk to me one last time (because her parents thought my mother was completely overreacting), and together we sat in the library and tried to figure out what we had done that was so terrible.

It is hard now to convey our ignorance. Neither one of us had ever heard of homosexuality. Neither one of us knew there was such a thing. In none of our most feverish scenarios did we conceive of Illya and Napoleon doing the things together we knew men and women did, and we never thought of ourselves doing those things with one another.

Nicky said that her mother said that maybe my mother was worried that if we kissed each other we wouldn't want to kiss boys, and then we wouldn't ever get married and have babies. We discussed that, but it seemed farfetched to both of us—what did our Game, where we weren't even ourselves kissing one another, but pretending to be a man and a woman getting married, what did any of that have to do with growing up, getting married ourselves, and having babies? We both wanted to do that. We were genuinely, sincerely, baffled. We had always known that exposure of The Game would mean ruin, and if we had been caught tying one another to the bedposts with our winter scarves, well, that we would have understood. But this particular Game had been so normal! We parted, having reached no conclusions, and being kids, with no transportation or phones or anything of our own, our friendship ended there.

Some time after that, I fell in love with John Lennon and the Beatles. That passion consumed me through high school, into college, and out (within the same semester). I moved to Greenwich Village to be closer to John Lennon, and actually encountered him and Yoko several times. I have never been interested in writing Real Person fan fiction, so I satisfied myself with writing long drippy poems to him, all of them dwelling on his perfections, the inability of anybody else to comprehend or love him truly, my sorrow at the separation forced on by us cruel fate, and, later, the beauty of his love with Yoko. To this day I love the Beatles, and in many (doubtless sick, crazy, wrong) ways, John Lennon was the one great love of my life. And yes, I know how that sounds.

But at the same time I found a job, got married, and had children. We moved out to the suburbs, and my husband went to work for my father's company. He had been a drummer with a rock-and-roll band before our marriage, and he didn't know what hit him, bless his heart. It was a desperately unhappy, emotionally abusive marriage, and I was very isolated on Long Island with small children and no car.

But I had a neighbour. I had a new best friend, and that best friend, Patty, enjoyed watching *Star Trek*.

Oh. My. Word. *Star Trek*. Kirk and Spock. Rescuing one another, expressing, occasionally, a tortured kind of friendship for one another. Good guys. Working for the good guys. Sometimes embracing; sometimes fighting. Always best friends. My fangirl self, buried for a long time under the day-to-day life the adult world seemed to demand, sprang to full blown consciousness, and with it came a kind of joy, a kind of playfulness I had completely forgotten about. I loved *Star Trek*! I loved Kirk and Spock! And, as I discovered on picking up a copy of a paperback book called "*Star Trek Lives*", so did a lot of other people! Normal people; not sick, not crazy, not losers nor geeks... well, maybe geeks, but then maybe geek wasn't always a bad thing!

Star Trek—or, more precisely, *Star Trek* fandom—changed my life. That is a fact. Before I encountered that fandom, I had one kind of life. Afterwards—after that first convention at the Statler-Hilton Hotel in New York City—I had another life. A different kind of life, a better kind of life.

It didn't come right away. I returned from that first convention with a bagful of fanzines. Fanzines. Other people, people I had met, people I liked, people who seemed to like me, were writing stories about their favorite TV shows, too. It wasn't a miserable, solitary aberration after all. It was a joyous, shout-out-loud shared aberration!

And more. More. One of the fanzines I picked up was titled, simply, *Thrust*. And on the front cover—on the FRONT COVER, like there was nothing wrong there at all, nothing crazy or sick—was a spectacular illustration of Kirk and Spock, naked, writhing together in mutual passion.

It may be impossible to convey to Young People nowadays what that meant. With the Internet, nobody has to be that terribly alone. No matter what your interest, passion, hobby, fandom, kink—there are other people who share it, and you can find them and talk to them if you like—but even if you don't like, you know they exist. How to express how it felt to be one hundred percent convinced, to the very core of your being, that you are deeply and fatally flawed, and NOBODY ELSE in the history of the world has ever, ever been sick like you are.

And then you learn that there are others. And they're not flawed, they are vibrant, talented, normal people living regular lives, and they are reaching out to you! To me! They reached out to me! They said: share our dream, share our fun, join the party! And when I wondered if I could ever write something like the stories in these zines, they said: Sure you can! Go ahead! Send it to me and I'll read it!

I went home from that convention on top of the world. And while I am not going to do a Jerry Springer episode on you, let me say that my then-husband liked me better beaten down and humbled, and feeling like worthless shit. Because when I came home not feeling that way, but feeling optimistic and happy and self confident, then I thought maybe I deserved to be spoken to more nicely, and treated with some respect. That didn't fly with him. We were too young to get married anyway, far too young to have had children, and motherhood changed me in ways that fatherhood didn't change him. We both felt cheated. The marriage ended in the wake of my new self-acceptance, and I was free.

Free. That was my word for it. I had two children under four, and one on the way. I was living on public assistance and trying to get a college degree because when I looked at my future as a single mom with a high school diploma, it was a rather discouraging view. I didn't have a car, so I took buses everywhere, two children in tow, gigantic pregnant belly making it hard—so very hard—to stand on the bus. We were poor—got cardboard boxed Thanksgiving turkeys from the local church and very thankful to have them poor. And I was—we were—free.

No early morning fights and smashing of objects because he had to get up and go to work, and hated me for it. No frightening deadline of five-thirty every evening, when he would come home, with our entire night hanging on the mood he was in. None of that. Just me and my kids.

And my typewriter.

I had a manual typewriter I used for college papers, and my first *Star Trek* stories were pounded out on that. But when I actually made it through my first semester of college on the Dean's List, my parents bought me an electric typewriter. This was a big ticket purchase at the time, and it was one of the very best presents I have ever received.

Somehow, I made time to write. I was a full-time student, full time single parent, and eventually had a full-time job, but whenever possible I sat there and wrote. I wrote about Kirk and Spock, about pon farr[1] and forbidden love. I played a game (not The Game, but enhanced

---

[1] The Vulcan mating time, detailed in the ST episode "Amok Time"—ed.

by my adult knowledge and experience with human sexuality) with and about them, and it was all great fun.

At that time, the time I first got into fandom, the slash thing was a HUGE thing. (Slash was the word for what we wrote, read, dreamed. It signifies the '/' between the initials of whoever it is you are writing into a love/sexual relationship. Kirk and Spock are K/S.) The anti-slash contingent in *Star Trek* and science fiction fandom was actually bigger than the slashers, but our hearts were, if not precisely pure, stalwart. Once freed, we were not shutting up again, even though I am sure many wished we would. It was genuinely offensive to many fans to suggest that a respected, normal, manly man like James Kirk, or Spock, might be "that way". It was considered a gross insult to the actors themselves, and there were frequent threats to 'out' us and get us kicked out of fandom by sending slash zines to the actors—Shatner, Nimoy, Kelley, et al. There were "fandom wars", and "zine wars", and it was all very exciting, but for me the writing was the thing, the main thing. I realized, as I wrote, that I needed this. I realized, as my skills improved, as they were honed by talented editors and perceptive readers, that my writing is essential to me, and that without it I am less. Less of a person, less of a mother, a student, a daughter, a friend. I needed that spark. I still need it.

I was immersed in that world for several years. I wrote many stories, and they were published in fanzines. I received fan mail, and won awards. Patty and I put together and published our own zine, and sold it at conventions. We were never really BNFs (Big Name Fans, like, for example, the authors of *Star Trek Lives*) but within the smaller K/S community we were accepted, welcomed, appreciated, loved. Patty and I have remained friends to this day, despite time, and distance, and very different lives appreciated, loved. Patty and I have remained friends to this day, despite time, and distance, and very different lives.

I graduated from college with a degree in Elementary Education, looked around at the job market, the home prices, the congestion and the noise, and decided to move—with my children, now ages fourteen, eleven, and nine—to the mountains of western North Carolina.

This effectively ended my personal *Star Trek* involvement. The move, with all its inevitable disruptions, loss of familiar routines (and no conventions!) squelched my creativity for a while. I didn't notice. I was busy. I was working, and trying to settle in to my new community, and dealing with a fair amount of culture shock. There were some extremely difficult, terrible years while my son went through adolescence. Any day that didn't have me crying out loud in public for some reason was counted as a good one, and enough.

It wasn't.

I seem to have to learn this lesson over and over again.

A few years later, for no reason that I can remember, I started playing The Game again. The Game for real. With Illya and Napoleon—lovers now, thanks to my experience with K/S.

There are similarities in my two slash fandoms. Each pairing consists of a leader, both by nature and in fact, and a cool, intellectual, improbably sexy partner. Their abilities complement one another's and, together, they are greater than the sum of their parts. Both pairings include the "alien among us" trope that is so important to slash. The associated trope is the friend, the one who sees through the Russian/Vulcan façade, and extends the warmth of human contact to someone who—just like we, the readers, writers, fans—needs it. It wasn't that much of a stretch at all, to switch back from the game to The Game. And it rose up to take me away with all its old force, and then some.

One day I was at a church yard sale and saw an old portable manual typewriter. My electric one had long since been pawned. I bought this one for five dollars, and took it home. I set it up on a folding table facing the window, and forced myself to sit down. It felt incredibly daring, because somehow all those years in *Star Trek* fandom had not prepared me for this, this setting forth of my Game in all its long pent up glory. "Napoleon Solo stretched, and rotated his shoulder muscles," I typed, and had to stop. It felt so bold. Well, nobody else will ever see it, I comforted myself. There was not, to my knowledge, a *MFU* fandom like *Star Trek*'s. I certainly had never seen a *MFU* fanzine at any of the conventions I had attended, even though almost every other pair of male buddies had them. Starsky/Hutch, Holmes and Watson ... many more shows I had never heard of, actors I didn't know. But not so much as a photograph or flier about Illya and Napoleon. So I felt free to write, free to finally set down all the elements that had filled my imagination and mind and heart for lo those many years.

But it turned out I wasn't alone. Again. There was an active *MFU* fandom out there, and even a slash fandom. Other people were slashing Illya and Napoleon. That knocked the wind out of me all over again. I don't know why, but it did. I think I had accepted that while *Star Trek*, of course, was a very popular show still, with reruns on every station, and huge conventions, who besides me even remembered *MFU*? It had been equally popular at the time, but not anymore. But I was wrong. Again.

Meanwhile, I had written all of The Game into *A Trackless Domain*. With my discovery of this previously unknown fandom, it ended up being published, filling six volumes. I could have stopped there, and fully thought I had stopped there. But then I added another large series, an offshoot of *Trackless Domain*, (an AU's AU, ha ha) called *Child of Morning, Child of Night*. An evening at a "Medieval Feast" banquet/ attraction in Myrtle Beach sparked a novel set in an AU medieval landscape, and later there was another novel set in a dystopian future. And there are many short stories—some in zines, but mostly online. I mourn the departure of the fanzine, but it is fun posting online, too.

I am retired now after thirty years of teaching, and still writing *MFU* slash fan fiction. I love it. I have had a life, (thank you, Mr. Shatner), and enjoyed it thoroughly. I raised my three children and now they, with their spouses and children, live near me. I have done a lot of volunteer work in animal rescue. I have a home, a garden, and some hobbies.

But underneath all of that, in between all of that, runs The Game. The Game takes me merrily on long tedious car trips as Illya and Napoleon enjoy their honeymoon. The Game saw me through boring staff meetings, as Illya paid close attention and Napoleon tried to distract him. The Game helped me cope when the Ferris Wheel I was on stopped during a wild thunderstorm and blackout. I was terrified, but Illya and Napoleon took the opportunity to do some smooching in the pitch black, and that amused me so much that I was sorry when the lights came back on. (That scene is in "Sweet Delight", because as soon as I got home I wrote it down.)

And now here we are, in the midst of a pandemic. The Game has steadied and calmed me. I have not written of it, because I generally don't include current events. The Game is apart from all of that. But Illya and Napoleon have enjoyed their long hours together, and the stories keep on coming, brightening my day, easing the load, lifting the stress.

Although I now know I am not the only one, am I nevertheless a sick one, a crazy one, a wrong one? Why have I obsessed on the sexual relationship between two men—two fictional men—since before I knew there was such a thing? Why the terrible tortures, the intense hurt/comfort/rescue, over and over and over again? I don't know and don't really care to know. Maybe I am a sick one, a crazy one. But I don't think I am a wrong one, because to quote an old song kind of off-key, if loving Illya and Napoleon, Kirk and Spock, slash fan fiction and its readers and writers is wrong, I don't want to be right. I don't. For real.

Each of my passions, my fandoms, has shaped my character and my worldview. From Star Trek I learned that the beauty of creation is in its infinite diversity, and that if we work together we can overcome the terrors and problems of this world and move into a glorious future free of prejudice and war and inequities. The Beatles taught me that all we need is love, and John Lennon in particular still encourages me to imagine. And *Man from U. N. C. L. E.* , from my very young years, told me that at any time I, as an ordinary person, might have to step up and save the world, to be brave and resourceful and true. And I think that all makes me a strong one, a healthy, brave and loving one.

So live long and prosper, and let your freak flag fly.

essay © 2020 Cynthia Drake

ALLYSON M W DYAR
The Importance of Communication

"We wanted a publication where ideas could be discussed without fear. We didn't want it degrading into a slugfest where everyone resorted to personal attacks—we'd seen it happen in other letterzines—so we took precautions. As a result, the discussions ranged all over." — Allyson Dyar

I honestly don't recall what the exact definition of fandom was when I got into fandom. But I'd define it as a group of like-minded folks, or fans of a specific genre, sport, etc. By those lights, I first got involved in fandom by attending the first *Star Trek* Convention in NYC in January 1972. *Star Trek* was my "gateway" to fandom, and still is!

I had grown up in New York City until my family moved to New Rochelle NY in 1964. My family definitely didn't understand my "obsession" with fandom, despite my explaining it to them. (I think my mother finally understood when she came to a Lunacon with me. She met the writer of a soap opera column and started chatting with him.)

I really enjoyed communicating with other fans, so I joined the *Star Trek* Welcommittee, where we would answer mail and questions from fans searching for a sense of belonging. Eventually, I edited the Welcommittee Directory. This led to some interesting occurrences. One in particular comes to mind. When the original fiction book was published about Harry Mudd (I'm a bad Trekker as I don't recall the name of the book and my books are packed away), it listed my post office box. Despite the incorrect zip code, an avalanche of mail appeared. Fun times!

I also communicated with a number of folks via email, especially in those days with the *Star Trek* Welcommittee.

One funny story: Because my last name is Whitfield, and Stephen Whitfield wrote *The Making of Star Trek*, many people assumed we were related—in fact, most assumed that Stephen was my father. I later learned from Susan Sackett, Gene Roddenberry's assistant, that

Whitfield wasn't Stephen's last name after all. It was Poe. Susan gave me his address and I did write him, but never heard back.

Luckily, I lived so close to NYC that it allowed me to go to many *Star Trek* and science fiction conventions. Each convention allowed me to connect with old and new friends. I miss those days. (For the record, I hate the conventions as they are now; they just seem to be put on for money, not for the love of the genre.)

Later on, I became a calligrapher and contributed to many fanzines. My calligraphy seemed to be everywhere, mostly because I didn't turn anyone down! I also sold artwork at conventions as well as made convention signs.

I also co-edited a newsletter, *COMLINK*, which covered all aspects of fandom, not just *Star Trek*. It ran bi-monthly for over ten years. The articles we published reflected a broad range of interest, and we wanted a publication where ideas could be discussed without fear. We didn't want it degrading into a slugfest where everyone resorted to personal attacks—we'd seen it happen in other letterzines—so we took precautions. As a result, the discussions ranged all over: from the *Star Wars* universe (whether or not Darth was Luke's daddy, rumors surrounding *Return of the Jedi*, and comparisons to *The Lord of the Rings*), to the film *The Hidden Fortress* and its 10th anniversary. Also discussed was animation, James Bond, the campaigns to resurrect *Starman* and *Beauty and the Beast*, as well as several essays on fannish concerns like the dearth of young fen and men in media fandom, or censorship in fanzines.

It's my nature to stay away from controversy, but the biggest controversy I can recall was over the more adult oriented fanzines. I personally never had an issue with them but some folks did.

After I got married to a career Air Force NCO, it was much harder to keep up with things (the Internet as we know it was still a twinkle in an engineer's eye), so I more or less gafiated, attending a few conventions here and there, but really not keeping up with fandom.

Still, fandom gave me a purpose in life. It fulfilled my desire to "help"—and it also helped me get through the rough patches of my life, especially when I was in college in the 70s, going through what would now be called depression. Because I was willing to try things I'd never done before, especially public speaking (organizing convention panels, etc), fandom has definitely helped me in my work. I'm not afraid to speak in front of an audience.

Even though I'm still a big fan, nowadays I spend my time reading Facebook, Twitter, etc. It's so much easier now to keep up with everything, as opposed to the old days. I still have a lot of friends from those days. Unfortunately, a few of them have also crossed the rainbow bridge.

I think I can sum up fandom this way: my fannish friends became my extended family, and for that, I am extremely grateful.

© 2020 Allyson M W Dyar

ABBIE BERNSTEIN
The Power of Story

"I didn't realize until much, much later that all of this spoke to me powerfully. I only knew that Oz was as real inside my mind as anything I knew about, but hadn't seen personally. I also knew that I wanted to read every single word there was about Oz." —Abbie Bernstein

I have always been fannish.

I know that pretty much everybody has their own definition of "fannish," so here's mine: if I love a story, I want to contemplate every bit of it, every turn and inch and why and wherefore. I have a long, narrow attention span. I'm not fannish about many things, but once something has gotten into my heart, it seldom dislodges, even when there's trauma attached.

I also know that "always" means different things to different people. For me, it means as long as I can remember. When I was maybe three or four years old, my parents bought the unabridged *The Wizard of Oz* by L. Frank Baum on a set of LP records (this was before books on tape). It came with an illustrated copy of the book, which I am sure helped me learn to read, since the words on the page matched those I was hearing.

I do not know how many times I listened to that recording, walking in circles around the living room. Being a little girl, I loved that the hero of the story was a little girl. I loved how easily she made friends. I loved the Scarecrow particularly, because he was gentle and vulnerable. I loved that Dorothy had a dog. (My family got our first dog when I was about five, but I was well immersed in Oz by then.) I loved that women were major forces for good (Glinda) and evil (the Wicked Witches), and that nobody commented on this. I loved that all the animals could talk and seemed to live on fairly equal terms with the humans.

Something I especially loved, that had my imagination conjuring up every scene, was the idea that each of Oz's four countries—Munchkins in the east, Winkies in the west, Quadlings in the south, and (although not introduced until the second book) Gillkins in the north—had its own color. This didn't mean that everything was mono-chrome, but instead that each country had its own infinity of hues within that color. So you didn't have to be stuck with the first blue, yellow, red, and purple (and green, for the capital Emerald City) you saw. You could really examine each bit of every house, piece of furniture, item of clothing, blade of grass, and see how it subtly differed from what was next to it. There was endless possibility within each big choice.

I didn't realize until much, much later that all of this spoke to me powerfully. But Oz felt as real to me as the sun and the moon and England, and any other place that I heard about and just couldn't reach physically. I also knew that I wanted to read every single word there was about Oz.

My parents, who I don't believe ever refused to buy me a book I requested (they were thrilled they were raising a reader), got all fourteen of the L. Frank Baum Oz books, which were then being printed as a set. I read each one over and over, loving all the new towns and countries and possibilities.

I did have a three-day-long meltdown when I first got to the end of *The Emerald City of Oz*, when Oz closes its borders to outsiders. Now, this is Book Six out of fourteen. I could clearly see there were eight more books, and even at age six could understand this meant that obviously Oz reopened. But I took it personally. I wasn't inside Oz, which meant I was an outsider, and closing the borders meant that the people inside Oz, who I loved, didn't want me to know what they were doing anymore.

It felt like being cast out of Eden by God for the crime of being irrelevant. My family is Reform Jewish, so I have no experience of being condemned from the pulpit, but I imagine it's a similar sensation. The adults around me could see I was weeping hysterically, but I couldn't explain the problem in a way they could understand. I remember a friend's mother comforting me. I don't know what finally calmed me down. My guess is that I picked up the next book, grudgingly accepted Baum's explanation of how it was there could *be* another book, and eventually sank back into Oz. It was never quite the same after that, but I couldn't stop identifying with it, either.

I like the 1939 musical movie *The Wizard of Oz*. This, however, had almost nothing to do with my Oz fandom. Back in the days when it showed on TV once a year, my mom and I would trek across the street to watch it with the neighbors. It was fun, and pretty, and I liked the songs, but it didn't match the books, and I never forgave it for the heresy of having Dorothy's experiences turn out to be a dream. How dare they? Oz was real.

My mom, always on the lookout for ways to expand my world (and everybody else's, but that's another story), discovered the existence of the International Wizard of Oz Club. Founded in 1957 (before my time) by Justin G. Schiller, it has remained in existence ever since. Its newsletter, *The Baum Bugle*, now comes out three times a year. I don't know what its frequency of publication was in my childhood, but I read it eagerly. It was edited by Fred M. Meyer, who, in my childhood, I supposed had some sort of spiritual link to the Oz material. Perhaps he did. Again, I hardly had the ability to ask him about this.

At that time (1968-1971), the Oz club held several annual conventions in different regions of the country. Being in the west—Los Angeles county, outside L. A. city proper—we were in Winkie territory. Mom took me and a friend to several of these conventions. There are now more annual conventions, in more regions around the country, something I have since learned from Wikipedia.

And here is where I wish my recollections were so much better. Baum had made some silent films of the *Oz* stories, and these were screened at the conventions. I think this was my first exposure to silent movies. I was fascinated, though I was perturbed that the films didn't entirely match the books. I was also confused why this was the case, since Baum ought to know what he wrote. (Reader, I have since figured this out.)

I remember that the air in Cambria Pines, where at least one Winkie convention was held, smelled so wonderful that it seemed like something you ought to be able to eat. There was a full-color illustrated map of the Marvelous Land of Oz that included artwork of every single place mentioned in the books, plus directions to other countries mentioned in Baum's work. (His fantasy novels all took place in the same universe, so even if a book didn't take place in Oz, the other characters were aware of the land).

Some brilliant baker made cookies in the shapes of various Oz characters and castles, with icing in the colors of whatever region these inhabited in the books. There were presentations of scholarly papers, which I sat through, straining to comprehend not only what was being said, but what points were being made.

One lady very kindly made me a Patchwork Girl doll, and a neighbor made me a toy Saw Horse (for those unfamiliar with Oz, these are both major characters who appear later on in the series). Seeing that I already had "actors" literally at hand, I enlisted a friend, and we used these toys and a size-appropriate doll to do a little Oz play that I wrote. My dad made some poster-board backgrounds of various colors (for the various Oz counties), with a hole in the center of each one, so that we could put our hands through and manipulate the toys on top of a picnic table. I have no idea now what the story was about, and I have no doubt it was awful, but we were allowed to perform it at a Winkie con. Bless the Oz fandom folks for letting us do it.

There weren't a lot of other kids at these conventions. I wanted to interact with the adults—and I am drawing a blank on what this was like. I'm pretty sure they were kind, since I don't recall coming home feeling bad. I believe what I was hoping for, though, was that I'd encounter some grownup who could say, "Oh, yes, if you just keep this particular thought in mind, and study this, and know that, then you will be able to imagine Oz correctly and find new things about it all on your own. You won't be an outsider." Even more, someone who'd say, "I'm looking for that, too. Let's find it together."

This was a completely insane, unfulfillable desire, made more complicated by the fact that I wasn't conscious of it enough to speak it, and if I had been that aware, I doubt I would have dared say it then, anyway. I still love Baum's Oz books (there are now other Oz books by other writers, most of which I don't mind but do not love), and reread them from time to time. I don't think I left the fandom for any reason other than preadolescence got busy and complicated, and traumatic, as I mentioned earlier. I also had few human anchors to it, due to the aforementioned age gap.

This was, however, my first experience of organized fandom: a lot of people I didn't know, who had wondrous knowledge and physical treasures. I was afraid I'd have nothing to offer them, and I don't think I did, but they let me in because we all loved the same thing.

essay © Abbie Bernstein

KELLEY HARKINS
We Found Our Community

"While we had the movies and television, fans were often still isolated from each other. While the Internet changed much of that in the late 90s, this was long before that. That sense of community is one of the things that helped develop fandom and conventions into what they are today. Conventions themselves became our framework, as were fanzines, letterzines, and APAs. It was how we communicated and connected."— Kelley Harkins

Being born at the end of the baby boomer era, I didn't really fit in with them, and I didn't fit in with the next stage, whatever it ended up being named.

I was, however, a child of the media era, even though I spent a lot of time at the public library. Thanks to a wonderful introduction from my elder brother, I sank into the literary options of Andre Norton, Madeline L'Engle, and Ursula K. Le Guin. Books opened my eyes and imagination to so many possibilities.

The first story, besides the inevitable Nancy Drews, Dana Girls, and Black Stallion books, to stick in my mind was "A Pail of Air" by science fiction writer Fritz Leiber. It was in an anthology that Andre Norton had put together, and the visceral imagery of that story was just mind-blowing. It still resonates in my memory, and it was written back in 1956.

Now, I'm not even that old, clocking in about 58 at this point, but I was probably about 11 or 12 when I read "A Pail of Air". I had a good public library, being from a moderate-sized town in Pennsylvania that later became a poster child for pop music and rust belt mentality with Billy Joel's song of "Allentown". It always bewildered me that they gave the key to the city to him, since the song is a dark tale of a manufacturing world passing from mainline existence.

I subsisted on a diet of books, Saturday morning cartoons, and comics, until the mid 70s when the world as a whole started to get a clue that it "might" be ready for some women to show some power. It was the era of women's liberation and the ERA (Equal Rights Amendment), and more options were opening up for me than being the schoolteacher my mother suggested. On television we got Lynda Carter's *Wonder Woman*, and Lindsay Wagner's *Bionic Woman*.

Don't forget to note the woman in the title, just in case it wasn't clear these women weren't the "norm"—though they packaged them up neatly with Diana Prince being essentially a secretary and Jaime Sommers being a school teacher when not righting the wrongs of the world.

Strangely enough, while I watched *Star Trek*, it never quite clicked with me. I think I was hungry for that strong female role model, and while *Star Trek* has done that since then, it really hadn't at that point. So, in this time of malnutrition, George Lucas dropped the quintessential fairy tale of the modern era, *Star Wars*. Only this time the princess wasn't so passive, and I felt the same aching need for a larger world that Luke Skywalker did. Leia was already worldly wise and aware, and I absolutely admired her strength and commitment to her cause. However, Luke was 16 at the start of *A New Hope*, and I was 15, so it seemed natural to connect so fully with his hopes and dreams of a wider "world". That sense of optimism and excitement. Sure, Han had the talk, the charm, but that wasn't me, and to me *Star Wars* was strangely a very personal story. So that pushed me off the deep end. When I chose to write my own main character in that realm, I did so by combining the two icons in my mind, and wrote a young woman with dreams and hope of a better, bigger world, one where she strove to be a strong committed force for good in spirit and in influence.

That fall, after difficulties in my public-school experience, I was privileged enough to be offered a new path at a very different school, in a very traditional setting: of all places, a girls' boarding school in New England that held the bones of "northern goth atmosphere house" in the old mansions in Springfield, Massachusetts. There I found friends that weren't the norm and connected with those who had been to those biggest of geeky experiences: a convention. They also introduced me to the concept and idea of costuming.

I cannot tell you how many times I saw *Star Wars* that year. Going to the movies was something that was approved of by the school, and they shuttled us there on the weekends. My roommates and I transcribed the script from a snuck-in tape recorder so we could use it for reference or running the dialog amongst ourselves to relive those moments. So was born an obsession, all with the support of friends who "got" me. Together, we created alternative versions of ourselves that lived in that galaxy far, far away. Tian, Mayet, and Raiah might have physically shared a dorm room, but our spirits got to fight in much bigger battles.

One of our circle, Anne Marie, took me to my first convention, *Star*

Trek America 1978, in New York City. It was truly eye opening for a 17-year-old, and even more when I walked into the fanzine room. They had a whole room there for the selling of fanzines—mostly *Star Trek*—but thankfully *Star Wars* had quickly developed a following, and some zines were starting to put out *Star Wars* content.

Down the rabbit hole I went, along with my best friend, Lin Stack. She was as much a Han Solo junkie as I was for Luke. Her life experience was so different from mine, but together, it felt like we could take on the galaxy.

I read some of the truly mediocre professional novels that Lucasfilm and Del Rey put out, but none of them compared to the wonderful versions of the *Star Wars* universe that people I knew were creating. I devoured it all. We read Anne Elizabeth Zeek, Barbara Wenk, Judi Hendricks, Cyn Holmes, Jani Hicks, Karen Osman, Judy Lowe, and so many others.

Lin and I were inspired to create our own fan universe, with the soon-to-be traditional trope of female point of view characters. We weren't big name fans, but we had an idea and a dream. We connected with others that shared our passion and sure, there was drama now and then, but we mostly were there to support each other.

We decided to jump into the world of publishing with a zine called *Millennium*. Lin was a talented artist. I learned how to do layout and typography, and through these efforts made more friends as I bought my first Selectric™ typewriter. This typewriter was notable, as it allowed you to pop off the ball that held the type. Each ball had a different font, so it was easy to switch between courier and italic. Remember, this is the age before computer aided layout, so having a Selectric™ was the first step in being able to create print ready material.

Another step happened when we went to the first MediaWest*Con in 1981. We made the trek from the East Coast all the way to East Lansing, Michigan, a place I would never have considered a destination.

As is kind of traditional at all conventions, Lin and I didn't see much besides the hotel, but, boy, did fans take over that place. Doors were decorated, we had room parties, made costumes based on our favorite media, or even our own characters. There was an incredibly powerful intensity. I put faces to names I had read. I gasped at the amazing cover art that Judith Lowe did for *The Princess Tapes*, the detail of Karen River's stipple work, drooled over Gee Moaven's sensuous lines. There were the usual fixtures of most conventions—an art show, a masquerade, panels—but the small size and focus of all our interests made it something different, more intense. MediaWest had panels devoted to Brit fans, comic fans, buddy/bromance shows, even slash in all its varied shapes and sizes. There were competitions for door decorations and pangalactic gargle blasters around the hot tub.

To me this whole time frame was the realization that we could be more than we had been told by the world of guidance counselors and parents, who still suggested "safe" careers like teaching and nursing. I say this now as an older fan who has been and worked at many cons, including the past twenty years at one of the largest conventions in the U. S. , that there's something to be said for smaller cons that focus on a topic or subject matter. Not that MediaWest*Con was just *Star Wars*, no, but it was mostly media. While we were all readers, we were also at the forefront (just after *Trek*) of a new media fandom. Bear in mind there wasn't a lot of professional material out at this time, so we made up what we didn't have.

Lin and I had put together our first issue of *Millennium*. We did have the luck to find a GBC spiral binder, which made our zine one of the few that didn't fall apart! It's hard to imagine what a big deal that was now. Lin did most of the art, but we made connections and got other artists. That first issue was mediocre, and we knew it, but it was our first and we spent our own money to get it made. I think that was part of the key to it: that investment, monetary, emotionally, and perhaps a bit spiritually. Wanting to share and expand on these stories that had captured our imaginations.

I won't profess to scholarship as to female fandom before there was an active media presence like *Star Trek* and *Star Wars*. But the percentages of men to women from when I first started going to conventions and being an active part of fandom, to now, has shifted a great deal. It used to be more male-oriented than female, but now it's balanced out overall, and also gotten a lot younger. In my early 20s (very early), I was amongst the younger set in media fandom. Many seasoned participants had already dipped their toes into *Star Trek* fandom.

At MediaWest*con, Lin and I found our community. While we had the movies and television, fans were often still isolated from each other. While the Internet changed much of that in the late 90s, this was long before that. That sense of community is one of the things that helped develop fandom and conventions into what they are today. Conventions themselves became our framework, as were fanzines, letterzines, and APAs. It was how we communicated and connected.

Sure, there is a similar sense when sports fans gather at games and bars, but overall it seems to be more ephemeral. Many people will identify themselves as franchise sport fans, but in my opinion, it does not drive them like it drove us.

While *Millennium* didn't make a huge splash, it did passably well, enough that Lin and I were pleased and happy with our first foray into a world we had known little about, but craved to be more involved in. It wasn't enough to be passive and just read, we had to create. We learned more at our first MediaWest; we were able to sit and talk, go to panels both on publishing and writing, and entertain ideas that really sparked our imaginations. We came home full of dreams and ambitions fired and supported by friends, old and new, that we had made there. Some are still friends to this day.

After that, we rebranded, having found out there was another zine somewhere else that had also used the name *Millennium*, and we called ourselves, *Crossed Sabers*. Lin and I had always looked at ourselves as two sides of a coin, and we had bonded over Luke and Han, in the sense that we saw them in a similar fashion. Remember at this time we had little canon, so the possibilities were boundless. Lucasfilm seemed to have little comprehension of the expansive universe we now know as *Star Wars*, so with an entire galaxy to explore and hints of history untold, we had much to consider and imagine. Like many, we created our own story cycle, the *Janus Cycle*, with our own point-of-view female characters, since, besides Leia and Uhura, we just didn't have that many females to connect with. Particularly ones that had any real personal drive.

When this was done badly or for strictly romantic reasons, the "Mary Sue" wish fulfillment trope was there to haunt us. That somehow also morphed into the Wesley Crusher trope later on.

However, there were enough incredible writers and artists, all creating universes that fit so perfectly, they practically became canon for us. We wanted our own part, so while we decided our characters would not be romantic interests for Luke and Han, they would be part of their lives. Lin had her smuggler type, and I had my rebel one. In the long run, we didn't tell as many stories as we wanted to in that story world, but we learned a lot about ourselves in the process. We had our heroes and they were on their own "hero's journey", just as Lucas created the Skywalker Saga based on Joseph Campbell's work. We learned and were inspired as well, traveling on our own personal journeys.

We created our second issue, and it was a great improvement over *Millennium*, with better production quality and, I think, better writing and editing. We had a broader pool of talent to reach out to, friends we had made and people we admired, and finding talent in those just joining the fan fiction ranks. Lin had penned a short, few lines story on a flyer for *CS* 2, about that final plot thrust in Empire, and in that she got us connected with people that hadn't been in our wider circle.

Through that we met Jean Michelle, now known as eluki bes shahar, and thankfully she lived almost directly between us, so her home became a convenient meeting place, and I spent many weekends there, learning more from her. She had been in comics fandom for years, was an artist and done some graphic design work, so had an understanding that we were still trying to learn. You couldn't help but laugh at her wry sense of humor and fun cartoons, and her obsession with Darth Vader. One weekend she even came to my hometown, where we did a late-night talk show on a local AM station about *Star Wars* and fan fiction. I still have the cartoons she doodled that night.

It was okay that we all connected with someone different in the Saga. Somehow that made it all the better, and even when we meet someone who connected with the same person we did, like when I connected with Jenni Hennig, we found different stories to tell, but found validity in all the variations. There was no "this is the 'right' version" or "the canon version," but it was just our story, our version. The flyers we created were often welcome mats, doorways to new friends, giving us entry to new places and perspectives. Before this time, there really wasn't a concept so much as "universes" or serial story lines in the same universe that weren't the same characters.

To this day, I find it a touch ironic that George Lucas drew from many sources and has stated that *Star Wars* was inspired by the old movie serials, such as Flash Gordon and Buck Rogers. Television had the concept of spin off; clearly novels did to a degree, although it was accepted more slowly. This still is a growing concept in our day and age even as the financial model has changed to allow the "serial" or great arc of a universe. Now we see multiple stories and multiple main characters, and it's good for a franchise. While I might be biased, I do think we drew this into the mainstream by the fannish desire to keep worlds alive, even after their story was finished.

Fans, by their nature, often take ownership. This was true in those early days, just as much as it is now. You can see that in the mentality we all had that it was okay for us to add on, as long as we didn't profit. We did honor the creators, but refused to let things go. Unfortunately, this has led to a toxic level of "it's ours, don't fuck with it," mentality that has poisoned new work. We still feel the need for things to have the same tone as the originals. Never mind that our world has a billion stories in it of all different shapes, sizes, and colors, and they can all be fascinating and intriguing. The gatekeeper mentality is useless and, back then, I don't think we really had one. Yes, there were BNFs, but no one ever stopped anyone from creating their own versions. At times people were even willing to share their own universes, though generally we just enjoyed the freedom to play in the ones we did.

Copyright law hasn't helped a lot, and Lucasfilm, long before Disney's ownership, tried to figure out how to approach fanfic without alienating their fanbase. From their perspective, it makes sense for them to control the narrative, though I am not aware of any specific efforts by Paramount or Desilu to stop *Star Trek* fan works, even when they trod into the slash territory. This was all new territory to Hollywood. Copyright lawyers didn't really understand. Wasn't making money the whole point? Clearly not for fanzine publishers.

For the most part, Lucasfilm actually paid for our zines. We probably would have given them free copies if they had asked. I kept one of my payout slips for years, just to have a check from Lucasfilm. There was never outright support, but those payments seemed to encourage us.

Then, as we filled in the blanks, the inevitable happened. Out came an adult, clearly non G-rated story. It wasn't perverse in any sense, certainly nowhere close to what had gone on in some aspects of *Star Trek* fanfic, or in the fanfic world of today. "Slow Boat to Bespin", by Anne Elizabeth Zeek, was a slightly steamy version of the long flight from the asteroid field to Bespin between Han and Leia on the *Falcon*.

Partially because it involved main characters, Lucasfilm wasn't too happy. All fanzine publishers got a rather pointed suggestion that we should keep it G-rated, as that was what George Lucas saw in his vision of *Star Wars*. Of course, he was the one that showed planets being destroyed and the seamy underbelly of Mos Eisley. To my suburban teenage eye, it was an invitation to a wider world.

As you'd expect, there was a bit of a backlash from the fans and the fanzine publishers with some rather pointed satire pieces after that, poking fun at the G ratings and some of our own clichés. While fans complained and were unhappy with the mandate, they seemed non-committal on the whole, and willing to just ignore this "guideline." It seemed to me that Lucasfilm kind of shrugged and figured we were a small set of people that had a limited outreach to their larger fandom. Maybe they were right. However, we could laugh at ourselves and Lucasfilm, and still be passionate about our subject matter.

Return of the Jedi was highly anticipated (that is a vast under-statement), and while there were moments of brilliance, it wasn't as strong an entry as the first two films were. Lucas tried to appeal to multiple age groups, not seeming to understand that doing so weakened the film, creating such different tones that never really seemed to blend. It was divisive. Many fans drifted off, unhappy with the gray nature of Obi-Wan's perspective to Luke, or the childish vibe of the Ewoks.

During this decade, life kept naturally going on. My fascination with how these films were created and developed became a stronger element for me, and I started studying film and video production, as well as psychology, on my own and at several colleges. Earlier I pointed out that women were receiving more acknowledgement, up to a point, but it was a lot harder to nudge into production work. Women were often production assistants and continuity checkers, not directors, and as an editor, it seemed like you needed to know someone. Since most of the studios and production companies were in California, it helped to be there as you were beginning your career. I was not. You have only to look at the #MeToo movement to see that the entertainment industry was not hospitable to women, especially behind the scenes. I managed it, to a degree, in the dry instructional/continuing education field of production, doing everything from script editing, video editing, answering the phone, and bookkeeping. The production company I worked for, Back East Productions, was small, but it was good experience. It wasn't going to last though, with it being so small. It was the producer/owner and me for the most part, and he hired freelancers when he needed more. Finally, seeking stability for his own family, he ended up joining a production team with a pharmaceutical company, and I was out of luck.

Hoping to use a mutual connection from Back East Productions and a friend in the Society for Creative Anachronism, I took a leap of faith and moved to Texas, which didn't work out too well. It lasted about a year, and then I headed to Florida through a roundabout series of life events. This is kind of ironic because, while working at Back East Productions years before, I had been accepted to a highly competitive film graduate program at Florida State where there isn't a lot of financial aid for Graduate programs, especially in the Arts. During my time in Texas, the tech sector became a thing. I learned and grew more intrigued with computers and their capabilities. It felt like shades of the future coming to life. My brother (the same one who had introduced me to science fiction) had given me my first computer before that move, and we all know how rapidly home computers evolved, and the presence they have today.

Since I had no real media/production connections in the industry in Florida, I ended up developing my tech skills further, getting computer certifications and seeing the rise of nonlinear editing and digital effects. The Internet opened up communication and access to many. We saw incredible user-created content in text and imagery. This led directly back to Lucasfilm really understanding how *Star Wars* fandom had grown. Through parents, who had savored the initial trilogy, and their children, fandom began using the technology they now had in their hands to make their own stories; not that dissimilar from the fan fiction and art we created initially.

Through this growing awareness of the fans' interest, we got the Prequels, episodes 1, 2 and 3. They have elements of great imagination and brilliance, but still seem a bit lost on threaded narrative and focus. Some performances could have been stronger, and some threads were downright confusing. In hindsight, there's also a surprising number of cliché portrayals that border on insulting, if not outright inappropriate, choices.

My affection for the *Star Wars* universe hasn't faded, but it has evolved. The world has seen fan culture and "nerd-dom" become more mainstream. In the height of original trilogy time, we had maybe three or four media "universes" that went anywhere, and a lot of ripoffs that have become cultural touchstones, but often struggled to be financial successes. I have no doubt that *Star Trek* and then *Star Wars* were the impetus behind the force that genre has become in the industry. They opened the door into that wider galaxy. Science and NASA made it more real, and it was firmly in our lives as shuttles launched into the sky, and we had our own space station with a much more benevolent mission to dream about.

With that expanding range of material, I still was and am passionate about creating and sharing our imaginations. Creators and fans have thrown open the gates and shown us new worlds.

Through these connections, I met someone, married him, and live a happy geeky life, with it being a strong touchstone to who I am. That sense of community, though, has never left me; and in 1999, I was introduced to my first Dragon Con. Now understand that, as I mentioned before, most conventions were run by fans for fans. It was always about that, but as fans grew up and earned their own money, they wanted to embrace the things they loved, designing a culture that hungered for those connections to our love of the weird and wonderful.

I love Dragon Con. It is unique, and I don't say that as someone who has worked at the con for two decades, and done my best to encourage those bonds of family and understanding between yet more fans. Our financial power has gotten the all-too-greedy attention of the corporate world. Some for good, some for bad. Many fan-run conventions and brands throughout the world were purchased, and time with your favorite actor or the latest collectible has become a commodity. Dragon Con has refused to sell to these corporations, despite offers from corporate entities to buy out the current fan owners. It isn't perfect, it's run by human beings, but that acceptance, and that sense of community has become something different. A decade ago, DragonCon offered me a position as a director for one of the fan tracks, which I welcomed. A good chunk of my year is geared to planning and organizing about 60 panels and events for 80,000 people, who have all found their own communities within our microcosm.

Those connections are fandom's life blood. They are what makes it so natural to start a conversation with someone in line about a shared passion, possibly even learning or sharing something new with a new friend. I've even been lucky enough to mingle all my past lives skills into teaching at a college that caters to geeks of all shapes and sizes: from music lovers, to Disney, to the latest computer game or Marvel movie. Thank you, Full Sail University. I will never forget the day after *Game of Thrones'* "Red Wedding" episode, when I couldn't walk more than 15 feet before someone else asked me what I had thought about it. It's a blessing to not have to hide anymore. Full Sail understands and appreciates that I take off for Dragon Con every year.

In looking back, now that I am nearing 60, what do I see, and would I have done anything differently? Yes, and no. Of course, there are regrets and paths not taken. Being in that transitional world, fear stepped in and derailed me periodically, but overall, no. I found a way to express myself at a time when the world wasn't quite sure what to do with women, let alone a woman with an imagination. We formed connections that still bind us. It has made me more aware when I see my students, or fans at a convention, that we have this common ground. I still have many students that are amazed that I am a geeky person, and I don't hesitate to let my geek flag fly. Helping others see that they are not alone, that there are others like them who understand their passion, gives me a mission. Whether in my job, or my hobbies, and even in my class, I am happy to bring it back to *Star Wars* and what being a part of the fanzine community has brought me to today.

essay © Kelley Harkins

LINDA DENEROFF
Crucial Work Behind the Scenes

"My definition of fandom is people who share my interests. In that sense, I have many fandoms. I guess science fiction literature was my 'gateway drug', but really it was serendipity all the way."
—Linda Deneroff

I was born in the Bronx, New York. Growing up, my family never understood my fascination with science fiction, but in the early 1980s I got my father to give up nagging me when I told him that through sf fandom I had travelled, learned photography, and published a fanzine.

There's a saying, "the golden age of science fiction is 12," and it certainly was for me. A librarian introduced me to *Red Planet* by Robert Heinlein and, after that, I devoured every sf book I could find in my public library. In those days, you had to be in eighth grade to be allowed to take books out of the adult section, so for a year I was relegated to the children's section, but it held books by Asimov and Heinlein and Clarke, among others. I was hooked.

I also watched some *Twilight Zone* (1959-1964), but at that time we had only one television, and my parents usually wanted to watch something else. I caught *Superman* (on reruns), and a few other shows I don't remember. I also watched whatever sf movies were on TV, but that might have been later on: *The Day the Earth Stood Still*, *This Island Earth*, and a bunch of really bad 1950s sf films. (Many years later, a boyfriend introduced me to the 1927 *Metropolis* and the 1936 *Things to Come*, and I was blown away by them.)

In 1966, *Star Trek* premiered. My parents had just purchased a color television, and *Star Trek* was going to be on Thursday nights at 8:30. By this time, my father (who repaired black-and-white vacuum tube televisions as a hobby) had collected two or three black-and-white TVs that people had thrown away. So, the trick for me to watch *Star Trek* in color was to get the TV at 8, before my father could get to it. (And if there was something else he really wanted to watch, I was relegated to the black-and-white TV. I remember having to watch

"Amok Time" in black-and-white and being annoyed about it.) But I was still a solitary fan; none of my friends were into science fiction, and I still didn't know about fandom as a social group.

I knew about sf conventions, of course, through the magazine, *Analog*, but I didn't know they were something a nonprofessional could attend, and I had never heard of fanzines. But by the end of 1971, I had been introduced to both, and my fate was sealed.

I was 21 in 1971, and in that magical year I met the people who would become lifelong friends. I wrote about that many years ago (for *COMLINK*, I think), and how it was a chain of events—meeting one person who introduced me to someone else, etc. , and all of them introducing me to new aspects of fandom.

I was standing in a registration line at Lehman College in New York (probably in the fall of 1970) and complaining to a friend that my mother had insisted I go to a school dance, thereby missing what I considered to be the best episode of the third season, "The Paradise Syndrome."

A woman tapped me on the shoulder and asked if I was a *Star Trek* fan. Of course I said, "Yes," and she told me that she had a copy of the *Star Trek* blooper reel. We got a room at the college and invited people to view it, but the room wasn't big enough. We ran it three times, and people still wanted to see it. We got a bigger room, and a bigger room after that, and finally the biggest auditorium in the college, and we still had to run it multiple times.

By that time, as it turns out, through another school friend I had already met the cousin of the person with the blooper reel (small world!), and through her cousin I was introduced to *Star Trek* fanzines and conventions). I attended my first sf convention in April 1971, Lunacon, followed by a comic convention, followed by Nore-ascon I (the 1971 World Science Fiction Convention). Then came that fateful first *Star Trek* con in January 1972. My friend with the blooper reel was involved with running it, and I won the trivia contest! After that I joined the "Committee," as it was known, and over the next four years, I wrote the trivia contests (plus one extra) for each subsequent convention.

While the show was being "stripped" (shown every night) in New York on WPIX-TV, it was cut to shreds, and you had to watch every show twice, just to catch scenes that were cut the first time. There was no such thing as videotape copies; if you were lucky, you might make an audio tape. But I took copious notes in the tiniest handwriting, which came in handy for creating those contests, which consisted of

100 questions each. (By the time of the fifth and final convention, I saw people with three or four 2-inch notebooks, answering the questions while they waited in line to register. And, later, the questions—and answers—were published in Joan Winston's book, *The Making of the Trek Conventions*.)

As I got more involved in fandom, I joined the New York Science Fiction Society (the Lunarians), worked on both Lunacon and the Committee *Star Trek* conventions, and started a fanzine (with Cynthia Levine) called *Guardian*. As often as possible I tried to go to conventions, particularly Worldcon, which meant travelling to different cities, including Toronto, Canada, in 1972, my first out-of-country convention.

Back in those days, there was no Internet, of course, but we had letterzines, and I contributed to *Halkan Council* (*Star Trek*), followed later by *COMLINK* and *Jundland Wastes* (both *Star Wars*). I was co-editor of *COMLINK* while the main editor was in Iceland. I also wrote some *Kraith* (*Star Trek* universe) stories with Fran Zawacky, but I found my talent was more in editing than writing. So Cynthia Levine and I created *Guardian*, which morphed from a wholly *Star Trek* zine to a multi-universe zine.

Then and now, I try to avoid fan feuds because they're stupid. For example, I remember the rivalry between *Star Trek* and a British sf show called *UFO*. I wasn't a fan of the second show, but I didn't need to condemn it just because I liked *Star Trek*.

The same thing happened between fans of *Star Trek* and *Star Wars*, but I liked both and wasn't going to take sides or choose only one.

One of the conventions Cynthia and I travelled to was MediaWest*Con in Lansing, Michigan. Unlike most *Star Trek* conventions, this one was for fans—no guests. It became a great place to sell your zines because people came from all over the country. And because it was a zine-centric convention, they gave out the Fan-Q awards, which *Guardian* won.

We printed eight issues of *Guardian*, but the one that generated the most controversy was *Guardian 4*, in which we printed two stories, both called "Slow Boat to Bespin." In one, Han and Leia did not have sex; in the other they did, but in any event it wasn't terribly explicit, and today I don't think anyone would bat an eyelash at it. Now, I don't have all the details because I never saw the Swedish zine that set Lucasfilm's teeth on edge, but the two zines coming on top of one another drove the company to have its lawyers send Cynthia and me a cease-and-desist letter. We were nearly sold out of the zine anyway, so we responded to Lucasfilm that we had no intention of hurting their product and would keep our zine PG (which it was, really). It should also be noted that Lucasfilm was actively purchasing four copies of every *Star Wars* fanzine. This was unheard of, since Paramount was actively trying to destroy *Star Trek* fandom.

But, as they say, all fandom plunged into war. Other fanzine editors wanted to know what Lucasfilm's standard for PG was. And how dare Lucasfilm try to control what fanzine editors printed. And anyway, no one had or made any money, so who cared? And of course Lucasfilm was not going to respond with hard-and-fast rules, because fans being fans, that would only encourage them to try and evade them.

The controversy eventually died down, as these things usually did, and Cynthia and I continued to put out issues of *Guardian*.

We had what I (she said modestly) considered high standards for *Guardian*. We were one of the first, if not the first, to print our zine perfect-bound as opposed to stapled or spiral bound. Each issue ran about 200 pages, and we also used oversized paper and double-columned the text so we could reduce the print slightly and get more on the page. Other zines later copied our format! After our first issue, I bought a Selectric II typewriter so I could work on the zine at home, rather than at my office. And by the final issue, Cynthia and I had each purchased a Kaypro 4 computer running C/PM (look it up, kids! It's an antique).

Just before I moved to Seattle, I compiled *ThousandWorlds Collected*, which gathered all of Maggie Nowakowska's stories into three volumes. I had met Maggie in Brighton, England, at the 1979 Worldcon, and she had contributed a fabulous *Star Trek* timeline that Cynthia and I published in *Guardian*. I loved her *Star Wars* stories, but they were published in various zines and sometimes, given small print runs, hard to find. So I asked Maggie if I could do a collection of them, and she said yes. At the same time, Bev Clark was publishing *Skywalker 5*, which was going to be a *ThousandWorlds* novel. I arranged with her to use *Guardian's* printer (they were relatively cheap and did fantastic work). The printer would print 300 copies of *Skywalker 5*, and then print another set with new *ThousandWorlds Collected* covers (and a few different pages) that became the final volume.

The strangest "fan feud" wasn't really a feud; it was a dispute started by two fans who thought George Lucas needed to re-film *The Empire Strikes Back* because Darth Vader could not possibly be

Luke's father. Oh, the letters that went back and forth via the U. S. Mail! Part of the problem was these two women thought that we were being sarcastic when we were being serious, and that we were being serious when we were actually sarcastic. It finally died down to nothing, but somewhere in my files I still have my copies of those letters.

These days my fannish interests lie more with Worldcon, where I have been the Secretary of the Business Meeting of the World Science Fiction Society ("WSFS") for the last ten or so years, and that takes up a lot of my summer. In addition to those duties, I was liaison to an astronaut, Story Musgrave, at the Worldcon in 2012 (Chicon 7), one of the nicest people I have ever met! In 2015, I was not only the Secretary of the WSFS Business Meeting, but I was the WSFS Division Head. In 2019, I was a Fan Guest of Honor at Spikecon, the 2019 North American Science Fiction Convention ("NASFiC"), which is the national convention held when the Worldcon is outside North America. Since I generally think of myself as a "behind the scenes" person, I was flabbergasted to be asked! I also attended Dublin 2019, the World Science Fiction Convention, in Dublin, Ireland, that year, so I was really busy. This year the Worldcon, called ConNZealand (because it was supposed to be held in New Zealand), was held virtually, and I sat glued to my computer for five days, attending panels on Zoom.

I left the Lunarians science fiction club when I moved from New York to Seattle, but these days I go to Vanguard meetings (a social gathering of sf fans) and Seattle Tun (another like-minded social gathering)—which again are held via Zoom in these days of COVID-19—and I attend some, but not all, of the various local conventions in both Washington and Oregon.

Most of my friends are in sf fandom, though thanks to Facebook, I've reconnected with some school friends. I'm also on a couple of internet email groups, the largest of which is probably the SMOFs (Secret Masters of Fandom) email list. The name started as a joke, but it's hung on. In December there's usually a SMOFCon, which is a convention for convention-runners.

The thing that has changed the most, to my way of thinking, is how much more popular science fiction is today. Part of it, of course, is that we are living *in* a science fiction world. It used to be said "it was a proud and lonely thing to be a fan", but when I moved to Seattle, I was amazed at how much more open people were about science fiction and fandom. At my job in New York, I never told anyone about my being a science fiction fan. In Seattle, people would ask when I was attending my next "conference". I think that has a lot to do with *Star Trek* and *Star Wars* popularizing the genre, of course, as well as the arrival of Comic-Con and other really large conventions.

Why did I join "fandom?" That's a tough question to answer. I think part of it was that I'm an introvert. I don't make friends easily, and I don't find interesting things that other people do. I've never been interested in the bar scene, and even in my job I worked mostly alone. On the other hand, I love to read, travel, and take photographs—and fandom still fulfills those things for me. I don't know, obviously, what I'd be doing or even where I'd be if I hadn't joined fandom, but I'm certainly glad I did.

interview © Linda Deneroff

WANDA LYBARGER
Living a Dream

*"The atmosphere was electric with everything seeming possible. Fans
wanted to take part. It's the kind of wonderful creativity when the
castles in the air build ever higher, each contributing and adding to
it; not one-upmanship, but a joyous flocking to "put up the barn"
together. Invention and ideas seethed everywhere, especially in those
convention rooms and hallways, over a meal or drinks or coffee and
into the wee hours, when we could solve anything."*
—Wanda Lybarger

I was born in New York—one of those rare birds, a native of
Manhattan, more by chance and circumstance. My maternal
grandparents lived in Brooklyn, and that I remember best. I was an
Army brat, so where I was born is kind of irrelevant. My dad was in the
Army Corps of Engineers, so he never had normal tours of duty. He got
sent wherever a levee needed sandbagging and so on. We'd be two
weeks in one place and a month or half a year in another, never long
enough to make any friends, not even school yet. The moves took us
all over the States and to France, with visits to Italy, Belgium,
Netherlands, Germany, Denmark; I was a baby in Japan and don't
remember it. I had 32 moves before I was even school age. I mostly
remember riding somewhere or waiting in cavernous train stations
for somewhere. But thanks to Fort Benning, we finally settled for good
in Columbus, GA when I was nine; so I grew up in a medium-sized
southern town, very 1950s suburban with my mother at home, as was
just about everyone else's mother, and doing things like Girl Scouts.

I was still solitary because I'd never learned how to be friends with
other children. I read, fascinated by archaeology, cultural ideas,
ancient religions; the more adult matter I read, the less I had in
common with kids my age. I was bored by stories about the world
around me. I was reading science fiction in the third grade. I
discovered Ray Bradbury's *Martian Chronicles* in 1955 (published
just prior to my coming back to America to elementary school). I
didn't want stories about going to proms or trying to get the sandlot
for a baseball team; I wanted other time periods and other cultures in

40

the world. I wanted to be transported, my imagination given enough food to soar. And it was about the same time that I began to be focused on art, to the exclusion of any other desire.

I was a "weirdo". I waited, not always so patiently, for popular culture to get around to accepting if not embracing the fantasies I saw. *The Lord of the Rings* was first published in America while I was in college; by the time I graduated, the book stores were full of wonderful, affordable large paperbacks of artists like Frank Frazetta, Roger Dean, the Tolkien calendar art of the Hildebrandt brothers and Brian Froud. The artwork of Europe was filtering in with magazines like *Heavy Metal*, full of works by artists like Jean Girard (Moebius). Fantasy had arrived in the mainstream.

I'd been somewhat aware of fandom before I jumped in, by reading some of the professionally published stuff on *Star Trek*. I loved *Trek*, but was satisfied with the novelized scripts.

When *Star Wars* arrived, the effects, the pell-mell speed of the action was so immersive, coming out of the theater was like emerging from a dream in deep sleep. The story was so much like a wonderful game you could act out on the playground, the compulsion to join in was irresistible. You were clamoring for a passport to that "galaxy far, far away".

That compulsion probably had the most to do with my hunger to read the fan fiction, the continued adventures of characters I already loved and identified with. And of course, Han Solo had me the moment he slid into that booth on Mos Eisley.

I became rather desperate to make contact with a fanzine. My search fell through a number of times, but finally I found a classified advertisement for one in the back of *Starlog Magazine*. I sent for the zine; it was a little thing put out by a couple of friends, who'd written and illustrated nearly the whole thing—and about what you'd expect from a couple of teenage girls, best buddies, who wanted to print a zine. But *Starlog* had scads of classifieds for other zines, and I started writing to them. That much of the fiction wasn't very good was irrelevant. They satisfied my absolute hunger for more adventures.

Though illustration had never entered my mind in the past, I found I wanted to draw for these stories and sent samples of my ink and brush work. It happened to be at a time when artists were in fairly short supply. All the good ones were always booked up, or not doing *Star Wars*. I was welcomed quickly for my art and sent stories to illustrate.

I was also very lucky in the fact I came into fandom about the time printing was becoming affordable. Until then, zines were either photo-copied—at a time when even those machines were hard to find—or done on a mimeo machine. My style of art, with strong areas of black and dynamic thick and thin lines, would never have reproduced well on either method; mimeo in particular required a very controlled, thin line and open areas, or you'd have a nightmare of smeared ink. The printed sheets were still hand collated and stapled. It was a number of years before regular binding came in, often comb bound. When color printing for covers became feasible, it was like someone opened the floodgates.

I stipulated firmly that I wanted only Han-centric plots and no "kills" or graphic sex—this was when Lucas was sending out cease and desist letters left and right and everyone was shocked and unnerved. We'd been lulled by the permissiveness Paramount had begun to accord *Trek* fandom. Lucas was very different, and pretty paranoid. He'd relentlessly copyrighted everything down to Han Solo's belt buckle. Fans were either angry—as Lucas seemed ready to either shut the fandom down at the gate or impose strictures so tight nothing could practically be done—or genuinely worried and not wanting to get in trouble with the law. Lucas' cease-and-desist orders were worded to be intimidating. But fortunately, I suspect some of his own people, veterans of the circling and posturing that Paramount and the *Star Trek* fans had gone through, set him straight. We got breathing room. I didn't want to get dragged into trouble with Lucas, but I also didn't want to illustrate problematic stories, anyway.

My "gateway" fandom was simultaneously *Star Wars* and Harrison Ford. Jane Firmstone and Kelly Hill, the editors of the Ford zine *Facets*, called me up after I'd sent them my art samples and invited me to share their room at the first MediaWest*Con in 1981. There had been two conventions previously in Lansing but this was the first one officially called MediaWest. It became the premiere fan and fanzine-centric convention for many years. I was taken aback by the invitation, as I didn't get long-distance calls out of the blue, but on a very unusual—for me—impulse, I said yes. Red eye flights, three plane changes, then a taxi and bus ride later, I met Jane and Kelly and was enfolded—the only word for it.

Later that day another artist, Martynn, arrived from Pittsburgh; she'd also be sharing the hotel room. I had sort of briefly met Martynn on the phone. I'd called Jane over a story concern, and she'd advised me to talk it over with Martynn, who had been drawing for zines for a number of years and knew the ropes and pitfalls. She couldn't have been warmer, friendlier or more helpful, with plenty of solid advice. She not only calmed my mind, she gave me a basis for dealing with editors thereafter so that I was always on fair terms with all of them.

We all stayed up, getting acquainted. . . in between collating Jane and Kelly's own zine, which had to be ready the next morning to take to the con and sell. Headfirst into fandom, and I never truly came up for air for over 35 years.

It was the headiest time of my life. That first con, we ended up with eight in the room—some in sleeping bags—and were "green room" for the "townies" changing hall costumes. I could liken it to the famous scene in the Marx Brothers movie *Coconuts*, where all kinds of people keep coming into a ship stateroom, with no one leaving until Harpo is sleeping atop the seething mass! I got through the con on no sleep and a lot of adrenalin, came home wiped to the bone—and loved every second.

I'd not only met people who shared my passions, but I was plunged into a world of so many fandoms, hall costumes, masquerades, a banquet with awards, an art show, a dealers' room where you could buy things I'd never imagined existed, and just a whole lot of quirky, enthusiastic people: inventive, spontaneously creative, smart, and easy to meet. Not one soul talking about a mortgage, or so-and-so ditching so-and-so. They talked about books, movies, TV, stage.

The convention would secure an entire hotel for a long holiday weekend; like gypsies, we were safely among our own kind and could play freely. Every room would stand open with partiers spilling into the halls, mingling with the overflow from the party next door and across the way. VCR tapes, and later DVDs, played in machines, all showing clips and episodes from the fandom of choice. The only entrée required was an interest in that fandom: grab a fistful of popcorn or pretzels and a Coke, sit on the floor in the corner, and be happily proselytized into whichever passion of the folks throwing the party—or wander on to the next room and another fandom.

Costumed characters strolled the halls, some so beautifully realized they were camera-ready. It was, I suspect, like the hallucinatory, surreal experience of Mardi Gras in New Orleans, fueled by short sleep, irregular meals, and an overload of sensory stimulation. No wonder we couldn't wait to get back there next year. We'd never live so intensely the rest of the year.

I could have been starry-eyed very easily. Fortunately, I didn't get into fandom until I was 30 and had my balance. I've warned many a young fan coming in behind me that fandom is only a microcosm of the larger world and you have to act accordingly; not be too open and trusting, don't lead with your heart or your chin, and though these were passions, not to take everything so seriously that you couldn't see a measure of moderation and signs to be wary.

But in the main—the early days of fandom, during the huge influx of so many more drawn in by *Star Wars* than *Star Trek* previously—were kind of innocent and open. *Trek* was a large fandom and had already begun to get organized, but it was more focused, still very much in the camp of Science Fiction. *Star Wars,* with its fairy tale plot line and the budget to depict the trappings of the environment in what was then state-of-the-art effects, appealed to a larger base. The world of *Star Wars* was so vividly realized, it became a genuine social phenomenon. It ignited passion in such a broad swath of the population, it had to be constantly referenced in the mainstream, and thus embedded itself lastingly into the popular culture. For many, it's become a lifestyle even yet. And it swept *Star Trek* up along with it, so that fandom became even bigger.

The atmosphere was electric with everything seeming possible. Fans wanted to take part. It's the kind of wonderful creativity when the castles in the air build ever higher, each contributing and adding to it; not one-upmanship, but a joyous flocking to "put up the barn" together. Invention and ideas seethed everywhere, especially in those convention rooms and hallways, over a meal or drinks or coffee and into the wee hours, when we could solve anything.

The entrepreneurship that also came out of that brainstorming had to tread a careful line. Media fandom has always celebrated stories and characters that are copyrighted. Fans operated in a gray area, citing "fair usage" dependent on the sufferance of studios. It took some years before the owners realized, in allowing fans some latitude, they were getting a huge free PR machine. We were building their core audience for them. They've always had a slight tug-o-war with fandom; they woo us. San Diego Comic Con has gone from a little comics lovers' venue to a trade show for the entertainment industry as well as the place for every author, artist, and actor in the world; it's a monster. But they don't own us, we're free agents; we feel as proprietary over the works as they do, and with a sense that our love is the purer for not thinking of it only as a franchise. And so the little dance twirls on. . . In the meantime, fandom consolidated into a true subculture, with little vendors popping up to address the needs of the "citizens." In an era when the lemonade stand had gone the way of Norman Rockwell, these were the first notions of business for many, especially women.

All that is what fandom was for me. As for a definition, I'd have to go with the opportunity to live in a lifelong dream, though that's what it became, not what pulled me in. I came along just at the tail end of the golden age of periodical fiction and magazines like *Collier's* and the weekly version of *Saturday Evening Post*, which featured excellent fiction, all illustrated by the last great illustrators—artists I had idolized, followed, and saved clippings of their work. By the time I was old enough to seek work, that venue had all but vanished. I was lucky to get jobs in art departments, a lot of them, and did a considerable variety of art, but none of it was story illustration, no chance to flex a lifetime of study and preparation. Fandom made me be in demand—my technique was fast, and I often got tapped to step in on a story whose illustrator didn't come through in time for publication.

I got to live my dream in fandom. I got to apply the lessons I'd learned from master illustrators, to the point where editors quickly stopped trying to direct me and just left a story in my hands, knowing I'd recognize what scenes and actions needed depicting and how. I counted my ledger, which I kept. I illustrated for over 60 different zines and I stopped counting the art when, not counting covers, I passed a thousand. I even found time to contribute some fiction as well.

Artist Sue Perry Lewis (as she was named then) got me into costuming, and I loved that. I never entered the masquerades, being happy to walk around in a hall costume because I didn't want to tie up precious "con time" in rehearsals; so I never got into the growth of that part of fandom, its politics and evolution. I entered work in the art shows. One year at the World Fantasy Convention, I didn't attend and only sent my work. Unfortunately, I have the dubious distinction of one of mine being the only piece of art ever to be stolen from their show. I wish I could take it as a compliment, but it was the year *2010* hit the theaters and the planet Jupiter was a large feature in that painting.

My memories of fandom in the main are happy ones: many conventions, including World Cons and Dragon Cons, so many people with whom I interacted well. I'd spent a solitary life until fandom, an only child raised as a "short adult." Though I was long an adult by the time I entered fandom, it gave me the chance to experience a heady youth I'd never had. I had more acquaintances and so many who knew me only through my artwork, it could get hard to keep up. But I met and have kept some of my dearest friends, a close circle of perhaps six or seven, with maybe another ten still close but not interacted with as frequently. We met through a shared interest, but by now, after nearly 40 years, we've shared births, deaths, weddings, divorces, job woes, personal issues, all that friends can do.

I never "dropped" a fandom, though I've had a few dry up and go dormant on me. When I stopped going to conventions, I pretty much stopped doing illustration as well. *Star Wars* was going subdued, print zines were becoming fewer, and for all I'd loved fandom, navigating the high drama, politics, and upheavals in such a necessarily volatile environment had taken its toll on my energy and desire to deal. My home and work circumstances had evolved, and I was no longer in the same place in my life. I became my parents' help, and then my aunt's 24-7 caregiver. I had to be a "grownup."

Now retired and on my own, I have some time to sit back and greet a new film or show, with the same old enthusiasm and excitement I did before. I never actually stopped being a fan, just one active in fandom. I have kept an admiration for and an avuncular interest in Harrison Ford, and to a lesser extent the other "crushes" of those years, but I never expected to take to heart another actor. Along came *Pirates of the Caribbean*. In the long run, I placed my passion and affection in the Jack Sparrow character rather than the actor Johnny Depp. That was the last fandom I contributed art to, doing some illustrations for one of the few remaining print zines, and also a series of *Pirates of the Caribbean* cartoon strips. The latter I published in another zine as a portfolio collection, and also posted to the Internet within a fan group, Black Pearl Sails, and ultimately on its archive site.

Having "broken the ice" with Jack Sparrow, I started taking note of Tom Hiddleston, both as his Marvel character, Loki, and the actor in his own right. I realistically don't expect paragons, but it matters to me if the people I admire are worth admiring.

Besides movies and TV, I have time again for books like *Night Circus* by Erin Morgenstern, *The St. Mary's Chronicles,* and the *Invisible Library* series. I continue to cherish C. J. Cherryh's *Foreigner* series as I have for years. I'm thrilled—and relieved—to see one of my favorite books, *Good Omens*, which I've loved for 30 years, be made into a nigh perfectly done mini series.

After all these years—nearly 40—I'd only been peripherally aware of *Doctor Who*. But being taken with and following the actor, David Tennant, from his role in *Good Omens*, I've just discovered his years of tenure on *Doctor Who* as the Tenth Doctor. The show itself has captivated me, and I'll likely work my way through all the Doctors from the show's revival in 2005. (I might eventually go back to take a look at the "Classic" doctors, 1963—1987, too).

Last year, I undertook a major clear out and organizing of my houschold and belongings. I donated all my own carved marionettes to the Center for Puppetry Arts in Atlanta. A 23-piece, carved wooden Nativity I'd made over several Christmases for my mother is now on permanent display in the library at La Grange College, La Grange, GA. Most of my wood portrait dolls are in the hands of friends and some private collectors. I sold my band saw and tools. With arthritis, I no longer have the hand strength to carve. I may be a spectator now, but I find that I'm still a fan. I guess you never really stop being one.

interview © Wanda Lybarger

ROBERTA ROGOW
Like-Minded Obsessives

*"What really turned me on was the opportunity to write and be
published in a real, live magazine that other people read! When I
picked up fanzines at that first* Star Trek *con, I knew I had found my
place. People liked what I wrote, were willing to comment on it... I
learned my craft through those comments."*
—Roberta Rogow

My background... born and bred New Yorker... born in Brooklyn,
raised in Queens, educated in Queens public schools, even attended
Queens College CUNY (1958-1962), and majored in Music and
Theater. I was going to take Broadway by storm. . . only I didn't.
Instead, I married Murray Rogow, a PR hustler like the guy in *Sweet
Smell of Success*, but a lot nicer than the character Tony Curtis played!
I was a Bourgeois Bohemian housewife for seven years, then I got my
Master of Library Science at Columbia University, and got a job in
Paterson NJ. Moved to NJ in 1971... but I still consider myself a New
Yorker. My daughters, however, insist they are Jersey Girls.

My Family... Jewish Radicals in the 1930s, met at Brooklyn College.
My father, Stanley Winston, spent 40 years as a corporation lawyer,
then did what he always wanted to do and became an actor, with his
feature role as Uncle Louie in *Tony'n'Tina's Wedding* Off Broadway.
When he couldn't read lines any more (at age 90!) he became the
bodhran drummer in an Irish pub band, which he did almost to the day
of his death at 95. My mother, Shirley Winston, was a psychologist, got
her PhD in Psychic Healing, was a pioneer in that field. She also loved
science fiction... the two of us ran a semi-pro-zine (we paid for stories!)
from 1987 to 1992 until she got ill and could not continue.

When I got into fandom, my parents would take the kids while I
went to a NY convention... the girls were jealous, I was having fun and
they were with Grandma! So I started bringing them to conventions
with me. Louise is now a computer programmer in Virginia who has
just started working with computer animation for podcasts and
videos; Miriam works for American Express at the San Francisco
Airport. Miriam writes fanfic online, Louise is into cosplay (she goes to

Steampunk cons as "Lizzie Borg-den"). As for Louise's offspring, he's working his way through videogaming. So I guess the fannish bug penetrated the entire family.

Murray was bemused by my fanac... he was the Enabler, the Mundane who put up with it all. Of course, it helped that my fanzine sales were a definite addition to the family income!

Fandom for me is community. Whether it's people who *do* something (like filk) or *like* something (like *Star Trek* or Anime). They come together to discuss their obsession, and find like-minded souls, support each other, and defend each other against an unfriendly Outside World.

Gateway fandom... For me, *Star Trek*. I had watched the show from the beginning, then the re-runs. I ran into Devra Langsam, one of the leaders of the *Star Trek* Convention Committee, at a library conference, and she mentioned there would be another one. Murray suggested I go... and I was off and running! Of course, I knew about science fiction fandom, from reading about it in magazines like *Galaxy* and *Analog,* but I didn't realize I could be part of it.

What really turned me on was the opportunity to *write* and be published in a real, live magazine that other people read! When I picked up fanzines at that *Star Trek* con, I knew I had found my place. People liked what I wrote, were willing to comment on it. . . I learned my craft through those comments.

Of course, there was more. I did needlepoints, I made costumes, I wrote and performed my parody filk songs.

I started *TrexIndex* because I read half a story, couldn't find the rest, and as a brand-new librarian, I was annoyed there was no index like the Readers' Guide to tell me where the stories were. I did the *TrexIndex* for 10 years, until things got too complex. Now there is computer access, and *TrexIndex* is obsolete.

I started my fanzine *Grip* as a way of introducing new writers into fandom. Even then, the fanzines were being produced by top-flight people, many of whom became well-known writers and editors in the SF/Fantasy field. *Grip* wasn't very polished, but it was fun... and did what it was supposed to do, got people writing and drawing. I did it from 1978 to 1996, then the bottom dropped out of the fanzine market. People were able to get their fannish fix online, and I had a contract to write a Real Book... so that was the end of that.

Communication... this was BC—Before Computers. Mostly telephone... and wow! Were my phone bills high! My husband was furious, and I spent far too much time on the phone. Snailmail, of course. I even took a PO Box to handle it, so I wouldn't get crammed up with mail. Letter-columns in fanzines, and a few fanzines that were simply letter-cols. And conventions, but at that time, those weren't within my pocketbook or time. I was a working Mom, remember.

Conventions... this was the time of the Great Schism. There were the SF TruFen, who decried Trekkies as being middle-aged hausfraus and silly girls going nuts over Spock, and the Trek people, who considered the SF types snobs who never really read the books they were so hotly defending. Eventually, they met in the middle, but in the late 1970s/early 1980s, there was a real divide. And then the money people got in... Creation Cons, for one. They brought in actors, not writers... and that raised prices for con-goers, many of whom were youngsters on strict budgets.

I was much older. A lot of the people in *Star Trek* fandom were married women with children, in their late 30s and even 40s, but there were plenty of "kids" in their teens as well. The main difference was the gender divide. SF ran to males, *Trek*/Media ran to females. When the Nerds realized there were Nerdettes out there, they produced... Nerdlings! Who are now running the cons!

Controversies? Oooh, there's a hot-button topic! I was very intolerant of K/S and other "slash," what are now called "ship" stories. I didn't doubt that there were same-sex couples on the Enterprise (I even put one into a story), but Kirk and Spock weren't among them! A lot of those stories were really graphic... and some verged on sadistic. And I could not deal with *Blake's 7*; I thought the whole premise was immoral and said so. I lost several friends along the way.

I've mellowed considerably since then. Age has its virtues, and one is that one learns there are several sides to most questions... unless one becomes ossified in beliefs. I prefer to think I've grown nicer.

Friendships... I've had many over the years. I keep in contact via Facebook and I am always happy to pick up friendships at conventions. I've kept in touch with Jacqueline Lichtenberg, Devra Langsam, and Crystal Paul. I met Kathy Sands around 1983. I've made a whole new set of friends since 2004, when I took over filk programming at Lunacon... and once I started being published as a mystery writer in the 1990s, I found a whole new fandom. So I've been around the block a couple of times.

Life being what it is, I don't have regular meetings with these people. I really regret not being able to see people except via Zoom... but I'm still here!

What I'm doing now? Writing mysteries set in SF or alternate history universes! I don't do fanfic any more. . . but the last filk I wrote was for *The Mandalorian*. So I keep up my fannish connections.

I've attended several virtual cons this summer. I'm planning more, come Fall, and I suspect this is where fandom will go for a while.

interview © Roberta Rogow

LESLIE FISH
Activism and an Eyrie of Hope

"Fandom gave me a friendly and intelligent community, and then a career. Primarily, it put me in touch with a lot of good friends, good ideas, and arts I loved. I have hundreds of memories of fandom. Including a lot I can't mention in public."
—Leslie Fish

Leslie Fish has been a well-known filker, writer, blogger, and word-smith in fandom for decades. What's less known about her is that she comes from an immigrant/Native American family, knew (Senator) Tom Hayden in his prime 1960s protesting period, and the reason why she's always armed. She wrote on her blog,[2] "I've been a writer and singer all my adult life; I've made my name and fame and living off of words—and I know their definitions, and powers, and limitation.

"To which, I will add that words and music may have a powerful *influence*, which is the ability to *make people listen seriously to what you have to say*—but they don't have *power*—which is the ability to *force people to do your will*. The only way words can have *power* is if you can back them up with a gun, of some form, held to somebody's head. I have gained a lot of influence in my life, but *I have never had power*.

"The only thing I ever said to somebody whom I had a gun pointed at was, 'Go away!' (which he did). And despite the temptation of it, I've never wanted power, either. It's not only the most addictive drug in the world but the most corruptive; power corrupts even the intellect. Heroin is safer!"

She was raised in New Jersey, "In suburbs within walking distance of Newark: East Orange and South Orange, respectively" in the 1950s. "I sometimes thought I'd die of boredom there. I couldn't wait to escape, and college was the best escape offered. I managed to get my grades up to the point where the U. of Michigan would take me, and off I went."

Her father was a dentist, from a Polish/Jewish and Hungarian immigrant family."Grand-Pop was called 'Icha Meyer' back in

---

[2] http://lesliebard.blogspot.com/

the old country, because he was the biggest Jewish guy in the village. They used to have him test draft horses; if he couldn't push the horse over, the customer would buy it. He also worked as a bootlegger, the liquor hidden in a farm-cart full of produce, drawn by a small horse. One night the Czar's revenuers (this was Russian Poland) caught him and demanded to search his cart. He humbly acquiesced, but he also unharnessed his horse—and while the revenuers were bent over his cart, he *threw the horse at them.* Once they were safely down, he re-hitched the horse and drove it on down the road. No, he wasn't arrested, and the revenuers left him alone thereafter.

"He-he-heh. Can you imagine what they reported to their boss when they woke up, and what he said to them afterward?

"What made Grand-Pop emigrate was the case of his watch. In those days, watches (all pocket type) were handmade, very expensive, and considered jewelry. Grand-Pop worked and saved for a long time to buy that pocket-watch, and then somebody stole it.

"Grand-Pop was still steaming over that theft when he went to one of the town's weekly dances. There he saw a neighbor showing off his new pocket-watch—which Grand-Pop recognized. An argument ensued. The neighbor threw a punch—bad idea—which Grand-Pop blocked and then counter-punched. That one punch killed the thieving neighbor.

"Grand-Pop had to get out of town fast. Fortunately, he had a distant relative who, rarity of rarities, had a government job. The relative got Grand-Pop off to the port city of Gdansk, where he caught the first ship he could find that was going to America. It was a cattle-boat, and Grand-Pop worked his passage to America shoveling cattle manure out of the hold.

"Perhaps this is where I got my lifelong allergy to bullshit.

"When he landed at Ellis Island, Grand-Pop knew no more English than he'd managed to pick up on the ship, and he let the immigration clerk translate his name to 'Fish', but he was determined to learn more. He spent his days at the American School, learning American English, American History, American Law, and everything else he needed to become a citizen.

"He spent his days pushing a wheelbarrow around the streets and alleys, looking for bits of paper and cloth, and when his wheelbarrow was full, he wheeled it down to the paper mill where he sold his load. This brought him enough money to pay for a bunk-bed in a six-man room and two meals per day.

"When he got his citizenship, and learned enough English, he moved up to a job in a leather factory, cutting soles for shoes.

"While at an open-air union meeting (forbidden, of course) he met and fell in love with a young Hungarian lady. It turns out (which I didn't learn until years later, when I met folksinger Frank Gasperik) that she was the sister of Frank Gasperik's maternal grandmother. They had to run away (to the city of Newark, if you please) to get married, because their wooing scandalized both families; Grand-Pop was Jewish (rapidly becoming Reform Jewish) while Grandma, being Hungarian, was Catholic.

"Anyway, the wedding was fortunate for Grandma, because it got her out of New York and her job in the Triangle Shirtwaist Factory, which burned down a few years later (in 1911), killing most of the girls who worked there. Around then Grandpa joined the Industrial Workers of the World (IWW), which likewise I didn't learn until years later, when I told Pop about joining the Anti-War movement in college. Eventually I joined the IWW myself, which I suppose makes me a hereditary Wobbly."

Her mother's family, a mix of French from Canada, and Chippewa, had been in North America a lot longer, according to Ancestry. com.

"My (Viking blood) came by way of the Chippewa, who allied with the Vikings (back in the 11th century) against the Iroquois—aka 'Skraelings'. The alliance lasted until a plague decimated the Vikings and sent them back to Iceland. The Chippewa kept the knowledge of metal-working (particularly copper) and those Archaic Scandinavian genes."

She says her musical talent might have come from there, as her great-grandmother was a Chippewa medicine-singer, who left family letters. "I never saw them. My brother got them." Great-grandma moved to the nearest big city—Elmira, New York—became a professional singer, and married a French-Canadian of whom nothing more is said, except that he gave her two daughters. Grandma went to work in a large department store and eventually became a buyer for Bamberger's. She also ran into a wastrel younger son of a European aristocrat family. "Scottish-Austrian, we suspect—or else north Italian. It depends on whether his name was 'Von Shelleau' or 'Fonshello'. Grandma's family was very secretive, intent on concealing the family's secrets—such as 'non-White blood', a big deal in those days. Her mother was a professional musician who played piano and eventually became a music teacher in the northern New Jersey school system.

A prolific reader, Leslie read comic books at three, such as *Bucky Bug* (a Disney comic.) "He-he-heh. Yes, that's the first book I can remember reading all by myself. I remember I was stumped for days over the word 'mules'." She read "more comic books, mostly—and I came to recognize the artistic styles of Wally Wood, Steve Ditko (original Spider-Man artist), and Jack Davis. I eventually graduated to print books, starting with *Star Rangers*, by Andre Norton.

"I remember how my mother taught me, with the Alphabet Song, alphabet blocks, and reading me *Grimm's Fairy Tales* every night at bedtime, while pointing out the words as she read them. I strongly recommend that system."

Her family never supported her interest in what's known now as fandom. She was "teased, scolded, and threatened for wasting my time on 'that jonk'. The only time my pop ever indulged me in 'that jonk' was when he took me to see *Destination Moon*, first-run in the theaters in 1950. The only reason I can figure out his doing it was that he'd heard somewhere that the script was written by somebody famous." That famous person was Robert H. Heinlein, since the movie was based off his novella of the same name.

Then, her father burned her comics.

"Ah, that's a story. Pop could never endure any challenge to his authority. Once he came upon me reading after I was supposed to be in bed (IIRC it was one of Albert Payson Terhune's books about collies), and Pop was so incensed that he tore up the book—never minding that it wasn't mine but a new library book. It took me months to pay back the library for that book. Then one day when I was sixteen, I came on him beating my little brother (ten years old) with a belt, and little bro' was wailing 'What did I do? What did I do wrong?' Seeing that this was unjust, I ran into my room and got my riding crop (I was doing a lot of horseback riding at the time), grabbed Pop's arm and threatened him with the crop while snarling 'Leave my brother alone!' Pop was so incensed that he let Petey go and turned on me instead.

"I let him get the riding crop away from me and chase me into my room, since that likewise got him away from my brother. Once in my room, Pop tried to hit me with the crop, howling 'How dare you raise a hand to ME!' (*WHAP!*) I easily fended off the blow, so Pop tried again, and again, but I blocked his blows every time. After a dozen or so abortive ME!-*WHAP*s, he paused to pant for breath.

"At that point it dawned on him that I was not only faster than he was, but he was *looking UP at me*. I was taller than he was. I didn't make a move against him, just stood there ready to fend him off again, but he looked honestly *scared*. He ducked past me to escape, and at the door he paused to collect his wits and give himself an excuse to

cover his pride. He yelled 'It's comic books that make you act like this!
I'm going to burn all your comic books!'—and ran out the door.

"My brother and I spent the next half-hour (while Pop was digging
into the liquor cabinet to work up his nerve) hiding all our comic
books in various hidey-holes—except for a few that we didn't care
about, which we left in an easily found space as sacrifices to Pop's
pride. Unfortunately, he found a few more of our hidey-holes, so we
lost some classic comics (which would be worth thousands of dollars
today) along with the throwaways.

"Pop carried his haul out to the back patio, threw them in a metal
garbage barrel, poured lighter fluid on them, and set them on fire.
Books being a little harder to burn than he expected, they took time to
burn. I used the time to trot up to my bedroom, come back with my
alto recorder, and play Scottish dirges over the pyre. Pop stewed and
steamed while he burned the books, but he didn't look at me.

"That was the last time that Pop ever tried to beat me, or my brother."

By junior high she got involved in the struggle for Civil Rights,
producing pamphlets and flyers in the "late '50s and very early '60s,
actually." This led to involvement in other struggles over the decades
for women's liberation, Gay liberation, and other causes.

"And don't forget the radical Labor movement—and the Wobblies,"
she adds. "I did my share of grass roots politicking too, but I'm a lot
less well known for that."

Then came college. She went to the University of Michigan in Ann
Arbor on early acceptance in 1962. The first night, she picked up her
six-string Gibson Hummingbird guitar and joined a picket line—it
was "a silent Stand-in For Fair Housing"—of the Students for a Demo-
cratic Society, better known in the 1970s as SDS.

It was on that picket line where she met Tom Hayden, social
activist and radical who was arrested as one of "Chicago Seven" in
1968, was a Freedom Rider in the South, and later a California State
Senator. At the time, Hayden was the president of the SDS.

Fish joined the SDS.

She also became an anarchist. "Probably around Junior year in
college, when my avid political reading—and ever-more-disillusioning
political experience—led me to a collection of essays called *Patterns of
Anarchy* (Leonard I. Krimerman, Lewis Perry, 1966), which I'd
recommend to anyone. Of course, I argued over all of it, but when I
saw its applicability—when I started discovering little Anarchist
enclaves everywhere—I was convinced.

"This is why I'm so royally PO'd by those thugs who dare to call themselves Anarchists when they're so obviously Fascist extortionists. I'd love to deport the lot of them to Liberia, or Mecca, or the Mauritanian slave market."

One night she helped take several young men across to Canada to escape the U. S. draft. "It's somewhere on my blog, The Underground Sailboat—about taking kids across the Great Lakes to Canada while I was in college. I suspect that the statute of limitations on that is long since passed."

The University of Michigan was when she started singing in earnest, writing folk songs. She bought a new guitar as well. "That's when I obtained Monster, a 12-string made from an old Martin by Jeremy Kammerer. I bought it at Herb David's guitar shop in Ann Arbor. I also drew the logo for his business, which the shop uses to this day."

She also adopted three kittens, naming them for anarchists: Makhno, after a Ukrainian revolutionary, Kropotkin, a Russian revolutionary, and Bakuninn, after the nineteenth century founder of collectivist anarchism. This led to her development of "an experimental breed called 'Silverdust', recognized by the International Cat Association. I bred them for intelligence, and they've got it—and they use it for their own furry purposes, which are not necessarily ours. They're brilliant thieves of people food."

In 2015, she defined them on her Facebook page as "derived from the Oriental Shorthair, which in turn descends from the Siamese, and these little creatures do indeed have the slender body-build, big ears and eyes, personality, and voice of the Siamese. There the resemblance ends, for the Silverdust has a roaned-grey silver coat, gold-green eyes, workable thumbs on each forepaw, a larger-than-normal skull with a larger-than-normal brain inside, and remarkable high intelligence."

She started smoking. "My Sophomore year in college, there was a serial killer somewhere in town who targeted co-eds that looked *just like me*, and because of my anti-war work I didn't dare carry a weapon. I took some basic Karate lessons, and also a friend suggested that I always carry a lit cigarette when outdoors, so I could use it to stab an attacker's hands.

"While I was carrying lit cigarettes, it was natural to puff on them. I did, and found that I liked them. I'd always suffered from low blood-pressure (so low I had trouble getting out of a bathtub) and low metabolism, but smoking perked up both of them."

She graduated in 1966, but did some post-graduate years in Ann Arbor. She spent a year doing anti-war organizing at Michigan State University in Lansing.

MSU was also where she discovered a new life-changing interest: *Star Trek*. The television series was first broadcast between 1966-1969, but lived on in reruns. "By then I was living in Chicago, working with Vietnam Veterans Against the War.

"It was the evening of the day when Nixon announced the end of the Vietnam War (March 29, 1973), and I was at the HQ of the local chapter of Vietnam VVAW. We greeted the news with a vast, exhausted sigh. I got up and strolled over to the U of Chicago Student Union, where I found a bunch of kids watching a rerun of the *Star Trek* episode, *The Mark of Gideon*. I was instantly hooked."

She began to write what are now called "filks", a term she didn't discover until 1977. She bought the 1966 and 1967 James Blish *Star Trek* adaptations, and started writing her own stories.

"In one of the commercially-published *Star Trek* books there was the address of the *Star Trek* Welcommittee (begun in 1972). I signed up with them, which garnered me the names and addresses of various fanzines, and an announcement of a ST convention in a city I could get to. At the con I found lots more fanzines, and off I went from there." She especially became a fan of the Michigan State University well-known fanzine *Warped Space*, first published in 1974.

Her long *Star Trek* story, *The Weight*, was serialized over eleven years in *Warped Space*, starting in issue #17 in 1976. She won a Fan Q (Fan Quality) award for Best Author, for the first part in 1977. The finished version, with some attendant short stories, was later published as *The Weight, Collected*, clocking in at 520 pages according to the Fanlore website.

She remembered one of fandom's earliest and biggest controversies. "I was involved up to my eyeballs in the Kirk/Spock controversy. It helped that I had a couple of Gay friends. After a few books on *Star Trek* had admitted in public that the relationship between Kirk and Spock was not just professional respect but love, a lot of fans asked why it couldn't go further. Trek fans being largely women then, we knew all too well that 'love' was often a euphemism for sex. Why shouldn't people in a progressive future society have no problem accepting a male-male love affair? This spawned the 'K/S controversy': could or couldn't Kirk and Spock be lovers? I took the pro-K/S side, and wrote a few stories ('Shelter', 'Poses', and 'This Deadly Innocence', currently available online at the Archive Of Our Own website) and several essays in support of the theory, which was ultimately accepted by Trek fandom in general."

After college, she moved to Chicago for 12 years. Among other jobs (including go-go dancer in a strip joint), she worked at the B&O Railroad as a yard clerk, writing a song, "The Grain Train", about these times. She was "the first woman to have a job in the railyard since World War II", but problems with police prevented getting a permanent job there.

"Before I settled down to being a full-time filker (when I could get work!) and writer (fiction and satire, sadly underpaid), I worked as an under-editor on three newspapers (including *The Industrial Worker*, a Union newspaper), two magazines, and one radio station—all small and local. Yeah, Kipling was right about 'The Press'!

"I took up shooting while I lived in Chicago, took the training, and always carry a firearm with me. That reminds me, I have to renew my concealed carry permit soon. I don't need it within Arizona, which is a 'Constitutional Carry' state, but I need it for travel elsewhere. I can shoot a pistol reliably within the 7 ring at 25 yards.

"One startling thing I learned from target shooting is that to hit the target reliably you have to control your breathing and heart rate, and to do that you have to put yourself into a Zen-like meditative state. Do that often enough, and you condition yourself to drop into that Zen state every time your hands close around a gun. It's a built-in guarantee that I'll never shoot in a panic. I wrote a song about that—"The Zen of Cool"—for a police training course."

She also started the IWW band, The Dehorn Crew, who ended up doing an album of her *Star Trek* songs, *Folksongs For Folks Who Ain't Even Been Yet*, in 1976. It was re-released as a single CD along with *Solar Sailors* in 2002.

Then, in 1982, she moved to San Francisco.

"I'd determined to leave Chicago after the Bad Winter of 1979, but—as the song says—'Getting out of Chicago is easier said than done'. Having the promise of a job (with Off-Centaur Publications) and at least a temporary place to stay in California, I joined a small convoy with some other fans and headed out.

"Alas, the Chicago weather was reluctant to let us escape.

"Ferocious snowstorms made us turn south first, all the way to Texas, before we could turn west. Adding to the fun was an independent truckers' strike and a lot of subsequent police cars on the road. We had to stop several times (usually at truck stops, crowded with striking truckers,) and wait for the blizzard to let up. At Amarillo, the cops were pulling drivers off the highway, and we had to sneak past a cop car to get back on the road. The storms finally let up when we got to Road Forks, New Mexico—and if anyone asks, the truck stop there is the most elaborate I've ever seen.

"When we got into California, other members of the convoy began peeling off and heading to their own destinations. I made the last 50 miles into Albany alone, riding over a stretch of double-decker highway where the tarmac was rippled into waves from decades of truck traffic, and it was like surfing on wheels. I found it ironic that that particular length of highway later came down in the Loma Prieta earthquake. I'm delighted that I've never afterward had to drive through a snowstorm; that epic drive was enough for a lifetime."

She met her future husband, Robert "Rasty Bob" Ralston in California. "Actually, it was back in the '80s, at a tree planting at Forever Forests in Ukiah. He was taping the event, and I got to carry his battery pack. He still has those recordings, though they're in pretty poor shape."

It was there that she met professional writer—and soon to be friend—Hugo Award-winning author, C. J. Cherryh, at a West Coast convention. Leslie listened to the (very) shy author sing at an open filksing, and afterward complimented the original song. The next day, Cherryh asked to meet Leslie at the hotel bar, and they hit it off. The upshot of the good manners: after some interaction, a request to submit to Cherryh's new series *Merovingen Nights*, according to a Fish's write-up on the Prometheus Music website. "The moral of which is 'Always be nice to neo-fans; remember, thou too wert a neo once'."

Then there were the unusual jobs—like a S&M Dominatrix. "*Snerk* I needed the money for medical bills (I didn't have health insurance then), and I must say it was educational."

In 1993, she moved to Phoenix, Arizona, then to Mesa, and finally to Buckeye.

"When I was three, my parents started spending their winters in Tucson, Arizona. There I learned to ride horses, and fell in love with them. I also fell in love with Arizona, and swore that someday I'd get back there. It took a few years, but I succeeded."

She started her blog *lesliebard. blog. spot* in 2010, posting life, political and fannish commentary. She has never given up going to fannish conventions. "Oh yes! I go to conventions whenever I can, and I follow the online 'zines likewise... I had to pull back from publishing in *Trek* zines when I became a professional filksinger and pro writer, because I had only so much time and energy in a day. I went to a lot more conventions, but they weren't purely *Trek* cons."

A friend remembered Leslie Fish leading parades out of the Statler Hilton: "I've been to so many Sci-Fi conventions that I can't remember which one that was, but of course it had to be a New York con. Yes, that would have been in the late '80s."

In 2013, she took a train to Lunacon, held in Rye Brook, New York, as Filk Guest of Honor. She was armed. "I covertly brought my firearm and sword-cane with me. I'm never unarmed. Back when I got seriously into Paganism in Chicago, I joined the Cult of Mithra and got to the third level of initiation. As such, I took a mighty oath never to be unarmed—never to oblige other people to do my defending for me. I've stayed true to that oath."

In November 2011, she married "Rasty Bob" Ralston. They moved to a house in Buckeye, Arizona, and bought the lot next door to start an orchard. Mother Nature attacked with windstorms, and then gophers. Lots of gophers.

"Grrrr! I'm still at war with the goddam gophers! They're Pocket Gophers, and their holes are too small for my cats to get into, though my little furry familiars do manage to catch one now and again. They destroyed our attempt at a vegetable garden, and it seems there's nothing they like to eat better than the sweet succulent roots of the fig tree. They destroyed three fig trees in a row, until I gave up and switched to pomegranates, a couple citrus trees, and a pecan. Grumble-grumble-grumble."

Unfortunately, two of her "Witch Cat" kittens died of scorpion bites. "And now I've declared war on scorpions, too. Whenever I can, I scatter Pyrethrum Dust and Neem Oil all over the ground. Those are two organic poisons which won't harm warm-blooded animals, such as cats. I highly recommend them (just not during the flowering season, lest they kill bees). I also live just down the block from a beekeeper who sells excellent honey, available at the local stores. Buy local!"

She won a Special Prometheus Award in 2014 for a novella—*Tower of Horses*—based in Marion Zimmer Bradley's *Darkover* series, published in the anthology, *Music of Darkover*, edited by writer Elisabeth Waters. The Award is given by the Libertarian Futurist Society.

One interesting thing happened in 2016 when she was earning $140 for two days' work as an election clerk in an Arizona primary. "By Arizona law, whenever there's a controversy about a particular ballot, it has to be inspected by two poll workers *of different parties*. Since my tiny district had nothing but Republicans, I was much in demand as the only Libertarian.

"I haven't followed up on that job because my back won't take the hours of standing around anymore. I did, however, find it quite educational. Take it from me: there is *not one* state in the union that does not already have mail-in/absentee ballots. The way to cheat on elections with mail-in ballots is simply to send out a lot of them that never arrive (say, being sent to no-longer valid addresses, or to voters who have died), so they can be snatched up and used by the unscrupulous.

"Other than that, it's remarkably hard to cheat on elections in Arizona; there are so damn many layers of security, it's amazing. In Chicago, however, election-cheating is an art form. I'm probably still voting there—Democrat, of course—all these years later."

Her work is still available from Mary Creasey at the Random_Factors Ltd. website as well as on Amazon. Her filks have been covered by many other singers over the decades. Her most famous—but personally most disliked—filk is *Banned From Argo*, the racy story of the original *Star Trek* crew on shore leave. "After it came out on my first album, and later on tape, I was asked to sing it—usually several times—at every convention I went to. I got so sick of playing that damned song that I finally put the brakes on it; no more than once a year, please!"

Many of her "fannish" friendships go back as far as thirty years. She comments that fandom, "gave me a friendly and intelligent community, and then a career. Primarily, it put me in touch with a lot of good friends, good ideas, and arts I loved." She has hundreds of memories of fandom. "Including a lot I can't mention in public." Her "gateway" fandom was the original *Star Trek*. When she entered fandom, it was "small."

Asked if she'd do it all again, she gives a resounding, "HELL, YES!!!"

Her favorite filk is 1975's "Hope Eyrie", about the 1969 landing on the Moon. "Hope Eyrie" won her a Pegasus Award in 1984 for the Best Original Filk Song. "It's been sung by dozens of musicians, ever since I recorded it on that first album. I believe there are half a dozen versions up on YouTube, which is fine with me.

"If I can be remembered for only one song, let it be that one."

interview © 2020 Leslie Fish

ELUKI BES SHAHAR/ROSEMARY EDGHILL
Born in the Mid-50s, and Still Fannish

"Trek fans invented the fannish prototype. They developed the social networks, the letterzines, the fanzines, letterzines, apas, conventions, and fannish meetups. So when Star Wars came along, the template was already there. You didn't have to struggle with what you should do with your deep fannish love of the movie, you already knew." —eluki bes shahar

I. FANFIC: THE EARLY YEARS: COMIC BOOKS, KATO, AND OPEN CHANNEL D.

My first fannish venture was a *Batman* comic book I created around the age of four. I drew it and I wrote it. (It was frustrating, because the crayons would just not make the tight lines I was looking for.) I don't quite understand where the *Batman* thing came from, but I do know that I was two years old when it started. I could walk and see through the windows of the drugstore, and all the books were all on spinner racks in those days. I put up an unholy fuss, and as a result I got out of there with the 1958 *Batman Annual*. So, boom, fannish from a very young age. I never stopped reading comic books—or Batman!—but I was mostly reading Marvel from c. 1964-1983. After that, I was driven out by the cost: I just couldn't afford to buy the books any more.

I also remember when *X-Men #1* was published, and being subject to my mother sneering "Get rid of all of that junk, it will never amount to anything!" And I sneered back many years later when I wrote two *X-Men* tie-in novels.

After *Batman*, and added to Marvel, came a severe crush on *The Man From U.N.C.L.E.* and *The Green Hornet*. I wrote fanfic for both of these. I still didn't have any fannish contact. My actual-kind-of fandom journey started later, but meanwhile...

II. *STAR TREK*: TO ME, MY X-MEN!

I saw most of Original *Trek* on its first airing. I saw most of the second and all of the third seasons, so it was probably 1968. My first episode was "Journey to Babel." And by the time the reruns came around for the summer, I adored *Star Trek*. I transcribed the episodes—wrote them down as the show was playing and then corrected it later and copied it out—not for anyone, just to have it. Tape recorders were sort of a thing of the future, then.

Being twelve, I was Embarrassingly Fannish. Of course I did what a lot of Very Young Fans did, and sent story ideas to Paramount. They sent back a letter (terrifying to a twelve-year-old) about how they couldn't read any unsolicited material.

Fast forward to 1976: I went to New York to attend a comic book convention (or: "comicon"). The PTB[3] were showcasing the reboot of the *X-Men*, written by Len Wein—*Giant-Size X-Men #93*. I was unimpressed.

Then I picked up *X-Men #94*, written by brash young newcomer Chris Claremont. Friends, I fell. And I fell HARD. *X-Men* became the fandom that ate my life.

Of course, the internet didn't exist, then. So I wrote detailed five, six, twelve-page critiques of the current issue and everything about it—with analysis and questions—and would send them off to the *X-Men*'s publisher. There was a lot of that at that time; they had addresses in the back of the comics you could write to and they had in-print letters pages. So I wrote, and all the time thinking the letters are disappearing into a great black hole...

Until one day, when I picked up the phone, and the voice on the other end said: "This is Chris Claremont in New York. Do you live anywhere near Chicago?" I was in Indianapolis at the time. Indianapolis is not anywhere near Chicago. But I said: Yes! Of course I do! And so I went to a con in Chicago to meet him—I think it was an SF con, but I don't really remember much about it.

With one thing and another, c. 1976, I packed up and moved to New Jersey. I started submitting to the only comic books that took outside submissions: the black and white comics of the Warren Magazine Group (*Creepy, Eerie,* and *Vampirella*). I sold about a dozen stories. But then the entire publishing company folded up. So I tried writing actual text short stories and sending them off to, erm, absolutely no acclaim. For my last submission, I got a return postcard from *Magazine of Fantasy and Science Fiction*—it was acid green with some Virgil Finlay art on the bottom and pre-printed rejection. All they had to do was write my name on the front, fill in the title of the story, and throw it into the mail, right? Only somebody at *F&SF* had taken the time and effort to run it through a typewriter and add the following words: *Find another hobby.*

---

[3] "Powers That Be" (ed.)

III. *THE EMPIRE STRIKES BACK*: THE EVEN-DARKER PHOENIX[4]

So at that point I pretty much figured writing wasn't for me. I went off and minded my own business, living a quiet, happy life of suburban desperation...

And then, for reasons I do not understand, I decided to go to the first showing of *The Empire Strikes Back*. It is a thing inexplicable because *Star Wars* had not particularly impressed me. I said, yeah, okay, space opera movie, fine. The guy in the black cape was cute, and that was about it. But when I saw *Empire*, it was like a religious experience. I was transformed. I wanted to live in that universe. I wanted to create that universe. I wanted that universe completely around me.

I saw *Empire* one and two times a week for its entire first run over that summer.[5] That was the first place I made contact with fans, because they were standing right there in the line with me. Eventually, we would recognize each other from previous showings and start talking.

Now, *Star Wars* fandom had a huge advantage when it began, because *Star Trek* had already paved the way and the social frameworks were still in place because the fandom had never died. *Trek* fans invented the fannish prototype. They developed the social networks, the letterzines, the fanzines, apas, conventions, and fannish meetups. So when *Star Wars* came along, the template was already there. You didn't have to struggle with what you should do with your deep fannish love of the movie, you already knew.

At that time, fannish groups were regional because you could get together easily. Four-hour phone calls were horrendously expensive, the Internet still didn't (widely) exist, and there were no cell phones. Computers, even at the beginning of the 1980s, were not a big part of Real Life. Nobody I knew had one, and few of us even owned electric typewriters. Your fan peeps were people nearby. As far as I ever discovered, all of the fannish groups thatgathered together face-to-face in real life at that time were generally gathering around the idea of putting out a fanzine of some sort.

Thus it was with me.

In 1981 (still before the Internet!)[6] fanzines were physical objects,

---

[4] This is a riff on the *X-Men* "Dark Phoenix" *Saga,* which most of you won't have heard of. But that's okay because nobody's going to read this.

[5] Movies used to run in the theatre for months at a time. Sometimes over a year, as in the case of *Star Wars.* (ed.)

In 1981 (still before the Internet!)[6] fanzines were physical objects, text and illustrations put onto paper and then reproduced by some mechanical means, with editions of anywhere between 100 and 1000. (I never did anything like a thousand. My own zines ran about 100-150 copies.) All hand-collated and hand-stapled, unless you went to the print shop and had them do it, and very few of us had that kind of money. Everything would have been so easy on the computer! But computers, internet... not a part of any of this. We produced our fanzines much in the way they would have produced them in the 19th century.

Two methods falling out of favor at the time were the dittomaker (aka spirit duplicator) and the mimeograph. Both were *literally* from the 19th century (which was when their technology was invented). Neither was art-friendly. Both required you to type out your text (without a single error!) onto a dittomaster or a stencil.

The quick-print type shops were just coming in, but most fans found them too expensive to use. The idea was to break even with the cost of creating a zine (the cost not to include any of the labor costs), and once you'd given out your free contributor copies (postage was another semi-prohibitive cost), you tried to sell the rest for—if memory recalls—somewhere between five and seven bucks. There was enormous pushback against more expensive zines. They were supposed to be labors of love. A lot of leftovers from the hippie/commune cultures were a part of fandom in its early period.

IV. HEY, KID: WANNA DO A FANZINE?

To get contributors for zines (if you weren't just publishing stories by your geographically-local friends), either you put out the word among your circle of correspondents—dear Lord, did we ever write letters in those days!—or you would run a notice in another fanzine, and you would get submissions through the mail. And then you would, or you wouldn't—I did, I made enemies—edit these submissions. And then you sent copies of the stories out to the fan artists who you had begged "illustrate it" and continued to beg, prod, and eventually threaten so the illustrations would arrive. The earliest illos in the zines were all one-pagers, as that was the easiest to drop into place, but the ambitious editors among us would sometimes re-type the entire story to make it fit around smaller illustrations. Some overachievers

---

[6] https://en.wikipedia.org/wiki/Eternal_September. Yeah, that was 1993, but it took some time to get rolling.

even did a double column method and justified the left-hand column by counting spaces. On a typewriter.

So by this point you would have what was called in the professional trade a "mechanical." That was the whole zine pasted together—frequently with the original art pasted in—and ready to be printed. You could take it to a print shop like Quick Print or Insta-print (if you had money and probably a car); you could use the IBM copier at work (if you didn't get caught); or you could use a Gestetner (if you had one).

My New Jersey group of *Star Wars* fans had one.

A Gestetner was a major investment expense for anyone at that time. They cost, I think, about $600 used. Our Gestetner was—so I was told—one of the last Gestetners with all metal parts, so it produced a sharper design, the parts didn't break and wear out, the tolerances didn't go skating off. I don't remember how the machine worked. But when you would print out all of the pieces of paper you needed to print out, you'd run them through the machine twice because you were printing on both sides. Then you had a collating party if you had friends, or a really boring weekend if you didn't.

The zine covers (no matter the method) were usually printed on a more robust stock—card stock, in fact. Sometimes this was the only element of the zine that would be done at a professional printing shop. Most of them were black ink on white stock, but a few of them were on colored stock. I remember one zine, in the early eighties (*Imperial Entanglements*, by Karen Osman) did a gorgeous cover of black and blue on metallic silver stock. Wherever your cover came from, at that point you had collated your run, added your front and back cover, and then the whole thing was fastened together in a variety of exciting and entirely idiosyncratic means. One zine run had the edge sewn up with yarn. Another one did ribbons with a bow. Ours used a type of fastening called a brad. It was yellow brass and it had what looked like a nail head and then a long piece, which you put it through the hole and bent the long pieces as flat as they would go, hoping they hadn't ripped your hands to shreds while you're doing it.

Later, I ended up among the New York (Brooklyn) fen, specifically Anne Elizabeth Zeek, Devra Langsam, Joyce Yasner, and Barbara Wenk (three of whom had been on The Committee running the early *Trek* cons). It was HEAVEN. And since these were fen who had been there in the embryonic days of Original *Trek* Fandom, I got to hear a number of the old stories...

V. *STAR TREK*: THE TRUFEN STRIKE BACK

As soon as the "True" SF Fans realized that we (female media fans) weren't going to be assimilated into their print-driven bro culture, it was War to the Knife. They said, "They're just a bunch of girls, they have girl cooties, they couldn't make it in real fandom." Even though originally fandom loved having these *Star Trek* people, because it was all girls and there were practically no girls in "True" Fandom. I mean, these girls might even look at them and possibly talk to them. But soon it started to be "They're taking over, the *Star Trek* stuff is taking over!" Apparently they couldn't seem to see that you could do both: *Star Trek* and SF.

In fact, I wrote a story on precisely that subject: "My Object All Sublime," that was professionally anthologized. There is a man who dislikes *Star Trek* a lot as "Junk SF" and thinks that if only it had never existed, there would be so many more science fiction books published.

So, he borrows a time machine from a friend—as one does—and goes into the past, and builds a VCR, which is immediately pirated and there are thousands of them in use everywhere by 1967. When *Star Trek* is first shown, there are a thousand VCRs waiting to receive it, and the time traveler thinks everyone will stay home with their tapes and the purity of science fiction will exist.

But no, he comes back to the present and finds out that all those media fans did tape their *Star Trek*—and became professional romance writers. So there's even less science fiction in the world now. His time machine has vanished, and he's "alone in a world slowly turning pink."

VI: Fanfic Today, Literature Tomorrow (and hey, THE INTERNET FINALLY GOT HERE!)

But all heavenly things come to an end, and my end was the third *Star Wars* movie: *Return of the Jedi.*

I'd been planning to take another swing at pro writing anyway, I said: No more fanfic, I'm going to put all of my precious bodily fluids into pro fiction.

I got out for 20 years. But once in, never out. Since I got back, I've written more than one million words of new fic in my new fandom. And no, I'm not saying what it is. Never Cross the Streams.

Do you want to know what the lovely thing with fanfic was, back in the day? There was no gatekeeper and it didn't matter how little money you had: you could get yourself out there—if you didn't publish or submit to a zine, you could still just send your story to all your fannish friends. There was very little barrier to entry and geographical confinement was at a minimum.

And now, with websites like AO3, barrier to entry is close to zero and fandom has become even larger.

With the shift in both culture and technology, you see the same thing happening with writing/publishing in general, because you can now write a book and publish it on Amazon. There is no longer any gatekeeper in either fannish or nonfannish writing. If the Big Five (as of this writing) professional publishing houses don't want to buy your book and publish it, you can do it yourself.

But fanfiction is not, or not merely, self-publishing. Of course, in a piece of fanfic you're scratching your own itches first, but it's also become a culture of expectation. There's a book called *Rogue Archives*—a book entirely about internet fandom—discussing how the steps differ when you write for yourself expecting to be your only reader, versus the stuff you write for other fans to read.

And here ends my tale. Go write something.

_____

interview © 2020 eluki bes shahar

MAGGIE M. NOWAKOWSKA
A Nerd Before it was Cool

"Star Wars made it impossible to have wilting heroines without a snigger about the silliness of that gambit. It broke the looking-backward habit for our fairy tales, and turned us around facing the real future, the life we were living now. And boy am I glad it did."
—Maggie Nowakowska

I wasn't born a fan. . . but pretty damn close.

It's all my mother's fault.

When I was four years old, Mom put *The Golden Book of Astronomy* in my hands, began teaching me to read, and told me that one day I would travel to the stars.

When I was six, after school, Mom drove me to the local branch library and with my first library card I took out a different kind of science book: *Space Cat Visits Venus.*

Was Mom happy? You bet.

A lifetime later, I still have the first science fiction paperback I bought myself, Ray Bradbury's *The Martian Chronicles*, and, a few years ago, I found a reprint of that *Space Cat* book.

In my basement office, I also have:

• Boxes of *Star Trek* and *Star Wars* fanzines (eh, a few other fandoms, too) stacked under a really long desk.

• Binders of fanfic manuscripts lining my bookshelves, most of the stories finished and placed in zines; some not.

• Two file drawers packed with 40-year-old letters — pages and pages and pages of letters — from fannish friends and zine editors.

• An awful lot of boxes (some even labeled properly) filled with convention badges, program books, and neat fannish toys that can be bought at science fiction conventions.

And there are some old costumes tucked away in drawers, most of which wouldn't fit me today. Someday I'll have a quilt made out of all the genre and convention t-shirts I've saved. Maybe two quilts, probably three.

I'm pretty sure Mom would approve, even if only to mutter, as she often had when alive:

"Well, at least she's never been bored."

SOME FANS run conventions; some sell their crafts, create wonderful costumes and weaponry, write and perform filk songs; some love gaming and others like to recreate fantasy universes or medieval festivals. Most of us love books, movies, small-screen drama series, and will sit for hours, talking about our favorite universes and characters.

From my mid-twenties on, my experience in media fandom, my fanac, has been grounded in words. I wrote to letterzines, loving the conversations with people I'd never met but who loved the same universes and characters I did, who read the same books I had. I wrote letters, long, single-space pages, sent to pen pals who wrote back many pages to me. I wrote—still do write—fanfic based in those universes and concerning those characters and the adventures they have. I had stories printed in paper fanzines for years, and now I've put some stories online.

Only recently have I realized that I have been doing this all my life. As a socially isolated, socially awkward girl in the 1950s, with a mother who expected me to study all the time and become a scientist, I had to amuse myself. Making up stories about the characters in books, movies, and TV shows was fun. I never imagined that anyone else liked to do the same. Fandom would enrich my life beyond all expectations, but it took me a while to find it.

Life, in fact, would have been easier if I had gotten obsessed with all the science toys Mom bought for me. I'm sure she would have been a massively involved science fiction fan herself — if she had ever found someone to talk with about all the wonders of science and the SF books she loved to read as a kid.

Similar problems for both of us.

WE LIVED in Cleveland, Ohio, above the family business: a working-class tavern on the steel-age industrial edge of the Polish immigrant neighborhood where both my parents grew up.

(During the 1920s Prohibition Era, my grandfather supplemented his steel mill work by helping rum-runners smuggle liquor from Canada across Lake Erie to Cleveland. When booze became legal again, a state liquor license was my grandfather's reward. After running three bars, he finally sold the fourth, Cricket Tavern, to my mom and dad. I think I got my adventurous genes from him.)

In the 1930s, my mom, Irene, had been an out-of-sorts teenager, a girl who read *Doc Savage* books and whatever science fiction/adventure stories she could find. Irene didn't want to quit school at age 16 as her family expected; Irene wanted to go to college.

Then World War II began. Irene joined the Women's Army Corps for a year, worked for a defense company till the war ended. Irene turned 25 in 1945 and her younger brother became the first kid in the family who attended a university.

Irene continued to work after the war. In '46, she married Stanley and eventually they had two children. Life was busy. Stanley would open the tavern at dawn for night-shift workers just clocking out; truckers coming off the state highway, looking for breakfast and a shot of liquor in their coffee, would join them. When Cricket Tavern's business partner suddenly walked out, Mom took over tending bar in late afternoon for the factory day-shifters wanting a quick beer before heading home. At two a. m. , she closed "The Store" a few hours before Dad would show up to reopen it at six.

In-between raising kids and work, Irene read the science news and followed the rockets that began to roar out of Cape Canaveral. It was a fact, she told anyone who listened, that one day everyone would have their very own computer on their desk.

And she assured her oldest child—me—that if I didn't want to be an astronaut, being a nuclear physicist would be alright, too.

Most important, she repeated, don't let anyone ever tell you that girls can't be scientists.

Naturally, I read science fiction, just like Mom.

OUR NEW house south of the city, about a fourteen mile drive from the tavern's old neighborhood, was so much nicer than our upstairs apartment. And so very different from the in-city neighborhood. Brecksville was a post-Revolutionary War village that had grown up around a stagecoach stop on the way from the Ohio River to Lake Erie. Small churches ringed a town square with shady elm trees and a grand band gazebo. The people who lived there kept chests filled with clothes and books and papers from the Civil War era in their attics. War veterans from 1781 were buried along State Route 21, the main drag from Cleveland, through Brecksville, to the state capitol in Columbus.

We didn't have much in common with other families on our street. As tavern-owners and the American-born children of Catholic immigrants, Irene and Stanley were exotic aliens—and, besides, they worked too many long hours to be social. My brother and I were driven to our parochial school in the next town over, not bussed to public school with the kids down the street. We really didn't know our neighbors at all.

But Mom and I had a shiny new library to explore! By the time I was 8 or 9, I had worked my way through the last of the science fiction juveniles shelved downstairs and joined Mom to cruise the adult science fiction section upstairs.

We saw all the 1950s flying saucer movies in the theater. We watched *The Twilight Zone* and *The Outer Limits* on TV and talked about the stories for hours. Seeing *2001: A Space Odyssey* in a huge downtown theater in '68 was a major mother-daughter occasion; when *The Prisoner* aired in the U. S. , we followed its mysterious plot avidly, a two-person debate club parsing every scene for the rest of the day.

We were solitary science fiction fans together, Mom and I. She read her news, her books, and waited for her daughter to grow up to be the first woman on the moon.

I read the same books and became the class weirdo in grade school, the class wonk in high school, and in college, with *Star Trek* premiering my freshman year, I became a certified egghead, a nerd.

THINKING ABOUT reading alone, I'm going to digress.

I once heard Harlan Ellison—SF writer, critic, script-writer, provocateur—talk at the University of Washington. He mentioned how he discovered SF fandom in the 1940s when he was a teenager living in Cleveland. One day a librarian, having noticed that he took out stacks of SF books each visit, asked Harlan if he knew that a group of local boys had formed a science fiction reading club. He didn't, but he found them soon enough and the rest, he said, is SF history.

Afterward, chancing a chat with Ellison, I told him that not so many years after his librarian story, I too had taken out stacks of SF books each time I left my childhood Cleveland library. My librarians looked at my selection and wondered if I would rather read Nurse Barton books? Or some new Nancy Drews?

Mr. Ellison had a reputation for being snarky with people, but he wasn't that night. He believed my story and pointed out that the World SF Convention had been held in Cleveland in 1966.

And if I had known about that con back then, I told him, I would have been there with bells on, and my mother with me!

He laughed; he even commiserated. It almost made up for my old frustration.

MY EARLIEST fantasy worlds weren't inspired by science fiction at all.

Mom was the crucial source, as always. An early tech adopter, Irene owned a television before she had a daughter. The picture tube was small, but it sat encased in a grand double-door cabinet with wood stained golden yellow and a black rabbit-ears antenna on top. I vaguely remember watching shadowy images of lots of grown-ups making lots of noise (at the first televised Republican convention in election year 1952, I was told later). I learned about polio from news film of kids in iron lungs. More happily, I remember the TV as the magic black & white machine that dropped all the early TV westerns—*Hopalong Cassidy*, *The Cisco Kid*, *The Roy Rogers Show*, *The Gabby Hayes Show*—in my lap.

I think I was 4, maybe 5, when I realized that I could make up my own westerns. I entertained myself by inventing some bad guys who caused trouble, a surprise hero—me—who saved the day, and the big pay-off at story's end when peace had been restored. That successful hero—me again—rode next to Roy Rogers on his jeep, Nellybelle, in a victory parade through any number of dusty western towns.

As I grew older, *Have Gun Will Travel* gave me an imperfect protagonist who played chess, and because Dad had taught both his kids the game I had a perfect entry into Paladin's 1870s San Francisco hotel. By then I also understood that, unlike Roy Rogers, sometimes a good guy got hurt. So *Gunsmoke's* Sheriff Matt Dillon would get shot, a flesh wound in his arm, or would badly sprain an ankle. Then, naturally, he needed a clever deputy at his side to help save Dodge City from the ungodly.

Unfortunately, the American frontier had a limited storyline for a budding pre-teen girl. One night, working on a new story, I realized that I couldn't finish it. As a practical kid who preferred science to magic, I knew that during the "real" Old West, people with breasts didn't get to be smart, clever sheriffs. The Western universe was closing up on me. I was devastated.

Then, I remembered my science fiction books. SF characters had unlimited universes to explore, with thousands of planets to discover. I could imagine myself flying from star to star, introducing amazed Terrans to new peoples and civilizations. When the dust settled, I would pat an adoring kid on the head, tell 'em to be good, and fly off into an alien sunset, a galactic western hero like Shane, always moving on.

I was sure that life would be different for girls in space.

I didn't write down any of these stories until the early 1960s, which is probably all for the good. Still, looking back on those years, I can see a novice writer going through all the familiar developments of an everyday fanfic author.

Self-insertion stories (the heroic rescues, the parades at tale's end) were fun and great exercise, and they fell away over time. (Everyone ends up with at least one by-the-book Mary Sue story—or more—deeply filed away, don't they?)

Plot lines became more complex, demanding research to make an imaginary world richer. (I wanted to get Adam Cartwright off the Ponderosa and traveling across Europe in the 1860s. In czarist Russia he'd meet a mysterious woman from the Byzantine world. Together they'd have adventures, ending in terrible trouble in French Indochina. I planned for a cliff-hanger, with a mother and two young children arriving at the big house on the Ponderosa late one night. Ben Cartwright would come down the stairs, grumbling as he tied his robe, throw open the door—and meet his grandchildren, one even named Benjamin. Adam, he'd be told, would come when he could, if he could. Tears all around and continued next season.)

However, no matter how clever I thought my stories had become, I was still telling stories to myself.

When I turned 13, in preparation for high school, my parents gave me a typewriter. Force bless that old machine; my handwriting was terrible, especially when scribbling in binders hidden by textbooks propped open on my desk in class.

I suspect that Dad knew that I would be typing something other than homework. He told his own Harvey the Rabbit stories (from the old James Stewart movie by the same name) whenever he drove me and my friends around town, and the girls always asked for more next weekend.

Years later, rereading the few letters I have from him, I realized that Stanley, who was a lovely writer, was the reason why I would never be the scientist Mom wanted. Dad didn't share our love of science fiction, but he was all the way with me on whatever I wanted to do. I wrote him into my *Star Wars* fanfic; the year he died, so did his Corellian indie spacer avatar, both of them broke at the bank, but rich with friends and the respect of others.

IN HIGH school, I met some girls who were writing Real-Person fanfic about their favorite singing group. Four twenty-something young men traveling around the world singing was so far outside my perception of reality that I had no qualms about joining the fun. My world and theirs would never cross, after all.

We read our stories to each other over the phone in the evenings after school. My friends wrote about the characters' romances and families; I sent the boys to Borneo, where a storm would drive their small plane unto the jungle. Not the Wild West, not some other planet, but a place so distant from home that it might as well be Mars. I handled relationships by challenging them with the need to survive long enough to get out alive.

I loved the writing and filled three binders by the time my friends drifted away from such play in senior year. That was sad, but I was hooked. I had discovered how much fun it was to share stories with other readers, to riff off their ideas for the next chapter. I wanted to keep roaming a new universe with others who shared my interests.

It was 1966 by then and, oh, I was so ready to discover *Star Trek*, fanzines, and the worlds of fan fiction.

STAR TREK premiered as I was packing for college. At my first school in Iowa, I had to reserve the dorm TV for *Star Trek* by sitting through an hour of *Daniel Boone*. When I transferred to Ohio State, *Star Trek* was flat out "not cool" at any time in my dorm. I had to find the Catholic Newman Club to watch *Star Trek* on an old TV in its basement while the boys from the pool room stood in the doorway, sniggering about pointy-eared aliens.

At the end of *Star Trek*'s second season, I started writing about Mr. Spock as a Star Fleet Academy cadet. Wanting to explore interclass sports, Spock signs up for, and wins, an annual, notorious, student starship race across the solar system, embarrassing the Vulcan Embassy and his Ambassador father.

My friends weren't interested. Oh well. Back to telling stories to myself. I finished this one only in daydreams.

Star Trek really wasn't terribly popular during its original run. "Just college kids and eggheads watch it" seemed to be the general consensus. I heard about a letter campaign to save the show, but I didn't make contact with whoever those fans out there were. Maybe I lost the news article, misplaced an address. Maybe I was just clueless about what was possible.

I graduated in 1970 with a major in Communications and a minor in Film. I moved west (Dad was happy) to Seattle (where that singing group lived). *Star Trek* started airing in syndication, and the locally edited episodes were. . . irritating. Worse, the show was being aired out of order. How would anyone follow the development of the relationships among the crew? How would they understand how Spock changed and grew over three years?

Even friends who liked *Star Trek* considered my fussing a bit intense.

I tried a more sociological focus.

What about the young kids watching *Trek* after school? Would they love the show as we had, reacting the way we did? Would the girls be inspired to read science fiction, or young women to study the sciences?

I was a radio copywriter and producer at that time (able to hire that singing group, btw), and a free-lance business writer on the side. I could write an article that explored those questions! That doing research with other young women who were watching *Trek* anew would allow *me* to watch my fav TV show to my heart's content... was just incidental.

A DIGRESSION: A few years later, I found work at a local publishing company. One day, my boss told me that she had been worried to learn that I was a *Star Trek* fan. A couple of years earlier, a new employee had come to work wearing pointed ears. However, she said, I seemed fairly normal despite my odd taste in TV shows.

I did not mention that I was writing *Star Trek* stories to her. End of digression.

WITHIN A year, the article was forgotten. I was too busy enjoying the company of local fans. The Puget Sound Star Trekkers (PSST) were organized enough to hold yearly Star Trek mini-cons at Seattle Center. One day when I was visiting the PSST Starbase, another fan handed me a thick stack of papers, stapled in batches with illustrated covers and boldly inked titles.

"Look!" he said. "Here are new *Star Trek* stories to read! One even has a 'green blood' story—y'know, Mr. Spock gets hurt."

He called it a fanzine. I flipped through it, scanning the short stories, glancing at the poetry and cartoons, transfixed by the longer story that, I would learn, often closed out printed zines.

"It's fan fiction," he continued. "What do you think?"

I didn't have to take home an armful of fanzines—but I did—to recognize what I held. After all the lonely years of making up stories for myself, I knew. I don't remember if I said it out loud, but what I thought was, *Oh, hell, I can do this!*

IT TOOK me a few years to get active in fandom—there were so many zines to catch up with. And conventions! At the PSST mini-cons, I met George Takei; during a bigger convention at a downtown hotel, I met and talked with David Gerrold and Harlan Ellison. I was thoroughly giddy with joy. Truly, I had found my people, and there were so many more of them to meet!

It wasn't long before I started writing a new *Star Trek* story and discovered that putting a zine together was a lot like publishing the hunting-and-fishing weekly newspaper where I currently worked. Zines had editors, too, and print deadlines, especially when publishers wanted to have their zines come out in time for the zine mecca MediaWest*Con over Memorial Day.

Good stories are marvelous, but it was worth a writer's time to pay attention to the mechanics of how to reach your readers. Print zines costs were all up front and came out of a fan publisher's pocket, money that was only repaid when people bought the fanzine. If a writer wanted a story in a particular zine, word count and deadlines were the writer's concerns as well. An editor might reject a submission—not because it didn't tickle the editor's fancy, but because the zine budget would only support a specific number of pages. Or because the writer couldn't manage to meet the edit/rewrite turnaround deadlines before the zine had to be at the copy shop or printer.

(My editors are spitting out their coffee now; I was not known for writing short stories, and one of my *Star Wars* novels ran two, er, three years late.)

MY FIRST *Star Trek* fan fiction submission was accepted for the fanzine *R&R* in 1976. "Dragon Ears" was a short story about a young Spock on shore leave, going climbing, meeting an alien who challenged Vulcan logic. The editors even accepted the illustrated title page offered to them. Was I surprised? Yes. Was I inspired? You bet. I started outlining and typing like mad.

Next year, *The Guardian* printed my speculative timeline for the *Star Trek* universe, from the 20th to the 23rd Centuries. *The Other Side of Paradise* thought my pseudo-history crossing early Vulcan and *The Lord of the Rings* was funny and took it.

I was now a published writer of fan fiction, of "fanlit!" I happily started a file of ideas for more *Star Trek* stories.

A DIGRESSION on "Who's a Fan, Huh?"

I'm at a regional science fiction convention. In the Dealers Room a fan sits behind a table, making 2- and 3-inch buttons. His sign says:

> CHOOSE A SAYING FROM THE POSTED SHEET!
> MAKE UP YOUR OWN BUTTON!

So, I tell him, "I want a button that says, 'I was a nerd before it was cool'."

The young man looks me up and down, says, "No."

"Huh? Why not?"

He sighs. He looks me up and down again, making a point that clearly I'm not getting.

[Note: It's Easter weekend and I'm at a SF con with 700 people in a small airport hotel with a stuffy dealer's room crammed into a second floor meeting room. I am carrying SF books in a convention swag bag. I'm wearing a t-shirt with an obscure SF reference. I am a nerd. What else could I be?]

Finally, he says, "Girls can't be nerds," in the same voice that male SF fans would say, "You're just here for *Star Trek*," or "Media fans don't read," or "Where's your boyfriend?"

"Well, you just lost a sale," I tell him, laugh, and walk away.

THEN CAME May 1977 and *Star Wars.*

I sat in the theater that night in May and realized I had found my special universe. I was in my late 20s. I had done my first stint as a grown-up for seven years after graduating, had spent my time in one career and was about to move into another. I needed change in all aspects of my life.

I was ready for *Star Wars.* Don't get me wrong: I loved *Trek*; I just didn't see myself in the *Trek* universe, in the military, in a uniform. I *could* see myself flying my own *Millennium Falcon.* In a universe where ordinary haulers could travel from Alderaan to Tatooine in a piece of junk like the *Falcon*, I would be right at home.

(Hey, I come from a tavern family, right? Our customers included a lot of independent haulers. Of course, I would want a star truck for my own.)

The previous fall, I had picked up the first edition of the SW novelization. Unfortunately, I had flipped to a page that, taken out of context (and without SFX), read like one long cliche and covered mostly bang-bang, shoot-'em-up noise. I put the book back in the rack with a shrug.

But the May *Time Magazine* cover story on the movie presented the film glowingly, and I kinda wished I could go opening night. However, I still worked for the publishing house. That Wednesday evening I was packing for my company's first appearance at the annual American Bookseller's Association convention in San Francisco. We flew in on Thursday and set up our publications table on the mezzanine, right over the Ballantine Books exhibit space with its big *Star Wars* display.

I spent the weekend listening to all the buzz below about the new movie. On break, I went down for a look and, although I did not secure a ticket to the special matinee sponsored by Lucasfilms, I did score a French neckline *Star Wars* t-shirt.

From above, the most fun was watching the Ballantine booth where, in the middle of the aisle, stood a very tall someone in a black battle suit with a flowing black cape and huge black helmet. This dark vision didn't move, didn't have an sign introducing him. He just stood there, his black mask looking straight at the book-buyers coming at him, silently defying anyone in the crowd to pass. No one had any idea who or what he was, but as they got closer, they stopped talking, their eyes went wide, and they quickly swerved around the strange creature. Looking over their shoulders as they passed, they hurried away. Clearly, my boss and I thought, this movie had to be good if only for having such an impressive-looking character.

I saw *Star Wars* a week later and my life changed. It was a kids' movie, it was a bit corny. It was unlike anything we had seen before: its pace, its joyous acceptance of cherished space opera clichés, its assumption that everyone in the audience understood the lovely twists Lucas put on those conventions.

My god, the secondary hero was not automatically won over to the good guys' side! The hero himself was as goofy as those in the audience probably were. And the heroine! She was allowed to handle a weapon, to even aim and hit a bad guy with it; she was mouthy without the usual accompanying sniggers, and she certainly wasn't self-conscious about her out-of-American-norm behavior. She was short, not skinny, and she dripped intelligence. Nor did she end up hanging off a hero's arm or married or whimpering.

I really want to emphasize how physically exhilarating Star Wars was as a movie. Until then, most SF films had been made by people for whom the whole idea of space and technology was a grown-up wonder, or a joke. They were still in awe of outer space, or terrified by it, and the movies reflected their attitudes.

Star Wars really was something new, a movie that broke movie-making rules, giving the audience thrills and showing them wonders not seen before. The SFX were not just "we'll get them really good some day", but truly accomplished improvements on an art form.

One day at work, enjoying some downtime, I started writing a *Star Wars* vignette about a climatic lightsaber battle between Luke Skywalker and Darth Vader. Han Solo would be there, too, distracting Vader, enabling Luke to regain the saber he had lost. Solo would die heroically when Vader struck him, but Vader would lose his momentum and then his own life to Skywalker. Leia would become President of the new Republic Senate. The End.

A friend read the vignette, liked it, but told me flatly that I could not kill off Han Solo if I wanted to remain in fandom. I wrote to the editor of *The Other Side of Paradise* anyway, asking if she had heard of anyone planning to publish a *Star Wars* fanzine.

She had.

Skywalker, edited and produced by Bev Clark, came out in April 1978. It was not only one of the first dedicated SW fanlit fanzines, but was taken to 20th Century Fox to prove that fanzines with fan fiction were a boost in publicity, not a threat to the company's bottom line.

Bev was my first real editor in fandom. She and I both liked intricate plots and action in our fanlit. As friends, we hit all the fannish highlights: we wrote the familiar long letters to each other, could phone each other late at night because we both lived on the West Coast, and could talk about *SW* and fanlit endlessly.

The zine *Skywalker* became a classic, one zine in the Lucasfilms' zine library that always had to be reordered because copies were seldom returned, or so the fan club's director told me years later.

Bev Clark died at 54 in 2007. *SW* fandom lost a founding Geek Elder and her wealth of first-hand *Star Wars* fandom history. Readers lost an insightful contributor to letterzines. I lost a good friend. Bev introduced me to the woman I've lived with since 1979; in return, my wife and I introduced Bev to an Air Force vet we knew, a fanzine illustrator and indie cartoonist, who she married. We all had planned to watch the remaining *Star Wars* movies together. I miss her terribly.

WRITING IS a solitary task, even in the middle of as many people as enjoy media fandom. Since becoming an active fan, I've written hundreds of story manuscript pages and a thousand-plus page novel. I've illustrated my own stories and other writers' stories, and won three Fan Q Awards: two for my *SW*-based *ThousandWorlds* universe, and one for a filk.

But I've never met most of the fannish people I've written to or interacted with through the mail.

Sometimes we end up at the same convention, which is great. I like conventions and have been to a lot of them. Anything can happen at a con, especially the large ones. In 1977, Bev and I went to SeaCon, the SF Worldcon in Brighton, England. We had the good luck to meet Gary Kurtz casually before the con's Masquerade and talked with him about fanfic. With other fen, we helped strike the Lucasfilms/*Star*

Wars con exhibit, and to this day I run into people who met me in Brighton.

I don't remember too much about LACon II, the '84 Worldcon, when Bev and I were asked to talk about fanzines and fanlit at a Lucasfilm's *Star Wars* event. As I gathered my notes to go up to the podium with Bev, I broke the large scarab necklace I wore. Stone beads scattered across the floor. *That* I can't forget.

Fandom reaches around the world. In 1991, I was amazed to be invited as *Star Wars* Fan Guest of Honor at Italy's annual SF convention in San Marino, Italy. Gave a speech, even, and moderated a *Star Wars* panel as Mon Mothma.

Convention panels can be fun/a challenge/a way to learn something you didn't know, and an endless source of fannish gossip about good moderators, inept moderators, people who talk too much, and panel members who fly way off topic.

NOWADAYS, MOST of my fannish energy supports the efforts to document how long women have been in active fandom through fanzines, whether writing, artwork, editing, or publishing; by organizing and running conventions; when making costumes and when filk singing; women have shared their creative efforts. Some have found their careers through those activities; some have gone pro with their writing and art.

Conventions are family reunion sites for women whose own people had never heard of girls being interested in that sort of thing.

WHAT MOM would have made of my life in fandom is hard to say. I remember her sounding a bit envious when I told her about going to conventions. She knew some of my fannish friends, knew that Susan and I were living together and that we had lots of "projects." I wish she had come to one of our fangroup's annual *SW* parties. She would have enjoyed the blue milk and roasts made up to look like critters you'd see on Tatooine.

Still, Mom never did reconcile herself to having a daughter who was a writer and a tech artist instead of a scientist. Or that I didn't go back to school to become, at the very least, an engineer.

When I took a job with The Boeing Company at its Kent Space Center campus, she resigned herself to be happy—close to space work was close enough.

Mom saw *Star Wars* after she sold the tavern and moved to Seattle, our last SF movie seen together. Although she said that she enjoyed herself, like many *Star Trek* fen she thought the movie was a little silly. When I gave her my first *SW* fan story to read, she said she liked it, but didn't recognize herself in the Jedi I modeled after her. No matter. I know that she's flying off in space somewhere, in some other quantum universe.

The measure of a primal experience, of a paradigm shift, is how difficult it is to remember what you knew, how you felt, before your world changed. You look back and say, "How could people say/feel/look at things that way?"

I could not have imagined the turns my life would take because of fandom. Everything changed for me when I crossed its boundaries with "real" life. I'm glad so many other people are still finding fun within it.

To paraphrase Ben Kenobi, you take your first step into a larger world... and when you do, there is no turning back as the same person.

essay © Maggie M. Nowakowska

KAREN SCHNAUBELT (aka TURNER, DICK)
Patterns and Blueprints

"In the 1980s, costuming panels were very popular at science fiction conventions, and often ran overtime and spilled out into the hallway afterward. My friends and I decided there was a need for a whole separate costuming convention. Costume-Con 1 was held in January 1983, and continues to this day."
—Karen Schnaubelt

I am originally from San Diego, and am now a displaced Californian living in the Pittsburgh, PA area.

I have two definitions of "fandom." The first is when I first become overwhelmingly enamored with something and feel obligated to make it my own by making art, fan fiction, costumes, etc. The second is when I first connect with the organized fandom for the thing I love (in the form of clubs or conventions).

The first can be done as a solo pastime, without interaction with other fans, but it can be lonely. The second is more fulfilling, when you recognize that other like-minded individuals exist and share your passion.

Once I'm a fan of something, it is pretty much with me for life. So, my list of fannish interests keeps growing by accretion. There's an ebb and flow, and sometimes I let old favorites rest for a while, but I always come back to them, eventually.

My gateway fandom was anime, in 1964, in the form of *Astro Boy* (aka *Tetsuan Atom*), followed very closely by the original *Star Trek* series, first run, in 1967, and that followed by reading science fiction books out of the school library, also in 1967. My first forays into literary SF were the works of Andre Norton, Madeline L'Engle, and Robert Heinlein.

My family teased me about the intensity of my interests, but was overall supportive of them. I didn't have to tell them about it; I was very open about everything I did. When I was 9 and 10 years old, I had two giant display boards in my bedroom, and they were covered in my *Star Trek* and *Astro Boy* fan art.

My dad actually got sucked into my fandom, because he saw my friends building *Star Trek* props with no blueprints. They didn't come out in a uniform manner, so he started drawing blueprints of the various *Star Trek* hand props to try to help them.

Next thing I knew, he brought home a giant roll of vellum and started drawing the whole Starship *Enterprise*, deck by deck, as an intellectual exercise. He was an aerospace engineer by profession and was accustomed to drawing blueprints for airplanes.

Eventually, these works were commercially published by Ballantine Books as the *Booklet of General Ship's Plans* (aka *Enterprise Blueprints*) and the *Star Trek Star Fleet Technical Manual.* Yes, my dad was author/artist Franz Joseph (Schnaubelt). My friends and I did a lot of the research and provided film clips to him of the various props and sets. The patterns I researched and drafted to make *Star Trek* uniforms are the ones that ended up in the book.

I found organized fandom when I was 18, and I lived with my parents until I was 27, so they got to experience the first decade of my going to club meetings and conventions and making costumes. Over the years, I did most of the typical fan activities: fan art, fan fiction, costume designs in the style of a particular universe. Filking came later, in 1973, as did actually making costumes versus drawing them.

I draw in a very anime-ish style, and have never had any formal art training. As an artist, I can get my ideas across, but I am not a fine artist like my dad was. I sold some drawings of the *Star Blazers* anime characters at a Baycon art show in the 1980s. I mostly do art-to-wear type entries when I enter art shows now.

Fan fiction and fan art were my primary forms of expression during my junior high and high school years. I found like-minded people at school and befriended them. While our classmates were dating, attending football games, and worrying about what to wear to the prom, we wrote fanfic, and traded, read, and edited each other's stories. I later co-authored fan fiction with my friend Jan Hedlun, and we both came up with ideas and both wrote passages of the same novel. I am now a technical writer/editor by profession. My command of the English language and its often convoluted grammar definitely stems from writing a million words of fan fiction.

Some of my fan fiction was published in a San Diego fanzine called *Menagerie,* in the mid-1970s. I also self-published a fanzine, named *Intercepted,* for Gerry Anderson's *UFO* television series, also in the mid-1970s. In those days, photocopying was still very new and very expensive. We published fanzines using ditto or mimeograph machines, and corrected errors with "corflu." The machines were temperamental, and had to be monitored every minute. I can still smell the ink and the ditto fluid. Later, I was a contributor to a fanzine of erotic *Blakes 7* fiction called *Avon's Gadget Works*, published in 1987 or 1988.

I continue to read fan fiction on fanfiction.net and AO3, but I have not written anything, besides drabbles for my own consumption, in a long time.

In college, I found the local *Star Trek* club through one of my classmates when she saw a *"Star Trek Lives!"* bracelet I was wearing. I went to my first convention only 30 days after my first club meeting. The first conventions I attended were *Star Trek* and media conventions in 1973 (Bjo Trimble's Equicon 1, and the San Diego Comic-Con when it was in its infancy). My first general SF cons were Worldcon in 1978 and Westercon in 1979.

That first convention, Equicon 1, was a mind-bending experience. Jan and I went from thinking we were the last two *Star Trek* fans left on the planet, to knowing there were thousands of fans out there. I met fans from New York and Hawaii at the con, and we became pen pals. (Long-distance phone calls were heinously expensive then, and the Internet did not yet exist.) Equicon 1 was also the first time I made costumes to wear to a convention. Both were my original science fiction designs, one to wear on the convention floor, and one to compete in the masquerade. After that, costuming became my primary form of fannish expression.

Starting in the late 1970s, my friends and I were early adopters of doing anime-based costuming, including at the 1984 World Science Fiction Convention, where Nobuyuki Takahashi of Studio Hard saw American fans doing elaborate costumes both in the masquerade and in the halls, and coined the word "cosplay." I am pretty sure costumes I made were among the ones that left a lasting impression on him. (We had a Disney "Night on Bald Mountain" entry in the masquerade that had a Chernabog demon with mechanized wings. It had a 22-foot wingspan.)

In the 1980s, costuming panels were very popular at science fiction conventions, and often ran overtime and spilled out into the hallway afterward. My friends and I decided there was a need for a separate costuming convention. Costume-Con 1 was held in January 1983, and continues to this day.

In the late 1980s, I became heavily involved with *Blakes 7* fandom. I was on the periphery of two controversies in that fandom. One involved an early B7 convention where some of the committee members thought they were personal friends of some of the actors who were guests of the con, and said committee people threw a tantrum because they didn't get to spend one-on-one time with their favorite celebrities.

Another involved accusations of price-gouging by a prolific fanzine publisher, because photocopying prices in their geographic area were magnitudes higher than the cost of similar printing in other parts of the country. Eventually, the editor showed subscribers a price sheet from their printer, which proved that the prices to produce and mail their 'zines were fair. They also had full color cover art, which was quite expensive to print.

In the 1980s, fans didn't have the Internet to stay in touch with each other, but we had Amateur Press Associations (APAs), where maybe thirty people all submitted 30 copies of their entry (similar to writing a blog on a topic). An editor then collated the entries from the contributors, stapled them together into a booklet, and mailed them out once a month, or once every two months. I was a member of *SWAPA*, which was for general SF fans located in the Southwestern U. S. Later, I became a founding contributor of *CostumAPA*, an APA for SF costumers.

There were many flame wars in the APAs, because it was hard to tell a person's tone of voice in print versus talking to them in person. In comparison to the Internet, those flame wars were fought at glacial speed—over months instead of days—because it took so long to get the responses back and forth. The judging decisions at several Worldcon masquerades were heatedly discussed in issues of *CostumAPA*, complete with editorial cartoons.

I also belonged to a group called *General Technics* (GT), which was based out of the Chicago area. They were a discussion group, with their own publications, aimed at fans who were interested in scientific and technical topics. The modern-day equivalent would be *Ars Technica*.

When I moved to the East coast in 1990, I dropped out of the *Blakes 7* and anime fandoms completely, because my new significant other wasn't interested in them at all. I regret that decision now, as I missed out on the initial anime and cosplay conventions held in the 1990s. I am still devouring new (to me) anime series, playing catch-up on things I missed.

I am a huge *Fullmetal Alchemist* anime and manga fan, but that fandom has pretty much faded away due to the lack of new material being produced in the franchise. The last series ended in 2009, the last movie was in 2011, and while people are still writing fan fiction in that universe, it has gotten pretty stale.

I was also a huge fan of the original *Dark Shadows* (1966), *Beauty and The Beast* (1987), and *Lexx* (1996) while those shows were being aired first-run, but once they ended, I was done. I've re-watched them, thanks to the power of DVDs and streaming video, but don't feel a need to collect memorabilia, attend events, etc.

Gerry Anderson's *UFO* television series was my next big interest after the original *Star Trek* series was cancelled in 1969. I saw *UFO* in the early 1970s when it originally aired in the U. S. , again in the 1980s when it aired on a Northern California PBS station, and then when it came out on DVD. Sad to say, it has not aged well, and while I still love it, the amount of cigarette smoking and misogyny is pretty breathtaking.

I became complacent and blasé about *Star Trek* in recent years, but the new *Discovery* and *Picard* television series have really recaptured my interest and drawn me back into my primary fandom. The long form storytelling has revitalized the series for me, as they are now doing stories that take an entire season to tell versus trying to wrap things up in a single hour. I'm also very excited about the upcoming *Strange New Worlds* series, which will follow the adventures of Captain Christopher Pike and his crew.

I have both good and bad memories of nearly 6 decades of fandom. I certainly have lifelong friendships that I gained because of fandom. My oldest friendship in fandom (the aforementioned Jan) is forty-eight years, and many other enduring friendships top 30 or 40 years. I had a local group of fans I interacted with regularly in the 1970s when I lived in San Diego, and now, thanks to the power of the internet, we are having monthly Zoom meetings! Also, after decades of attending SF conventions, I have friends all over the country, and indeed, all over the world.

Some of the bad memories are because conventions tend to be stressful. There was a lot of relationship angst centered around conventions when I was younger and actively dating. In the mundane world, when you break up with someone, you never have to see them again if you don't want to. In fandom, you tend to run into them constantly at club meetings and conventions.

I wish I could relive the sense of wonder I felt when attending my first club meeting, or my first convention. That I, as the nerdy kid with the weird interests, now belonged. I had found my tribe. That was pretty wonderful.

My fannish participation has slowed down in recent years. I have had to deal with Real Life events (death of my parents, death of my significant other, health issues, and divorces), and I don't have as much disposable income as I used to, so I have to pick and choose what events I attend. I try to attend at least Costume-Con, and one big general SF regional convention (Arisia, Balticon, Westercon) per year. A Worldcon is too expensive unless it is nearby and I can drive to it. I haven't made it to many anime/cosplay/media cons because they are all very large, and I start getting overwhelmed when attendance reaches 10,000 people. Instead I enjoy them vicariously by watching coverage on the internet. I am still active in costuming, but not as productive as I was in my 20s and 30s. Still, I've won major awards in five different decades, and am shooting for a sixth.

Fandom has had an influence on my public life, too. I have been an active and prominent fan for 45+ years, and very open about my tendencies. But being fannish is much more socially acceptable and mainstream now than it was when I started. For most of my adult life, I have worked in tech fields, and those tend to have a higher percentage of SF fans as employees. The current company I work for is almost 100% fannish, and the sole manager who is mundane is bewildered by the rest of us when we talk about going to conventions, being on programming, competing in the masquerade, etc. In the 1980s, I downplayed my hobbies (particularly my costuming hobby) to my Silicon Valley employers, as I thought it might be seen as unprofessional.

Fandom has enriched my life by exposing me to art, literature, and a whole variety of people that I may never have encountered otherwise.

Fandom represents validations of my interests: innovative storytelling, appealing imagery, acceptance of technology and future-facing thinking, acceptance of differences in others (the whole *Star Trek* "IDIC" principle), and cooperative problem-solving. Fandom is the one place where I have felt unconditionally accepted.

interview © Karen Schnaubelt

SHARON PALMER / SMAP
Singing the Stories

*"Nothing is a better ice breaker for a bunch of introverts than a dog
or a cat or a ferret. I had friends who would borrow my dogs for
exactly that purpose. You'd see all these utterly serious rebels and
imperials in the blaster battle instantly dissolve into oohs and ahs as
a cute puppy came around a corner, then flip back into character
and head off down the hall looking for the 'enemy'."*
—Sharon Palmer

For me, fandom is when people gather (virtually or physically) to share their appreciation for a work of fiction (book[s], movie[s], TV show[s]) through discussion and debate, fan fiction, illustration, cartooning, costuming, prop/robot/whatever construction, singing, acting, and more ways than I can think of right now.

Although I have *always* loved science fiction and fantasy, I was a lone fan. I had no idea fandom existed until the end of my senior year of high school (1975), when I read the book *Star Trek Lives!* by Jacqueline Lichtenberg, Sondra Marshak, and Joan Winston, (the latter one of the founders of the first *Star Trek* conventions in NYC).

I was the eldest of three children growing up in the suburbs of Buffalo, New York, where Dad was the police chief of a small village and Mom ran a beauty shop out of our home.

I always got the impression my dad would have been fannish if he had had the opportunity. My brother has since attended several conventions and seems to especially appreciate the efforts of costumers. My sister eventually became a fannish viewer of shows like *Doctor Who*, but never felt compelled to become more involved.

But my mom was an anti-fan. Mom never understood the appeal of science fiction, going so far as to say that science fiction was stupid. As I headed to college, she announced to a friend of hers that, "Sharon's going to become a computer programmer like that Martian on *Star Trek*." Years later, she told me she still didn't understand the appeal of fandom, but she could see that it brought me joy and good friends, so she wanted me to know that she supported me.

I loved *Star Trek* and *The Wild Wild West* and all the Irwin Allen shows. I watched the *Flash Gordon* and *Buck Rodgers* serials on the

Sunday afternoon movies. My favorite cartoon was *Jonny Quest,* and the only soap opera I had any patience for was *Dark Shadows.* I also had a powerful attraction to spy shows like *The Avengers, The Man from U. N. C. L. E. , The Prisoner,* and *Mission: Impossible.*

By high school, I had fixated on *Star Trek* to the point that I put together my own little *Star Trek* handbook featuring the characters and the actors who portrayed them, the episode names, and mechanical drawings I had done of the Enterprise and the Galileo. My best friend Karen and I referred to each other as Spock and Kirk. The wall of my college dorm room was covered with *Star Trek* posters. Whenever I learned a new computer language, the first program I always wrote was one to calculate how many tribbles you'd have over time if left alone with unlimited quadrotriticale. My friends and I even won third prize in the "dorm tunnel painting contest" in 1977, with a mural of the Enterprise firing on a Klingon ship. Not bad for two computer scientists and two criminal justice majors at a college with a large art school.

My parents disapproved of comic books, so I didn't get to read them until college. I followed *Spider-Man*, *The New Teen Titans*, *X-Men*, *Star Wars*, and *Logan's Run*. I'd make my monthly run to the comic store and when I'd read them, I'd donate my comics to my friend "Doc", the evening on-campus paramedic, who said they did wonders for his popularity. In return, he introduced me to the works of Asimov and Tolkien. I was also invited to join a weekly game of *Dungeons & Dragons*. Role-play gaming has been a favorite pastime ever since.

Among my fellow gamers was an upperclassman nicknamed Spock, who cut his hair in the Vulcan way and favored the Mirror Universe goatee. He'd actually been to a couple of conventions! At the beginning of my Junior year, I went with Spock to my first con, *Star Trek* America '77, in NYC. I simultaneously felt out of this world and completely at home. I had a BLAST!

The dealers' room blew my mind. I discovered my first fanzines and spent the first evening reading issues 2 and 3 of *Contact*, a G-rated zine that focused on the Kirk/Spock friendship in original *Star Trek*. This was the very start of the fanzine trend that went from Kirk/Spock (friendship) to K/S (maybe a little more than friendship) to / or "slash" (definitely more than friendship).

I had heard about costuming. So, in the days leading up to the con, I made Andorian antennae out of paper maché. The night of the masquerade I pinned them into my hair, painted my face and hands blue with creme eye shadow, then went down to blend in with other costumed fans.

I went to my second convention, *Star Trek* America '79, alone. By a complete fluke of reservations, the single room I'd reserved turned out to be a double-double suite. Imagine my surprise when I met new friends and discovered that seven of them were sharing a room with a single double bed. I offered to let them share my room, but since we'd just met, they declined. Anyway, one of those new friends was Kellen Harkins, who has been instrumental in my fannish life ever since. In exploring the convention with them, I discovered filking. For me, "filk" is any music you find at a convention.

When I graduated from college, I moved to Maryland and worked as a computer scientist for the Federal Government. By pure serendipity, Maryland turned out to be a very active fannish center. I couldn't be happier.

Over my life, I have been to MANY conventions for many fandoms; from a tiny local high school-sponsored 500-person convention to DragonCon whose 80,000+ fans take over downtown Atlanta every Labor Day weekend. I've been to regional literary cons: Balticon, ConCarolinas, I-Con, Lunacon, Marcon, Philcon, and four World Cons. I've enjoyed conventions for *Star Trek*, *Blake's 7*, *Highlander* (including a cruise!), *Kung Fu: the Legend Continues*, *seaQuest DSV*, and *Stargate SG1*.

One of my all-time favorite conventions was MediaWest*Con in East Lansing, Michigan, a fan-run, multi-media convention with no guests. It was a convention of, by, and for fans. The dealerss room was filled with fanzines for every fandom under the sun. The masquerade, which I was privileged to judge three years in a row, was primarily recreation ("recreating" an already-established look or costume, what they now call "cosplay".) It was a weekend-long party, including such diverse activities as the *Star Wars* blaster battle in the halls, the *Remington Steele* formal soiree, and nuclear beach parties where they broke open light sticks, splattered the contents on the walls and turned on black lights. People decorated their doors to reflect their fandoms. Fannish music videos ran all night in the video room. The art show featured fannish art of all kinds, with a little section cordoned off for "adult" pieces. Every year they held the Fan-Q Awards for best zine, best art, etc. etc.

But the thing that really made MediaWest unique is that it was run by the Carletons who were/are active in dog shows with their Samoyeds. They worked a deal with the hotel so that con attendees could bring their pets. Nothing is a better ice breaker for a bunch of introverts than a dog or a cat or a ferret. I had friends who would borrow my dogs for exactly that purpose. You'd see all these utterly serious rebels and imperials in the blaster battle instantly dissolve into coos and awes as a cute puppy came around a corner, then flip back into character and head off down the hall looking for the "enemy".

I tended to avoid fannish controversies, though I witnessed many over the years. The only one I actively participated in was Clan Denial in *Highlander* fandom, protesting the beheading of our favorite character, Richie Ryan. I've never actively dropped out of a fandom, but they all fade over the years.

COSTUMING—yes, I'm old; it's "costuming", not "cosplay"—has been a part of my fandom experience from the beginning. I was an early member of the Greater Columbia Fantasy Costumers Guild and served as Treasurer, Vice President, President, and duly elected Deity. (Really. There was one year where we had trouble getting candidates and I was placed on the ballot as the alternate for every position. As a joke response they wrote me in as "Deity.") I've attended and competed at Costume Cons in Columbia, MD; Albany, NY; and Pittsburgh, PA. I have been a body in someone else's costume, done hall costumes and competition costumes, and have achieved the level of Craftsman, one step below Master. I worked masquerades up to the World Con level as pusher, catcher, runner, green room den mom, photo area coordinator, judge, judges' clerk, stage manager, and assistant masquerade manager, but most often as assistant stage manager. I can still be found as Assistant Stage Manager every year at Maryland fan-run conventions: Farpoint and Shore Leave.

FANZINES—I started as a fanzine consumer and I'm proud of my collection. Although my first fandom was *Star Trek*, my first fanzine contributions were illustrations ("illos") and filks for Kelley's *Star Wars* zine *Crossed Sabres*. I soon found I had a knack for cartooning and ended up with cartoons in a wide assortment of zines. I helped several friends assemble their zines, running around tables collating pages or ka-chunking the hole punch.

Then, Tish Wells asked my then-roommate, Nea Dodson, and me if we wanted to do a zine together. *CrosSignals* was born. As an all-crossover zine (I believe the modern term is "mash-up"), every story in *CrosSignals* had to incorporate two or more different universes. We got some wild pairings. (*Fraggle Rock* and *Doctor Who*, anyone?) We requested that authors give enough background for each universe that a reader who had never even heard of it could appreciate the story. We set up an editing process that worked for us. When a story came in, each of us read it, making comments in the margins in different colored inks. Tish, Nea, and I each had our strengths. Tish was and is master of plot. Nea specialized in dialogue and characterization. I specialized in word play and continuity. We sometimes argued in the comments, but best 2 out of 3 won. It was up to me to review all the comments and compose the acceptance/rejection letter to the author explaining what we wanted changed and why. I made copies of the letter and the marked-up document, then sent them the originals. We always told the author that they had the right to withdraw the submission if they didn't like our proposed changes. The vast majority of authors decided to take our suggestions and resubmit. Tish and I did layout and coordinated artwork, while Nea specialized in marketing. It worked for us. I'm very proud of our six issues. What I find amusing is that we were also noteworthy for producing a zine that featured contributions from several men, a rarity in fanzines of the day.

Then "real life" got busy and we found we didn't have the time to produce issue 7. We retired *CrosSignals*. We had agreed from the beginning that *CrosSignals* would be non-profit, but we ended in the black. So, our profits were split evenly between three charities.

I continued to contribute illos, cartoons, and filks to various fanzines in various fandoms, and even started contributing short stories and plays. It's a past hobby now, but working on fanzines gave me valuable experience, which I applied to managing technical documents at work, and creating concert programs for choruses.

Art—One of the things I had not seen at my first two conventions was the art show. The art show is an opportunity for artists to make a little money selling artwork they've created for fanzines and such. At the same time, it provides an opportunity for fans to purchase artwork that directly ties to their favorite fandoms. I've been lucky. I've never entered an art show without selling at least one piece, and over the years I've accumulated a fair collection of fannish art. In recent years, I've started carving and decorating wooden wands and walking sticks, and have even been commissioned to create custom sticks for costumers. I've donated several walking sticks for fund-raising events, and I'm contemplating creating a business to make and sell these.

FILK—My first contributions to fanzines were filks. In *Kung Fu: The Legend Continues* fandom, I was so notorious for my filks, I earned the title of "Mistress of Kung Filk". At Kung Fu Fest in Toronto in 1996, in front of the producer and several cast members, I got to lead attendees in singing filks fans had written for "Kung Fu: the Musical". The next day, Belinda Metz, one of the cast members, commented in her talk that as she was getting ready that morning, she realized she was singing, "Sing-wa, Chi-ru, Di-mok" (one of my *Kung Fu* filks).

But my biggest involvement in filk is being a member of the Boogie Knights, a filk group that takes modern songs and creates new lyrics based on history, mythology, or fantasy. I've been singing with them since 1987. Singing with them is so fun, and rehearsals are hysterical. In a strange way, singing with the Boogie Knights helped me get ahead at work. Shortly after joining the Knights, I was made a project leader at work and the new position required me to give presentations. At the time, I was painfully shy, but it dawned on me that if I could get dressed in medieval garb, sing silly songs and make a fool of myself in front of a large convention crowd of friends and strangers, what did I have to fear in dressing professionally and briefing strangers on a subject where I was knowledgeable and they weren't? It really helped.

The creative people behind the Boogie Knights are also involved in creating plays and/or radio plays performed at local cons under the banners of "Cheap Treks Productions", "Misfit Toy Productions", "Not Ready for Paramount Productions", and "Prometheus Radio Theatre." So through them I got a little experience with acting that encouraged me to get involved with community theater after I retired. Another way that fandom impacted my outside life.

With the Knights, I've performed at a wide variety of conventions up and down the East Coast. We've even performed at conventions just for filk such as Filk Ontario, Ohio Valley Filk Fest, and the Northeast Floating Filk Conventions.

One of the most mind-boggling experiences I ever had was at DragonCon where the late author Robert Asprin (who wrote filks himself) got down on his knees and did the "I'm not worthy" salaam to the Boogie Knights, saying, "Five-part harmony and funny lyrics in a filk circle? OMG, it's the f*cking Boogie Knights!" We stood there in total shock for a moment before all rushing to say, "Get up, get up." We were told that Asprin used to play our CDs and sing our lyrics around the French Quarter of New Orleans where he lived. He was a wonderful man and I miss him.

Guests—I've met many authors: Isaac Asimov, Robert Asprin, Jim Butcher, Peter David, Keith DeCandido, Michael Jan Friedman, Laura Anne Gilman, Bob Greenberger, Jody Lynn Nye, etc. , and count many of them among my friends.

I walked toward the dealers' room at my first World Con, saying to a friend, "I hear that Mercedes Lackey is here. I wonder what she looks like?" turned a corner and encountered a short, friendly woman who said, "I look like this."

At a tiny convention in Maryland in the early 1980s, I even got to meet Joan Winston, one of the authors of the book that introduced me to fandom: *Star Trek Lives!* We had a long, relaxed chat in a back hallway. I will cherish that conversation to the day I die, though I no longer remember exactly what we talked about.

I've also met many of the actors from my favorite shows, including the main cast of *Stargate SG1*, the entire cast of *Babylon 5*, and all of the original cast of *Star Trek* with the exception of Leonard Nimoy.

I was helping out backstage at Shore Leave when Peter Jurasik (*Babylon 5*'s Londo Mollari), commented that he never cared for sitting on bar stools to chat when on stage. So a friend and I brought up onto stage a high-backed cushioned chair for him. No sooner had we turned to take away the stool than Robert Krimmer, the actor who had played the insane Centauri Emperor, pranced on stage and draped himself across the "throne." Jurasik watched all this and made an aside to the audience, "I thought I eliminated that problem." Everybody had a good laugh.

At another Shore Leave, Bruce Boxleitner (*B5*'s Sheridan) had joined Jerry Doyle (Garibaldi) on stage and it was obvious that they were having fun together, but Jerry had a plane to catch. So that same friend and I headed onto the stage and, without saying a thing, started removing Doyle's things item by item until we finally snatched his microphone and escorted him offstage. Throughout, Boxleitner watched with amusement. BUT Doyle made his plane.

There's something unreal for me, as a child of the 60s, in sharing a DragonCon elevator with Batman (Adam West) staring down my cleavage for the entire ride.

Today—My memories of fandom are all good. I met my closest friends through fandom, and it has always amazed me how many of them share my interests in community theater and Renaissance fairs.

Currently, my number one fandom is *Supernatural* and I watch many others (such as the CW *Arrow*verse), though I have not been inspired to write or illustrate for quite a while. I'm a big fan of the Dresden books by Jim Butcher, and I have seen him at a couple of cons. I still write filks for and perform with the Boogie Knights. I still collect fannish art. I still work at the masquerades, but I haven't made a new costume in ages. My three go-to cons are Farpoint, Shore Leave, and DragonCon.

Fandom is my chosen family. It has enriched my life in so many ways. I've met fascinating people who have entertained me for years and gave me an opportunity to thank them for it. I've met many wonderful people who have never failed to support and encourage me in my creative endeavors. I've received constructive criticism from pros on improving my artwork. I've gained self-confidence. And I've gained the friendship of wonderful people. I have never regretted one minute of it.

interview © Sharon Palmer

We'd also like to share with you a bit of
Visual Fannish HERstory

Photos on the following pages are from our contributors'
personal and private collections, unless otherwise stated.

For a color version,
kindly visit the Forest Path Books website at:
http://forestpathbooks.com/ges-photo-supplement/

We costumed...

(1978) The First Terran Enclave, Seattle,WA **Maggie Nowakowska,** *far left*

Bjo the Dancing Girl
From *THE GENIE,* (1969)
*aka **Bjo Trimble***

Karen Schnaubelt and Fellow Costumers

Karen Schnaubelt and Fellow Costumers

(1985)
Nasfic/LoneStarCon 10
in Austin, TX, from the
winning novice group debut
of renowned costumers
Sandy & Pierre Pettinger.
Jenni H. *as 'costume dummy'*

Chris Edmunds repairing costumes (above banner by Fredd Gorham)

Cally from Blake's 7 - *aka* **Tish Wells**

(1989) Robin & Marion of Sherwood *aka* **Jenni Hennig** *(John Hennig as Robin)* at Herne's Con 1

(1980s) Marion at Scorpio Con *aka* **Jenni H.**

Jean Dewey in SCA garb

We sang and danced...

(2018) "It's the f**king Boogie Knights!
with **Sharon Palmer** (photo Tish Wells)

Space Heroes & Other Fools

*Julia Ecklar
Anne Harlan Prather*

Space Heroes & Other Fools

Vocalists: **Julia Ecklar** and **Anne Harlan Prather**
Back-up Music: **Leslie Fish**   Producer: **Teri Lee**
Sound Engineer: **Jeff Rogers**   Art: **Don Simpson**
Copyright © ℗1983, 1987 Off Centaur Publications
P.O. Box 424, El Cerrito, CA 94530   OCP-16   T18GA29

Leslie Fish and an example of her work.

(1983) Oola dancing
(*aka **Jenni H.***)

**Robert
Rogow's**
work

We wrote, edited, and published...

Karen MacLeod's collection of zines and an anthology. (She served as editor for all.)

Jacqueline Lichtenberg, the *Sime~Gen* novels, and her typewriter.

Barbara Wenk's "Mirror Mirror" con name tag (by Paulie) and her seminal *Star Trek* fan work *One Way Mirror*.

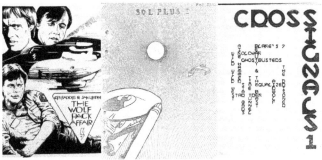

Guardian 6

GUARDIAN/**Linda Deneroff**, THE WOLF PACK AFFAIR/**Jan Lindner**, SOL PLUS/ **Jackie (Bielowicz) Kramer**, CROSSIGNALS/ **Tish Wells & Sharon Palmer**

CROSSED SABERS/**Kelley Harkins** (w/Lin Stack), FAR REALMS/**Jenni**, BATTLE FOR RYNAN/**Maggie Nowakowska**, JEDISTARDARKFALCONKNIGHT/ parody edited by **eluki bes shahar**

Cynthia Drake and friends

(1974) **Paula Smith** with Sharon Ferraro Editors of MASIFORM-D

Allyson M W Dyar & Carol M. with letterzine COMLINK

We made amazing art...

Dani Lane's portrait of Leia

Wanda Lybarger's illustrative style

The work of **Liz Danforth** (shown here signing Magic The Gathering cards). Find out more at: https://www.patreon.com/LizDanforth

5.75 + 2.50 postage

Fanzine flyer by
eluki bes shahar

Tish Wells and Salacious
at a fanzine table

We attended conventions and gatherings...

Kathy Agel
(photo: Tish Wells)

Bjo Trimble & Kavita

Bjo & husband John
(Photo by Robert Paz)

STAR TREK: The Motion Picture™

Bjo, William Shatner, & David Gerrold

Julie Bozza

Rosalie Blazej

(1984)
Maggie, Sandy, **Jenni**

Lin S. & **Kelley Harkins**

Carolyn E. Cooper

Liz Danforth at Avatar
Santillana del Mar &
Rillito

Jean Lorrah & Cuddles

Erica Frank

Abbie Bernstein

But most of all?
We were—and still are—
a Community.

JEAN LORRAH
We are Legion

"Why would I want to change anything? It's the only life I know."
—*Jean Lorrah*

I was a science fiction fan from the time I discovered the genre at age eleven in 1951. But for years all I did was read. Then, in high school, I discovered sf magazines. *Fantasy & Science Fiction* was my favorite, and I subscribed to it. I also regularly read *Astounding*, which later became *Analog*. Almost immediately, I attempted to write for them. My writing was not good enough to sell to the magazines—just a fact. Not every 14-year-old is Harlan Ellison! I also had this habit of writing from a female POV that was not acceptable in magazine sf of the 1950s—but the real reason was that I did not yet know how to write a story, and because I had no connection to fandom, I had no mentor to teach me.

I recall wanting desperately to go to the 1955 World Science Fiction Convention in Cleveland, only 60 miles from home, with Isaac Asimov as guest of honor. But my parents were not interested so I could not go, and missed that chance of connecting with original science fiction fandom. Ten years passed before I was able to connect.

I was in grad school when I became active in fandom, so my fanac was my own business. It was also whatever I could do on the cheap, mostly by snail mail (letters). I could not afford to travel, buy collectibles, costume (no talent for that anyway), etc. , as a student specializing in English, specifically Medieval British Literature. No one taught science fiction or fantasy, so medieval lit, folklore, and similar fields were where sf fans who went into literary scholarship in the 1950s and 60s hung out. It was only after I started teaching at a university that I began attending conventions. Even so, it was summer-only attendance, and three or four cons per year. But oh, it was such fun! Those were MY good old days, when I made friends I still have to this day.

Fandom, I think, to most people means being connected to other fans—and that did not happen for me until *Star Trek*. So, I entered as a fringe fan—and at the time *Trek* was the fringiest outskirt of sf fandom, mostly because of the skirts! We were 90% female, all intelligent, mostly college educated, but few of us were scientists. We were almost all in the humanities, and much more interested in personality and psychology than *pew-pew-pew!*, rockets, and space stations.

Male- and science-dominated sf fandom did *not* want us for those reasons—and for another much more important reason that everyone has forgotten now: we were the first *media* fans as opposed to text fans. Fans of a TV show thinking themselves somehow equal to people who read seven books a week?! How dare we! And who wrote and exchanged FICTION in SOMEONE ELSE'S UNIVERSE?! How DARE we! And who tended to write—ick, girl cooties—ROMANCE, and call it science fiction?! HOW DARE WE! Horrified men clutched their tattered first editions of *Amazing* to their breasts, and called the wrath of Cthulhu down on us.

So, I was not welcome in the science fiction fandom that ten years earlier I had yearned to enter. I was one of hundreds of *Star Trek* fans who overwhelmed sf cons by our sheer numbers: invading Amazons, without even realizing how we were perceived. I met dozens and then hundreds of like-minded women and a handful of men, got into the vibe, and by simply being there and doing our own thing, we became tolerated and then accepted. By the time *Star Wars* came along, media fandom had become a part of sf fandom, as had the modern fanzine full of stories written in other people's universes. The media companies recognized how this new kind of fandom helped to publicize their efforts, so few production companies tried to discourage or even control fandom—other than to prevent us from making profit off their trade-marked products, which none of the real fans had any interest in doing.

Paramount somehow had the sense to ignore the whole K/S craze— they probably thought it would blow over faster if they didn't get involved. Little did they (or we) know we were witnessing the origin of slash, which over the (gasp!) half century that has passed since those first shocking stories appeared, has become a staple of all fandoms.

In those early days it threatened to divide *Trek* fandom. The issue was not gay fiction per se, or about sexual content (*Trek*'s inclusive themes carried over into its fandom)—it was a feeling many fans had about respect for either the characters, who had never been portrayed as gay, or the actors, who might reasonably be upset at finding themselves drawn in graphic sexual poses, often with full frontal nudity. At the same time slash was burgeoning, the offset press made printing of illustrations cheap and technically excellent, and *Trek* fandom was rife with artists capable of drawing true likenesses and magnificent erotic art.

It was another first that could not happen until media fandom, where real humans were inextricably involved in the portrayal of fictional characters, and it was also something that could not have happened in the male nerd-dominated world of sf fandom, where nubile but anonymous women aplenty populated the artwork—never portrayed in the arms of human men, but always being threatened by aliens or monsters. One of the many things *The Big Bang Theory* got right about nerd culture is how far more open intellectual women are than intellectual men about sharing sexual fantasies. *Trek* fandom was the first time such a large group of creative women had the opportunity to turn their fantasies loose in a safe environment, and the technology to do it for a (relatively small) mass market. By the time *Trek* fandom began to merge into media fandom, both slash and straight eroticism had become an established element of fan culture. The vast majority of creators of media today accept that fanfic of every variety, including eroticism, is all good publicity, while attempts to suppress it produce only bad publicity.

My gateway to fandom was *Star Trek*. I wrote my million words of novice writing, learned to craft stories, and found mentors in professional writers such as Marion Zimmer Bradley, and especially Jacqueline Lichtenberg, who was a double-dyed Trek fan but also had her first professional publications in print when we met. Jacqueline and I have been writing together for forty years. Lois Wickstrom and I have been writing together for over thirty. I'm a few-good-friends kind of person, not a "hundreds-of-acquaintances" kind of person.

I try to stay out of fannish controversies. Specific fandoms come and go. I was into some, like *Blake's 7* (1978-1981), that came, bloomed, and faded away. Others, like *Trek,* the grandaddy of them all, may continue forever.

It was the 1960s, folks. There was no Internet. Long-distance phone calls (any call you have to put a "1" before today) *cost extra and were paid for by the minute,* so we communicated in writing, and *not* instantaneously! Email was twenty years in the future—unless you were a technician in some scientific institution *and* had access to the mainframe. The personal computer was ALSO almost twenty years in the future. Smartphones? We didn't even envision such a thing, and those who came closest thought of voice-only communicators linking only specific groups of people, not the world.

My work appeared in the first *Star Trek* fanzine, *Spockanalia*, in

1968. I was still in grad school and thus confined to what I could do through the mail. As more *Trek* zines appeared, I contributed to many of them, and published several of my own including, in 1976, the novel, *The Night Of The Twin Moons,* about Sarek and Amanda. That led to others in the *NTM* universe.

Fandom was ultimately my route into professional writing, including *Star Trek* novels. Fandom influenced my public life and enriched it. But fandom of the kind we had in the '70s and '80s is fading away. COVID-19 may put the final period to the age of the big conventions, but they were already dying. Today, fandom is 99% online. It's a different world. But it's still fandom.

The kind of active, creative fans we are make up only a small percentage of human population. Once we found one another through *Star Trek*, other fandoms followed, and the technology developed to make it now so incredibly easy for us to find one another. To be a fan of our type up until *Trek* fandom had been lonely. Such people were lucky to find one other person in their locale who shared their type of creative spirit. Most were isolated, except for what they could do by snail mail. Now even a small percentage of the world population is millions of people.

Now, we *know* we are legion, and others of our ilk are as close as our Google app.

interview © Jean Lorrah

LIZ DANFORTH
Falling into Freelance

"Is a fifteen-year subscription to World of Warcraft a 'fannish' interest?"
— Liz Danforth

I was raised in Tucson, Arizona, where my father was a civil engineer, the Director of Public Works for the city. He and my mother were big readers, and they modelled a love of reading and lifelong learning. That included reading science fiction—my dad had subscriptions to magazines like *Fantasy & Science Fiction* and *Analog*. They didn't read science fiction or fantasy as "genre" or "hobby," but simply as part of a voracious and ever-curious interest in all sorts of reading.

I literally learned to read from *The Hobbit*. I am old enough that that is weird. My folks had bought the British edition of *The Hobbit* and of *The Lord of the Rings* long before Ballantine put out the first American editions (and caused all the copyright issues that followed).

I remember seeing the book, with Tolkien's drawing on one side of the page, and my mother's finger tracing over the squiggly black lines on the opposite side. Every time her finger pointed to that shape, she said "the." I had my Helen Keller cup/water moment and became literate at that moment.

For many years, I thought that had to be a false memory. The hardback British editions I still own were printed when I was already in grade school, yet I had been reading before first grade. But late in her life, I asked my mother if it was possible, if she remembered reading Tolkien to me as a preschooler. She didn't remember my "Ah-ha" moment, but agreed that she had indeed read *The Hobbit* to me back then. But the earlier editions—what she would have been using? Turned out that those had been swiped by my older sister's high school boyfriend.

My tastes for games and gaming—which I consider part and parcel of fandom, not always a common association, but it emphatically was for me—also comes from my family, and especially my father. He was raised in a family that played bridge, backgammon, and cribbage, and did jigsaw puzzles together. In turn, game-playing was a common family activity for me as a child too. He even designed a city-planning game, and the family play-tested it before he submitted it to Mattel. They declined it, the silly gits, but certainly all this meant that I took gaming as a hobby in stride, once I discovered it was a hobby.

My father had long passed away when I began working professionally in the game industry. My mother had a little more trouble understanding what I was doing, but still approved. Her greatest difficulties were two-fold. For one, she would ask me "How do I tell my friends what you do? I am proud of you but it's so hard to explain!" To which I said, "Just tell them I'm an artist. If they press for more information, just tell them I draw barbarians, wizards, and dragons."

This led to problem number two, in the years of the Satanic Panic about games. She had become a born-again Christian and one time she had friends over from her church. They took great offense at the "demonic" art... mine... that she had proudly hung on her walls. They offered to help her "cleanse" and purify her home by getting rid of these terrible satanic things. Bless her socks—instead of my artwork, she threw them out of the house on their collective ears.

Like many geeks of my era, I was an absolute outcast all my years growing up. I was so far an outcast that even the other marginalized outcast kids of middle school wouldn't sit with me at the lunch tables. The fact that I was probably (re-)reading a *Man from U.N.C.L.E.* book didn't help, I'm sure.

When I found fandom late in high school, I found my tribe. I understood them and they understood me. They liked what I liked and, maybe more importantly, they liked what I did. They paid me money at art shows, and asked me to draw their RPG characters. That kind of approval had been rich in my home but nowhere else. Having reached the age to leave home, I found a new home in fandom.

I also found a career. A bachelor's degree (even granted cum laude) couldn't get me a professional job, certainly not in the years of the Carter recession. I also realized I'd have to get a Ph.D. to do the kinds of things I wanted to, academically, and I didn't have the vision or financial means to figure out how to do that.

Besides, people were allowing me to make a living as a freelancer! I kind of fell into it as a career, but that's what it was. I still use the academics I learned, and at times I wonder what person I would have been had I remained in the anthropological field. But I have to say, I have led a pretty damn awesome life, even if none of it has been exactly what I might have predicted at earlier stages.

I'd say *Star Trek* was my gateway fandom, although I can trace my fannish roots back even before that. (For example, *The Man from*

U.N.C.L.E. was my pre-ST obsession, but if there was a fandom for it back then, I didn't know about it.) I went to hear Ray Bradbury speak at the University of Arizona while I was still in high school. I was a big reader, remember, and knew his name. After I walked out with my family and a scrap of paper with his autograph, I saw a kiosk with a dittoed flyer advertising *Impulse*, described as "a new fanzine." I didn't know a fanzine from a magazine, but sent off my $5 to the Phoenix address, hopeful. So, I was appalled to receive back a handful of stapled pages, also ditto, and some uninspiring ditto-drawn illustrations.

I self-righteously wrote to the editor. Now we'd call it "a letter of comment" but then it was just a complaining screed. How I expected so much more, that I'd probably written better stories and drawn better art in grade school, and so on... and what I got via return mail was "Well, how would you like to be my co-editor then?"

I met Dyanne (D. Carol) Roberts, who was scheduled to start at the university in Tucson soon. We got along, and we co-edited *Impulse* for another dozen issues over several years. There weren't many ST fanzines then, and through that nascent community I discovered Westercons, Worldcons, the first Equicon, and was asked by Bjo Trimble to provide a drawing for her *Star Trek Concordance* (which I did). That was my first paid fan-related commission. I hung art in the convention art shows, big and small, local and national, and that made me realize I wasn't bad at it. People actually wanted to buy my art, and I could attend cons to have fun, but sell art to pay for the expenses.

Having moved to Phoenix for college and largely left *Star Trek* behind, I found the local science fiction/fantasy fan group through my then-boyfriend (a big Niven fan) who I met at a local con. The Phoenix Cosmic Circle was a group that met weekly for The Friday Night Inevitables. I took part in several APAs through that group (Amateur Press Association). There was AzAPA for Arizona's fen, (the "plural" of fan) and a nationwide APA focused on sword-and-sorcery writer Robert E. Howard's writings, called REHupa.

The Cosmic Circle was a lively bunch of writers, artists, filkers. It included a band of people hanging in the back corner playing games like Risk, Regatta, and Diplomacy, and often variants like Hyborian War. This was just before RPGs had been invented, and casual gaming like this was just another feature in the broader accepted definition of fanac. Although hardcore wargaming, Napoleonic, and Civil War games weren't part of fandom, what we now recognize as the more inclusive "gaming hobby" was nothing separate.

I fit into all those categories. I took part in writers' groups; I thought I would be a professional writer *long* before I would become a professional artist. I did art for the APAs and for friends, as well as writing blog-like essays galore, and I was a helluva guitarist-folksinger with my hair straight and halfway down my back. (In high school and early college, I thought I'd go into music professionally, and even got some paying gigs. Eventually I realized I didn't have what it took to make a go of it professionally. Besides, my bachelor's degree was in Anthropology, with a Zoology minor, and surely THAT would define my profession, right?! HA.)

The Cosmic Circle gang included, I should note, Teresa Nielson, now Teresa Nielson-Hayden, retired, of Tor and the *Making Light* blog with her husband Patrick. It really was a yeasty, creative, innovative group.

That included the proto-gamers. Among the friends I made there were Ken St Andre (usually the fellow cooking up the variant Diplomacy games), Bear Peters, Ugly John (Dan) Carver, Rob Carver, the Wilsons and the Deweys, and Steve McAllister who was often playing host to the Friday Night Inevitables along with his then-wife. So many others, some who went pro (like Teresa) and others into related fields.

One year... I'm guessing it might've been 1976?... the gang headed off to Westercon in Los Angeles. Ken had seen an early edition of Dungeons & Dragons (D&D) by then, thought it was 'way too complicated but had some good ideas, and made up his own game. (See "Diplomacy variants," above... he was always tinkering.) He ran off 100 copies at the university copy shop, distributed that first edition among a few friends, and gave the rest to Rick Loomis of Flying Buffalo, a small game company in Scottsdale, mostly running play-by-mail (PBM) space- and wargames. Rick sold those copies at the next game con and to Rick and Ken's surprise, it did quite well!

I didn't get the very first edition, but as Ken kept writing new supplements and expanding the rules, he had me start illustrating along with Rob Carver. I got introduced to the game at that '76 Westercon, and then played constantly with the gang after returning home. They couldn't keep generically calling it "dungeons and dragons" and Rob Carver suggested Tunnels & Trolls™, which name it has had ever since.

The first solitaire adventures were written for the game, before "Choose Your Own Adventures" or other solo adventures existed. Rick Loomis wrote the first one—Buffalo Castle—and he then commissioned me to illustrate it and many of those that came after. (I had already done a cover for Rick's *Supernova* newsletter, after Ken introduced us.) Eventually Rick hired me to work for Buffalo, first to transcribe play-by-mail turns over the phone and be the on-staff artist, eventually to run the Productions Department as the company grew and developed a robust publishing arm in addition to the PBM part of the company.

I worked for Flying Buffalo for seven years. We put out award-winning games, and our magazine *Sorcerer's Apprentice* featured fiction and nonfiction alike from Roger Zelazny, Manley Wade Wellman, Karl Edward Wagner, Fred Saberhagen, C.J. Cherryh, Tanith Lee, Charles de Lint, and many other names to conjure with from that time. We firmly believed in the intersection of fiction's ability to inspire games, and in the imaginative supercharging of games to inspire art and fiction. You have only to look at the early careers of Ray Feist, Kevin Anderson, and my co-worker at Flying Buffalo, Michael Stackpole, to see that the two "fandoms"—now so often disparaged as separate entities—have the same genetics at their root.

Rick was a marvelous boss because, while he couldn't pay extravagantly, he allowed all of us to work freelance for other companies in our spare time. I did, and made my name as a popular and reliable artist creating work for Iron Crown's Middle Earth RPG and card game (a return to my roots of literacy!), TSR's AD&D modules, GDW's Traveller, FASA's Battletech and Shadowrun, Steve Jackson's Melee/Wizard that became The Fantasy Trip, and many more. I was one of the early artists to work on Magic the Gathering, painting three dozen card arts.

Over the years, I worked for most of the major and many minor publishers in the industry, and became well-known enough to be inducted into the Academy of Gaming Arts and Design Hall of Fame 1995 (awarded 1996). The Academy was/is the creative arm of GAMA, the Game Manufacturers Association, which also ran Origins, one of the big game conventions for many decades.

And it wasn't just RPGs, card games, and tabletop games. I wrote scenarios (no art) for computer games including Wasteland 1 and 2, and Interplay's licensed *Star Trek* games, and a Tunnels & Trolls computer game through New World Computing that was actually put together for Japan, who loved *T&T* even more than State-siders.

When I left Flying Buffalo to go freelance, I knew everyone in the industry, and had a very long track record. As a result, I had all the work I could take and then some.

You might notice how little I talk about the common question I get asked in many interviews: about being "a female in a male-dominated industry." That's because it just wasn't much of an issue for me. I fully acknowledge that was not so for many others. Maybe I was lucky. Maybe the men I hung out with were, on the whole, progressives at heart before the term came into use, or they respected my ability to go toe-to-toe with them in the same activities they did, from hiking and backpacking, to fencing, to martial arts, to role-playing games and wargames alike.

I was admired for my singing and my art, but I also was unattached to anyone for most of the years I was in fandom. Yes, a boyfriend introduced me into the Cosmic Circle; we broke up after a few months. I had a hard crush on someone who wasn't interested in me, so I in turn encouraged no one and rarely dated. We accepted each other for who we were, period.

I probably should have gotten into the SCA (Society for Creative Anachronism) in the early days. One of my first Westercons (iirc) was in San Francisco, and the likes of Poul and Astrid Anderson were active in the scene then. I remember finding myself quite entranced with the whole idea, and got into a conversation with a costumed and beweaponed knight. When I said I was interested in learning to fight—because I'd been in martial arts and was a fencer since high school—he looked down his nose and said very sharply and slowly to be sure I could understand him: *Women. Do. Not. Fight.*

I lost interest in the SCA on the spot. I learned things changed, later, but that asshole ensured I never wanted to deal with what I learned was the endless political scrum and infighting of that segment of the fannish world. Today I have many close friends still playing SCA, but I never got into it.

I supposed you'd say I gafiated from "normal" fandom when I went into gaming, but I kept strong ties with "pure" fandom (if you must call it that). Rose Beetem, longtime chair of Denver's MileHiCon, is one of my oldest good friends to this day. I met her through her sister Dee, who also had an early *Star Trek* fanzine.

In addition, my longterm partner for many years was Michael Stackpole. I got him into fandom, not the other way around. I was already working for Flying Buffalo when Ken St Andre cooked up an Amber LARP (Live Action Role Playing before "LARP" was a word, and before Erick Wujcik invented the Diceless Amber Game.) Mike and I both found ourselves in the game: me as Random, him as Brand.

Stackpole and I met in person at a convention in Canada, and later became a pair. From the start, we kept our professional identities separate: he didn't want to be "Mr. Danforth" and I didn't want to be "Mrs. Stackpole", which was a risk for us both. We didn't hide that we were together; we just didn't make a big deal about it. We worked shoulder to shoulder as friends and shield mates as much as bedroom partners. However, it did make it very easy for conventions—gaming-focused or aimed at general fandom—to win a one-two punch with an author and an artist guest brought in together. So, we both had a hand in gaming, but we also kept our hands in conventional fandom and the pro communities with (for example) regular attendance at World Fantasy Cons too.

Was there constant background sexism in those early years? Sure. It was endemic in the culture, and I wasn't too hard on the eyes in my day. Did I have a handful of unpleasant encounters, including a promise to publish my work if I'd sleep with them? Yes, I got that question—once—and refused with extreme prejudice. Even the most unmannerly of my associates knew that when I laid down the line, I would not let them cross it. Mostly, in my personal and in my professional life, it just wasn't an issue.

Have today's misogynistic trolls changed the environment for the worse? Certainly, but you knew that already. I could trot out a few stories to make your eyes roll, but I have better things to do than feed the trolls. They, however, have to deal with the published fact of my name, my works artistic and written, and the copyright dates that prove I was an accomplished pro and working on some of their favorite games when they were still crapping in their diapers.

I did go through the stereotypical "Life in Progress" hiatus in my late 40s and early 50s. My mother grew ill and I was her sole caretaker. I had no help from my siblings, nor from my partner who had never gotten along well with my mother in any case. He and I split up a couple months after my mother's death, because (in his words) she was gone, so why hadn't I snapped back to being the person I used to be? (He never was good at death matters.)

My freelance career was already suffering because of the emotional toll and time-demands of caregiving, and when my relationship of a quarter century died, I kinda gave up. I thought my Artist GoH stint at Seattle's NASFIC fifteen years ago would be my swansong. I had been working part time in libraries for many years, so I decided to "grow up and get a real job." I got my master's degree in library work, and a full time library job in Tucson.

But I was not happy. The decades of "mastery, autonomy and

purpose" that had been the hallmark of my freelance career were weak or missing in libraries, as much as I value what libraries represent and endeavor to do.

I quickly knew I wanted out, and dropped back to part time work in order to rebuild my freelance career[7] from the ground up. I'd been gone from the industry long enough that (a) a lot had changed, and (b) many people no longer remembered who I was or anything about the games I worked on. I had to reinvent myself and began making headway...

...and then the Old School Renaissance[8] bloomed, and I was in the right place at the right time. I left the library completely, happily returning to full-time freelance. Once again, I am being asked to do more work than I have time to accept. I lost a good ten years I'll never get back, but I feel like I am back to being the person I was and still want to be. Others retire at my age, but I guess my "retirement years" got used up in that lost decade, so I'll work until I drop dead doing what I do. I remain friends and associates with most of the people I met through the Cosmic Circle gang, fannish and gamers alike. Nowadays, people who are fans of my work, whether it's T&T, Magic, the work I did on Wasteland or the other computer games, Traveller or Middle Earth, or whatever... near or far, friends by email or Discord or other social media platforms, whether I've met them face-to-face or not yet... many of them have grown to be people I invite into my house in a nanosecond, friends in every meaningful sense of the word.

One of my best friends today I met 10 years ago because we were both working a library event at the Pima County Fair. (My master's is in libraries... I could talk another novella's worth of talk about my library time.) Toward the end of the evening, she asked what I was doing after the fair closed, and I said (knowing her only as library-related and in accounting) that I was "seeing some friends online." She asked, "Doing what?" Cautiously I said, "Playing Warcraft." She looked at me sharply and said, "Warcraft? Or World of Warcraft?" Turned out she was a gamer, was keen on all the fanfic communities, and had played SCA for many years. We became fast friends.

Admittedly, I find it a little hard to relate to people who show little interest in things geekalicious, at least a bit. Still, things formerly "fannish" are so ubiquitous now, it's rare for me to run into anyone who

---

[7] https://blog.deliveringhappiness.com/the-motivation-trifecta-autonomy-mastery-and-purpose.

[8] A movement among players of tabletop role-playing games that draws inspiration from the earliest days of tabletop RPGs in the 1970s.

hasn't at least read Harry Potter, or watched *LOTR* or the Marvel Cinematic Universe (MCU), even if they're still confused about the supposedly "demonic" overtones of Dungeons & Dragons, which is now a pretty generic term for all RPGs amongst those who aren't very familiar with them. I usually have to reference Pokémon to explain Magic the Gathering to non-gamers but when I do, most people get it. They don't have to know the genre or the terms FIAWOL (Fandom Is A Way Of Life) or FIJAGDH (Fandom Is Just A Goddamned Hobby), but we still share something we all enjoy.

I continue to take pleasure in the same kinds of things I did decades ago. I thoroughly enjoy the MCU, and read fics from time to time as friends recommend this or that. I work in the field because I love all this stuff.

I hang my art when I go to fannish cons with an art show. I was one of the returning GoHs at MileHiCon's 50th anniversary last year, and was asked to be an Artist and RPG GoH at Poland's huge all-fandoms Pyrkon this year. That event hosted 55,000 attendees in 2019, but unfortunately, this May's planned convention got cancelled, like so much else, due to the COVID-19 pandemic.

As with everyone's lives, mine got overturned by the virus. Before now, for most events I attended, someone else picked up some or all of the bill. Alternatively, I could expect to make a good income selling autographs, prints, and sketches at *Magic the Gathering* tournaments around the world. Getting to travel, getting enough income to remain overseas and be a tourist, has been absolutely life-changing for me. Just in the last 18 months or so, I was in Spain twice, Portugal, Italy, and France. In May, I would have gone to Poland and the Czech Republic, and, I was scheduled to return to Barcelona again in November, and London in December. All have been cancelled. And I brought home a case of COVID-19 from my March trip in France. At least I was doing something I loved; you can't beat that.[9]

Over all those years and along the way, I made my share of mistakes, naturally. While I don't regret them, I wouldn't make the same mistakes twice if I could change it. I wish I had trusted myself more, trusted my talents and my ability to forge through difficulties. Trusted a few individuals less, and other people I wish I had trusted more.

But I am today the sum of the choices and decisions I made in the past. And I'm pretty impressed with what I have managed to accomplish

---

[9] https://globalhealthc3.org/heroes/liz-danforth/

accomplish, if I say so myself! I have grown men and women whose work I profoundly admire tell me that my art influenced them in their younger years. That is a legacy I never sought but am humbled to have enabled.

One man told me he came into his own literacy, and his desire to become a writer, because of looking at my art in the *T&T* solo adventures and wanting to know what the pictures were about, back when his language skills were not up to the job.

I had one woman say they knew they could work in the game industry because I had gone there first and been successful there. (I wasn't nearly the first, but that's a whole different conversation.) I am embarrassed every time someone tells me "You're a legend!" which I don't think should be right at all... but it does keep happening, and gets said sincerely.

I can only try to be the person they think I am, and keep doing the work that makes me happiest.

essay © Liz Danforth

JACQUELINE LICHTENBERG
All About Connections

"The muggle world thinks all this online activity is deplorable and bad for your health, that parents must limit kids' screen time. It's the exact same attitude the whole world had toward science fiction back then, and anyone stupid enough to be a fanatic about something so beyond practical reality as space travel needed a talking-to."
—Jacqueline Lichtenberg

I was born in early 1942, right during the aftermath of Pearl Harbor in the previous December. The world was in shreds, prospects bleak—and my parents bold, courageous, and looking to the future beyond the chaos.

I spent my infancy in New York, but during the war, I was sent to my grandmother in Arkansas until early 1946. Most of my genetic relatives are of the nonfiction-reading sort, but my mother was the explorer of imagination. In addition to fiction, she pushed vocabulary, elocution, body language, dress code, presentation as the key to success in the world, whereas her childhood had been the crushing poverty of the Depression.

She understood upward mobility and was determined I'd be upwardly mobile. But she also understood Reading Is Fundamental (long before the organization was founded,) and was appalled to be told by my 5th grade teacher that I was flunking reading. So, when I had the measles (before there was a vaccine), she brought me science fiction novels from the adult library aimed at teen boys. (I was a pre-adolescent girl, you see?) She also provided a dictionary and refused to tell me what words meant. One novel, *Battle on Mercury* by Lester Del Rey (1953), was fascinating. When I returned to school, I aced reading. It's really *simple*, you know.

She also connected me to a "pen pal" project where U.S. kids were assigned a foreign pen pal, to help them with English. I got a Vietnamese girl, and wrote 3-ounce letters, longhand on both sides of the notepad paper my Mom supplied. She footed the postage and the incessant trips to the post office to mail my international missives. I got replies almost every day—no idea today what became of that girl—this was years before the Vietnam war, which happened when I was in college.

So, my Mom got me reading, *and* writing. Whereupon, my Dad bought an Olympia manual typewriter (among the first portable typers made), and taught me to touch-type. (He was a teletype operator and did Morse code for the Army in WWII.)

These people unknowingly, and with good heart, unleashed a whirlwind on the world!

Reading science fiction magazines such as *Amazing*, *Analog*, *Astounding*, *Worlds of IF*, (some borrowed from the library, some bought with my precious allowance), I noted the inaccuracy of the illustrations—the words said one thing, the picture, another.

I was in 7th grade when I wrote a letter to the editor of *Worlds of IF*, a scathing, blistering indictment of artists illustrating stories they hadn't read (which gained me a professional artist pen pal, Jack Gaughan). At that time, magazines published letters of comment (LoCs), and because the world was nicer, safer, and kinder, they didn't need boldness or courage to publish the full name and house address of the person who sent the letter to them. My eloquent, adult-sounding, one paragraph, neatly typed without typos, letter—which I blasted out in about 10 minutes, and used my Dad's stamp to send, (three cents from Coast to Coast in three days)—got published. In 7th grade. I was already a PUBLISHED WRITER—in a letter column edited by a real, professional editor (Fred Pohl), in a real professional magazine that published stories like the ones I wanted to write (and get paid for).

Whereupon, my mailbox exploded with an overflowing torrent of letters from an organization called—wait for it—The N3F Welcommittee!

The N3F is the National Fantasy Fan Federation—founded by damon knight (small initial letters by his choice) in April 1941—who also founded SFWA (Science Fiction Writers of America.) N3F is on Facebook and still going strong.

I answered all the letters I got from the Welcommittee and became a dues-paying member of N3F when I saw that Pohl was a member. All the years growing up, my ambition was to become the kind of beacon light to new writers that he was to me, and have my name on the membership roster of N3F even while being known as a professional science fiction writer. Membership of SFWA became my goal. Now I'm a Life Member of SFWA.

Yep, my parents knew about my "fanac," but had no idea that science fiction fandom existed as an organization with a Constitution, elected officers and dues for membership, or that I was "that sort,"—or that opening fandom to the general public would become my career. They didn't "approve" of fanac because they had *no idea* it existed, but instigated and facilitated anything to do with reading and writing, with social networking (all by U.S.P.S "snail" mail, but exactly the same as on Facebook, etc. today, complete with flame wars), and supported anything I enthused about, simply because kids have to "go through phases" to become functional adults.

Little did they know this "phase" would be lifelong!

In 1955, I joined N3F as a reader and became a "letter hack," someone who writes letters to 'zines and everyone. When Alma Hill (a professional novelist) took over the N3F Writer's Bureau with intent to train members in professional writing, I joined instantly. The first lesson that I learned from her, and still teach, is "Writing is a Performing Art."

If you've ever played "Dark and Stormy Night" at a Con, where people sit in a circle and contribute scenes to a co-operative story, you know what a "Story Robin" is: a round-robin story. I participated in the N3F Letter Robins, which later generated the Story Robins, which I relished and always wrote way too much before sending it on to the next person on the list.

When I first joined the N3F, you could read all the science fiction magazines and all the science fiction novels published in a month, and have two weeks left over. It was *not* a popular genre. Keep in mind, society firmly believed it was impossible to put a physical object in orbit about the Earth, Jules Verne's spaceship to the Moon concept was silly, and anyone dedicating their life to that end had to be held in utmost contempt.

So, everyone you exchanged letters with, or fanzines, which then never carried fiction, only commentary on SF being published (as there was no radio or TV SF, and *X-minus One* came later), had read everything you just read. And they all had different opinions.

When I joined, I became an acti-fan (active fan), and started writing letters. Even though I was in 7th grade, my commentaries were gladly accepted and argued. I had no idea I was in a crowd of adult males. There were a few female names, but mostly men in their 20s and 30s. Some teens, but you couldn't tell the difference from reading what they were thinking. I had no idea that was odd until I was long out of college.

There were only a few hundred participants, maybe a couple thousand, and only in the USA. Everyone knew the most prolific letter hacks, and the 'zines contained a lot of personal life reporting (just like Facebook), along with Convention Reports because there were lots of local and regional conventions, and the Worldcon. Many Con Reports were so vivid you felt as if you were there (and 'zines were on spirit duplicator or hand cranked mimeo so they couldn't print full-color photos as we now post on Facebook.)

So, via cold print media, you felt you actually knew the people in person. Pretty much as with Facebook friends.

One of the publications I acquired by joining N3F explained everything. It was Dick Eney's *Fancyclopedia*: an encyclopedia of traditions, etiquette, history, and vocabulary of fandom.

Fandom was and still is a realm complete with BNFs, a history, tradition, unique language, and binding culture—everything a country or kingdom has *except* a physical location. Fans are at home on the Web because we're used to living in a neighborhood that has no physical location.

By definition, composition, subjects covered, and activity undertaken, "fandom" was a tight-knit community of creative visionaries who made their visions come to life for each other.

Fandom of yore has morphed from a small village size community into a worldwide, sprawling network. Fanfic, the most imaginative product of *Star Trek* fandom, has morphed into a significant component of what I now call The Fiction Delivery System—parallel to the Healthcare Delivery System. The Fiction Delivery System is the entire mechanism formed by the industries between the writer's fingertips and the reader's/viewer's eyes. During this COVID-19 pandemic, The Fiction Delivery System has proved itself to be as much of an essential life sustaining industry as healthcare.

Fanfic has become the feedback loop component of the Fiction Delivery System.

Readers buy, download, or stream a story, and that tells the publisher/producer and writer information about their marketing of the story, but not about content. Fanfic feeds back information about why the reader liked the story, and why they might buy another in the series, and what content they want most.

Long ago, 'fans' were thought by publishers/producers not to be worth listening to. Fans were too small a fraction of the audience to affect the profit margin. *Star Trek* Fandom changed that—and as I see it, that change is the most significant contribution of *Trek* to world history. It changes the entire retail landscape, not just of fiction but of all retail. Remember, Amazon started out selling only books!

I quickly learned the definition of fandom—a "domain" (as in Kingdom) of "fanatics" (as in fan).

Today's "fandom" is descended (directly, but as with genetics, has many lines of descent braided in) from the original science fiction fandom of the early 1930s New York, the Lunarians being one such organization.

I had been brought into the N3F in 1955 but fandom had not changed much. I communicated via letters (on paper, "snail" mail), had letters in fanzines, and participated in any activity having to do with writing. I was too young to go to cons until college, and then the workload forced me to gafiate, as studying Chemistry, with minors in Physics and Math at the University of California, took all my time for four years.

But even during that time, I did contribute to some fanzines, one in particular published by Irvin Koch, may he rest in peace, which got delayed for years. If not for that contribution and that delayed publication, *Star Trek Lives!* might never have existed.

The custom in fandom is that if you send in a LoC (letter of comment) that gets published as did mine in Irvin Koch's 'zine, you get a copy of the 'zine for free. (Everyone else pays printing and postage. Fanzine means amateur, volunteer-produced, not "nonprofit" where work is paid for in money). So, I got a lot of free 'zines in SF fandom, bought with coin-of-the-realm, words. That custom persisted into *Star Trek* fandom, as the 'zine and con' fandoms were initiated by long-time members of the Lunarians steeped in fannish tradition.

Though I had a long track record in fandom, I was not a BNF, only a wistful wannabe professional writer. I was always, throughout all this, studying hard to be a professional SF writer.

I did my degree work at the University of California, with the university thinking I was majoring in Chemistry. I was actually creating my own major in science fiction writing. All the best of the best SF writers I loved were chemists. Much later, I figured out that the Chemistry major requirements create a "jack of all trades"—another former chemist (geologist) I knew ran a large, prosperous store.

I learned the biographies of the SF writers I admired, and read lots of biographies from the library about writers and other people, since my Mom was a biography fan. One glaring fact leaped out at me. Professional writers didn't live their entire lives in the same place. All the good ones seemed to have spent some years living abroad, or globe-trotting, just traveling and knowing lots of languages

---

[10]https://www.goodreads.com/book/show/919580.Star_Trek_Lives_

and places. I decided I had to move abroad to complete my biography properly.

But I didn't have a clue how to swing that!

So, I got a job out of college working on a project that was mining the Great Salt Lake for potash and other agrochemicals. The California company had a contract with a similar company in Israel, and gave me a glowing recommendation to the head of the Israeli company, which was mining the Dead Sea for potash and agrochemicals.

I made some personal connections, and moved to Israel, where most people speak English, and I could hack the Hebrew, sort of. German worked, too. (Chemistry major at Cal Berkeley required German and I took all the courses because I needed the five-unit easy A grades. I'm good at languages, not so good at arithmetic.)

While there, I met and married my husband, who had just returned from Toronto to the Israeli company (which no longer exists). He was also a chemist working on the same project. We decided to move to New York, where he had family, and just as we were putting our apartment in Israel on the market (like a condo, you owned an apartment), Irvin Koch's fanzine, with a contribution from me, arrived at our apartment.

It had the whole front of the big, brown envelope covered with "FORWARD TO" markings.

It had gone to the address where I grew up, been forwarded to my apartment in Berkeley, forwarded back because I wasn't in Berkeley anymore, then forwarded to the Kibbutz in Israel where I had been on ulpan [a school for Hebrew—ed.], then forwarded to my apartment, then forwarded to my husband's apartment. My freebie 'zine chased me around the world, years and years after I'd forgotten about it.

And with it came Bjo Trimble's first write-in campaign to keep *Star Trek* on the air.

Had my Mom not brought me an adult book, and my Dad not taught me to type, and had magazines not published the addresses with letters, I would not have gotten Bjo's letter.

Bjo's letter campaign might not have happened had Gene Roddenberry not gone to WorldCon.

I wrote to Paramount that they had to keep *Star Trek* on the air until I could get home. There was no such thing as a VCR or home recording. Once aired, a show was gone forever—reruns cut many minutes of story out to make room for more commercials. You saw it when they broadcast it—or never did.

Thankfully, they acceded to my demand, and I saw *Star Trek* for the first time in my new in-laws' living room.

Then, of course, *Star Trek* got cancelled in 1969, and like all fen, I felt some horrible monster had cancelled the world. Humanity wasn't worth saving.

That's not hyperbole. Really and truly, that's how it felt, because *Star Trek* was unique—not just another TV Series, but absolutely unique in human history. Why couldn't "they" see that? (...Maybe they had seen it, and it scared them?)

I explained some of the reasoning behind my conclusion in *Star Trek Lives!* I held that *Star Trek* was the most important event in human history since the agricultural revolution. As I see it today, maybe that should be since the printing press, but I still think it may well be since agriculture. If fiction is food for the soul, the imagination, the will to live, then fanfic domesticates wild fiction from commercial sources. We fans grow our own!

Many people credit my Bantam paperback, *Star Trek Lives!* (which had been bought by that same Fred Pohl who published my first letter-to-the-editor, who bought my first professional short story. By the time we were marketing *Star Trek Lives!* he had moved from magazine editing to being a book editor at Bantam Books. *STL!* went 8 printings and still turns up in used bookstores) for connecting fandom to Hollywood, creating a feedback loop through which consumers of fiction can affect the content of fiction professionally created for profit. Keep in mind, Fred Pohl was a member of N3F and SFWA—he also wrote terrific SF novels.

In a commercial TV series' business model, the audience is not the customer. The audience is the product. Advertisers are the customer studios sell the product to. So I broke their business model.

Star Trek Lives! (with a foreword by Gene Roddenberry) forged the other half of the feedback loop: closing the loop, and letting creative energy flow from fan to pro just as electricity flows when you flip the light switch. It has taken decades for them to partly repair the business model.

Some of you may have heard of the key organization, the *Star Trek Welcommittee,* which I founded in 1972 to answer the fan mail generated by *Star Trek Lives!* I used the name of the group of fans who opened the door to fandom for me.

Who can say whether *Star Trek Lives!*—with its exposure of the highly respected credentials of fans (Ph.D.'s, teachers, librarians, physicians, lawyers, engineers, chemists, mathematicians, etc.) and their favorite activity, writing *Star Trek* fanfic—would ever have gotten into print had my mother not brought a preteen girl an adult male book because the preteen couldn't read at grade level? Given COVID-19 throwing us into solitary confinement, maybe my mother should be credited with saving a few thousand lives, or just sanity, in the century after she was born, decades after she passed away.

At about the time I was getting over the shock and grief of the cancellation, along came *Spockanalia* and *T-Negative*, the first two *Star Trek* fanzines. I wouldn't have gotten *Spockanalia* #1 if I hadn't been a member of N3F in the process of reconnecting to SF fandom after moving back to the States.

My faith in humanity was revived. If "they" won't do it for us, we'll do it ourselves! Now that's the essence of humanity for me. Agriculture. Creativity. Domestication. Community. We domesticated wild fiction.

At that time, I was launching my professional writing career, raising kids, and taking a correspondence course in writing for profit. The course was invented and taught by muggles. So, I did my homework assignments by inventing my *Star Trek* fanfic *Kraith* Universe and sending it to Ruth Berman's *T-Negative* Trekzine, and any other fanzine I heard of.

Star Trek, being a mere TV series, wasn't considered "real" science fiction by some of SF fandom. So I fixed that by writing *Kraith*. I also wrote a nonfiction "article" (nonfic pretending the *ST* universe is real) for *Spockanalia* which appeared in #4. The writing course promised you would produce a saleable story as homework for Lesson #4. I sold my Lesson #4 to Fred Pohl at *Worlds of IF*. I titled it "Operation High Time", the first professionally published story in my *Sime~Gen* series. Yes, the same Fred Pohl who published my indignant letter about illustrations bought my first story. I doubt he remembered my letter under my maiden name. "Operation High Time" got one of the most horrendously inaccurate illustrations *ever!!*

Kraith drew 50 creative Trek fen into creating and writing parts of my *Trek* "alternate universe", which got discussed in an article in the *New York Times*, featured in a Ph.D. thesis, and subsequently in many academic books and studies about fandom, fanfic, and especially women's fiction. All of *Kraith* is now posted online for free reading on simegen.com, and a fan of it is writing a new story for 2021 publication there. *Kraith Collected*, along with the *Sahaj* fanzines and Jean Lorrah's *Night of the Twin Moons* Trek 'zines, were used by grade school teachers to motivate students to come up to grade level reading.

Kraith forced me to attend my first science fiction convention—the 1974 WorldCon in Washington, D.C.—when I was nominated for a Best Fan Writer Hugo for *Kraith*. I didn't win because by then most of SF fandom (most of the people not remembering me as a kid) was rabidly anti-*Trek* fandom (because, supposedly, TV fans didn't read print novels and couldn't converse intelligently at a Worldcon about that year's novels). The Fan Hugo voting was madly split, for and against *Trek* nominees. Many fen saw Worldcon attendance burgeoning, but mostly with fans of actors in a TV series, not book readers. It was upsetting.

Fans being fen, you see, have to fight about everything. If there's nothing to fight about—we are imaginative enough to make something up. Fandom is a family squabble.

But before that Worldcon, there were the New York *Star Trek* conventions I attended — both the fan cons and the professional "shows" featuring stars on stage and noncontributors in the audience. I had become a sought-after guest and speaker at both.

At a fan con, attendees rent rooms in the hotel, hold room parties, rent tables in the Dealers' Room and sell things they have made with their own hands, and form groups in the lobby and traipse out to dinner to talk for hours then come back and traipse from room party to room party meeting old friends they've never met in person before. At a con, attendees bring the fun with them to share.

At a "show", people park their cars in the hotel lot, attend a program item or two where they expect to be given fun, and then take that fun away and go home at night as if there's nothing more. SF fandom was rejecting the "show" attendees, not actually the fan con attendees, but few knew the difference.

All the SF and ST cons blur together in my mind because this was the 1970s, and I was writing and managing submissions to *Kraith*, writing my own original science fiction, the *Sime~Gen* series with Jean Lorrah (now up to 15 books and still going with more than a dozen contributors, and a brand new Wiki), managing the five *Sime~Gen* fanzines that various editors were turning out, and researching and writing *Star Trek Lives!* I was also raising two girls. Considering how well my girls turned out, I'd do it again if it cost me my life!

Isn't it *odd* that some *Star Trek* fans created "the Internet"—the entire "virtual world"? Fandom has always existed in a virtual space, a domain without land, and now fandom has generated a realm where fandom just fits seamlessly into the virtual matrix.

You may be familiar with the old, and often told, story of the advent of "the Internet"—before there was such a thing as a "browser" or "the Web." A few college students on one campus wanted to play a *Star Trek* video game with some friends on another campus, so they connected two computers (clumsy, huge, university-owned, filled a room, spinning-tape-type "computers"—nothing you'd recognize today) by copper telephone line (not fiber optic, which hadn't been invented yet.)

Star Trek, therefore, can be credited with motivating the invention of what we term "the Internet." Today, the USA officially has a branch of the Armed Services called the Space Force. I wish my muggle high school teachers had lived to see that!

I hadn't thought of this connection between fandom, as it was when I got involved—I mean, there wasn't even a television set in our house then!—and *saving lives today,* as is happening all around with online contacts being the sanity lifeline. COVID-19 isolated a lot of people, but now we connect to the world by streaming TV and YouTube, as well as reading, writing, and discussing fanfic online. I attend a Twitter Chat, #scifichat, on Fridays, to discuss SF concepts, books, TV, everything. *Sime~Gen* has a Facebook Group. People have Zoom meetings with family. I have even attended a Zoom Funeral.

If it hadn't been for my Mom using science fiction to incite me to read, none of the rest would have happened so easily. If not for science fiction, the universe would have had to find another, maybe a less straightforward, way to create the Web, Web 2.0 (social networking) and Zoom, and forge a feedback loop from reader/viewer to commercial fiction purveyor. I'm pretty sure it would have happened somehow, even without *Star Trek Lives!* but it might have cost us more time and money, heart and soul.

Moms rock!

interview © Jacqueline Lichtenberg

DANI LANE
We've Conquered the World

"We would read a fanzine and then write a letter of comment (LoC), send it off and wait months and months for the next zine to come out and read our letter, then wait months and months to get the next zine and read any replies to that letter. No wonder we wrote and illustrated and created... we had all that time while we waited. I feel like the grandma who tells her grandkids about how she had to walk 5 miles to school in the snow... uphill!" —Dani Lane

I grew up back when you had only three television channels and, unless it was Saturday morning, you watched whatever your father watched. We saw plenty of war, western, and monster movies. And luckily, my old man watched *Star Trek*.

The best thing about *Star Trek* was that the stories could be about anything. They called it "Wagon Train to the Stars" but you didn't run into outlaws and Indians. You were up against Klingons and Romulans! At my age, I was supposed to love Pavel Chekov with his Beatles-style haircut, but I was much more interested in Mr. Spock.

I don't think I was overtly fannish about the show, but my parents must have noticed something because they bought me a paperback for Christmas: *Star Trek* 4. It contained six episodes of *Star Trek,* adapted by James Blish. It was my first science fiction book.

After that came high school and boys. I read books assigned in English class. I watched science fiction and monster movies. I met Don and married him when I was 17. As I was completing my senior year and my husband was working second shift, I had time on my hands. I recall that I re-read *Star Trek* 4 and had this stunning thought. If this was *4*, wouldn't there be *1, 2* and *3* out there? So I made my first of many trips to a local bookstore called Tom Sawyer's Book Raft. Not only did I find *1, 2,* and *3*, but also *5* through *12*! Not only that, but there was an entire section of the book store devoted to science fiction! That was 1974.

I started collecting books. I could have gone to the library, but I liked having the book to keep. I suppose you could say I was a fan then, but I don't think that part of my life started until 1977, and *Star Wars.*

133

I was reading *StarLog* magazine at the time and saw articles about this new movie coming out. I was intrigued by the pictures, but nothing they printed beforehand could have prepared me for my first trip to see that movie. Don and I went to see it, and while it wasn't unusual to wait in a line for a ticket, this line stretched all the way around the building. Once inside, and after the famous text crawled up the screen, I watched, amazed, as Princess Leia's blockade runner soared overhead. It was just gigantic!

But then the Imperial Star Destroyer eclipsed the screen, dwarfing the blockade runner. It just went on and on and on and on! We exclaimed in wonder with everyone else in the theatre that day. The robots, the blasters, the space ships... Luke and Han and Leia... Chewbacca, the Jawas, and the Tusken Raiders... I really fell hook, line and sinker for this movie. And my husband Don, who has never been a fan, went with me several more times as we took others to go see this cool new movie.

Star Wars played in the theatre longer than any movie I can remember. Over that summer, I saw it 50 times. I had a part-time job and, when I got out of work, I'd head to the movies before I had to pick Don up from his work.

From as far back as I remember, I have loved to draw. So I started drawing *Star Wars* characters. Not only that, but I started writing stories about Luke and Leia and Han. I went to work full time at Kmart and I fondly remember taking my lunch break in their cafeteria and writing feverishly in a spiral notebook. It was pure drivel, but I had to get the stories out. It was like an itch I couldn't scratch. I read about science fiction conventions and about fanzines, and decided that I would boldly go where I had never gone before.

There was a local *Star Trek* fan club, and they put on Babel Con. I ventured into the hotel, wandering around like a lost soul. I didn't know anyone and the whole experience is kind of a blur to me now, but I do recall the dealers' room and finding fanzines. I had read about them. I wanted them! I grabbed a ton of flyers and bought several *Star Trek* fanzines and that is the day I officially entered fandom.

Fanzines are a gateway into the underground of fandom. Not only do you get the stories, but letters to the editors, ads for other fanzines and other conventions, and there was information about other fans and clubs. I met with the *Star Trek* Club of Grand Rapids (STOCGR) and I began to correspond with some fanzine editors. I sent them drawings, and they published them, sending me contributor copies in return.

One of those editors called me on the phone and invited me to another convention in Lansing, Michigan. It was MediaWest*Con. She said that there were no rooms available, but I could stay with her and her friends. This was a very important step for me, and I should explain why.

By this time, my husband and I had two children. And Don did not understand this infatuation I had for *Star Trek* and *Star Wars*. When I told him I was going to go away for Memorial Day weekend to this convention in Lansing, he was adamantly opposed. When I insisted, he said, "Go ahead, but when you get back, your stuff will be out on the lawn." I wasn't expecting him to be happy about this trip, but those words were hard to hear. I remained steadfast, though. A week later he told me, "Okay, but I don't like it." And right before I left, he said, "Have a good time."

My first trip to MediaWest*Con was one to remember. I rode my new motorcycle, and when I tried to put it on the center stand in the parking lot, it fell over and pinned me underneath. My right foot was wedged under the brake lever, so when I tried to push the bike off me, it was crushing my foot. I flagged a man down who was driving by. He helped get the bike up and we put it on the stand together.

Limping into the hotel, I met my roommates in person for the first time. I didn't know it at the time, but they were Big Name Fans. And there were about a dozen of them sharing this room. I had a sleeping bag, and I put it by the door. I realized that I was coming down with a cold and starting to sneeze and cough. I was really worried that I would be an annoying roomie.

I got registered and finally went into the bathroom, where I unlaced my shoe to look at my injured foot. It blew up like a balloon and was beginning to turn purple. I couldn't tie the shoe as tight as before, but I could walk. And did I walk!

There were hundreds of people at MediaWest*Con. The dealers' room was huge, and just brimming with zines and books, stickers and pins, toys and swords and shirts. . . it was fabulous! But access to the people was even better. The panels were all about topics I recognized and wanted to be a part of. Rooms with their doors decorated and propped open were invitations to go inside and talk to anyone or watch what they were playing on their tv. I met people whose names I recognized from fanzines! Back in those days, the convention hosted a mass breakfast, lunch and dinner for the attendees and after dinner there was a play and entertainment. There were fans in costume and a competition. There were gatherings of filkers and impromptu groups in the lobby just talking and laughing. I learned about many more movies and TV shows that I thought would be right up my alley. And there was an art auction!

I went to the hotel room every night exhausted, sick, and with my foot throbbing. I pulled the sleeping bag over my head with my wadded up kleenex and tried to be as quiet as I could. Afterward, I rode home with so many plans of what to read and what to write and what to draw. When I got home I told Don, "Next year I'm getting my own room."

That was oh-so-many years ago, now. I've been to MediaWest*Con just about every year since. Don has come a long way. He rode with me to a WorldCon in Baltimore, Maryland, where I got a taste of anime. And when I was attending Legacy Con in Washington, D. C. , he let me take his brand new motorcycle. He sent me off to San Diego ComicCon a few years ago just as *Game of Thrones* was coming out. He still doesn't get this fandom thing, but he's supportive and a good sport. In fact, after 47 years of marriage, I think he's glad to get rid of me for a weekend!

I have written stories for zines and for the internet. I've illustrated stories. I've made music videos featuring snippets from movies and television fandoms that I have accumulated along the way. I have so many interests, so many friends, and so many wonderful memories. I have so many books and movies and television shows that I could withstand the COVID-19 lockdown a hundred times over.

I'm still a fan, but fandom has changed. What was once accessible only to those in the know, a sort of underground club, is now available to anyone on the internet. We used to communicate only by letter. I have a storage tub full of correspondence that I've been meaning to unearth and re-read. Our letters used to be pages and pages, either handwritten or pounded out on typewriters. We wrote to people all over the world! We would make the rare phone call, always counting the minutes so as not to run up our long distance bill. We would read a fanzine and then write a letter of comment, send it off and wait months and months for the next zine to come out and read our letter, then wait months and months to get the next zine and read any replies to that letter. No wonder we wrote and illustrated and created... we had all that time while we waited. I feel like the grandma who tells her grandkids about how she had to walk 5 miles to school in the snow... uphill!

MediaWest*Con has called it quits. It was a convention for us writers and illustrators, for us consumers of fanfiction. Now that we can publish a story with the touch of a button, now that we can surf the net for fiction about the characters we love, now that we can Skype our friends all over the world, what purpose does that kind of gathering serve? Still, I miss seeing my friends there.

But the fans that got us started are dying off, literally. I am witnessing the changing of the guard. I rather liked being part of that secret club, but I have to say that all those fans who have now grown up are putting out mainstream media that is making me smile. Everybody knows who Mr. Spock is these days. *Star Wars* and *Star Trek* are franchises that keep delivering, that keep evolving. It may not be my *Star Wars* or my *Star Trek*, but it will be my grandchildren's legacy someday. We have 23 Marvel movies in a cinematic universe I never thought would be possible. There is so much genre media being produced and streamed that it's hard to be that devoted fan of just one show, one book, or one movie.

Not only have we escaped the underground, I feel like we rule the world.

essay © Dani Lane

BARBARA WENK
An Importance of Characters

"I've heard our writing called fan 'lit' versus fan 'fic', which can be a good distinction. Out of information we gleaned from the show or the movie, fan writers built worlds that were complete. And no two worlds were alike; we made the show our own."
—Barbara Wenk

When did I get started in fandom? A long time ago—I was reveling in fandom in Ye Olde Dayes—back when we wrote our stories on a typewriter (and only the more well-off fans had an electric one!), printed our fanzines on a mimeograph machine, and collated the pages together in somebody's living room. And you know what? It was a total blast!

My first convention was Lunacon, 1969. Lunacon had 400 people attending that year, and was the second-largest science fiction convention of the year after WorldCon. So I entered fandom in time to be involved when the break happened between "True" Fandom and "Media" Fandom.

In True Fandom you'd read all SF classics, and usually all the current SF novels as well (there were far fewer SF novels published back then). In first wave Media Fandom, which was *Star Trek* purely and only, there was nothing else. It was all *Star Trek* fandom.

The important point is, those people in first wave media fandom had almost always read print science fiction. But when you got to second and third wave, many fans did not have a science fiction reading background. They had a regular American-person-reading background. So they were bringing in a wholly different culture. They didn't realize that some of these things they saw on the show had ever originally belonged to anybody but *Star Trek*.

People started coming into fandom who only knew the SF stuff because it had been on the show—like the Kzin, which appeared in the animated *Star Trek*. And so there was a set of fans writing stories with Kzin, and if you told them they can't do 'X' because Kzin females are 'Y', they'd reply, "Well, who says so?" And when you'd tell them Larry Niven said so, they'd say, "Who's he to say what Kzin did or didn't do?"

These fans didn't know Larry Niven had invented the Kzin in a series of novels. They'd never heard of "It's a Good Life" (*Twilight Zone*), only of "Charlie X". They'd never heard of the original "Arena".[11]

But these new fans led the way into a new fannish world: that of fanfic. And fanfic was new and different. Before *Star Trek*, writing fanfic about an SF novel was considered a waste of time. Why not write your own stuff, something you might be able to sell to a publisher? Media fanfic changed that – just as it changed what we saw on the screen to fit our own desires. You couldn't sell your media fanfic to a mainstream publisher, but that was never the goal. We wrote fanfic for us, and for our friends. Often fanfic was a communal project, involving several writers creating a new world to enjoy.

And since more fanfic writers were female, that fact shaped the way fan fiction developed.

One reason so much of the fanfic is, essentially, a romance, is because what fans (including me) were in it for was the kick of the emotional bonding between the characters. For us, it was all about the characters, and that's what we wrote about. You could see it with *The Man from U.N.C.L.E.*[12] fandom, *Blake's 7* fandom, *Doctor Who* fandom, and many others. Sometimes the characters became – let's just say, a little bizarre, as writers created their own versions of the people we saw on the screen. *The Professionals* – a British police series considered ultra-violent in its time (late 1970s) took this attitude to another level entirely.

Now, in *The Professionals*, the actors playing Bodie (Lewis Collins) and Doyle (Martin Shaw) are about the same size, and the characters frequently borrowed each other's clothes when one of them was all bloody or something. In the fanfic, Martin Shaw's character Doyle becomes smaller than Bodie; more elfin. and sweet. And we forget about the guy that Bodie always has to remind: Cowley wants to take him alive and don't shoot him, we need to talk to him, you know, but no. In the fanfic Doyle somehow turns into this twee elf who's too pure and sensitive to live. Also he turned upper class. Now look, here we've got William Andrew Phillip Bodie, and we've got Raymond Doyle. Seriously, which one of these two is upper class and which one isn't?

My point, and I do have one, is that between the TV images and the

---

[11] "Arena", which was also a *Star Trek* episode, was originally a short story by Frederic Brown, published 1944 in *Astounding Science Fiction.*(ed.)

[12] The 1960s TV show, not the recent (and totally pull-your-hair-out, gotta-be-an-alternate universe) movie. (ed.)

fanfic on the page, the entire vision and context of what we saw on the show morphed into something rich and strange. And sometimes not much like what we'd actually watched!

Slash fiction was part of the metamorphosis. This genre seemed to have a particular problem, where the people who wrote slash could only conceive of it working if one of the male characters was essentially feminized.[13] I like slash sometimes, but I want it with testosterone.

What really drove me bonkers about a lot of the slash writers is they would not listen to any amount of reason once they decided to slash a couple of characters. You know, all those slash stories about Kirk and Spock being stuck on a planet someplace when Spock goes into pon farr, so the only living thing around is Kirk? The K/S fans kept saying, well, in that case, Spock would have sex with Kirk and be okay, right? And I'd reply, the show says it flat out: "kill the male, take the female." So Spock would kill Kirk, and then Spock would die, right? And then they would start saying: but if, you know, Kirk was there, wouldn't they—? No.

But I digress. We were kind of starting to talk a little bit about what boys liked in fandom, versus what girls liked. Say you start out with some media—*Star Trek*—and both girls and boys view this item and both are incredibly engaged by this item. And so each of them says: I will do a fannish thing involving this show that has inflamed my interest and my passion.

The girl goes off and writes a 300,000 word novel about Spock's childhood. The boy goes off and builds a handmade full-sized replica of the *Enterprise* bridge. It's not totally that simple, but that's the basic difference. Oh, and both of sexes will do costumes—though that's relatively new. Costuming used to be mostly girls, with some guy often dragged along as an extra prop. Costuming could serve as the baseline for fandom.

So...I was there in the beginning, in the first days of the Trek conventions. Devra Langsam and Elyse Pines and a couple of other people had started the *Star Trek* convention, and it was amazing. The first year, they were expecting 300 attendees, and 3500 showed up— that's become part of the lore, hasn't it? I was one of the 3,500. There were so many more people than they thought they'd have, that the hotel wasn't really big enough for it. I'm trying to remember which year was which, but what I do remember is for the 1976 convention, I was on the committee by then. (This was all fan-run, with about 12 committee members and about 24 assistants.)

---

[13] The late Joanna Russ also did a talk on this at a Norwescon nearly 50 years ago. (ed.)

We spent approximately seven hours arguing over the following question: We were offering a four-day convention with major guest stars from the show. Could we legitimately charge the enormous fee of $20 for a four-day ticket? We finally realized we'd have to charge that, to be able to pay our bills for the con. And believe it or not, we had people calling and writing us asking if the $20 included a hotel room!

It was a simpler time: then you could walk into a hotel and just either leave a deposit or a travelers check or cash, and check out the next day. You didn't need massive ID or a driver's license. You just needed money. You certainly didn't need a credit card.

The *Trek* conventions were absolutely amazing, and a total adrenaline high. I still cannot remember which year it was—I think it was 1974—that Leonard Nimoy showed up unexpectedly. I was in the art show, helping put easels together. And all of a sudden you could hear, from a far somewhere in the hotel, the cry of "SPOCK!" and a sound like a herd of buffalo charging. I hastily shut the doors, and all of us working there just sort of cowered in the room until the excitement was all over.

The art shows themselves were such a joy! There was all sorts of art. Paintings, drawings, cartoons, sculpture, necklaces. Big stained glass—you name it, it was there all Trekked out. Needlework, a lot of fabric, a lot of fabric arts, custom name tags. (I'm still trying to decide whether I want to send my "Mirror, Mirror" custom name tag off to the University of Iowa fan archives or not.)

One year at the *Star Trek* convention art show, somebody had done a life size mannequin of Mr. Spock in uniform. It was sitting in a corner, and it gave a lot of people a shock. Somebody had also done a full size working model of the Vulcan lytherette (harp). And so we've got some pictures of D.C. Fontana sitting there next to the mannequin, pretending to play the lytherette and serenading Spock.

A side note on artwork: once there was a piece of Sarek/Amanda artwork called *The Brass Bed*. Alice Jones, an artist who did extremely beautiful pencil work, had done a set of illustrations for Jean Lorrah's fantastic series about Sarek and Amanda, *Night of the Twin Moons*. *The Brass Bed* was one of those illos, and it was up for sale at one of the MediaWest conventions in Kalamazoo. The opening bid was fifty dollars. There was a slight pause and the auctioneer said, "Do I hear any higher?" I said $125, which was my absolute top limit. And there was this dead silence in the room. People were like, she must be willing to go to thousands for this.

There were no other bids. I got it! And a few years later I sold it so I could take a week off (I was a temporary secretary in NYC at the time) and finish a story of my own, "And Comfort to the Enemy," which was published in Devra Langsam's zine *Masiform D*.

Conventions like our *Star Trek* cons weren't at all common. They simply weren't done. There was a year we think we had, something like over 20,000 people show up, and the fire marshals had to shut down the hotel for a while. At one point, I was there in the massive crowd holding a big sign, saying "this is the end of the line!" At one point the crowd was so jammed up in the stairwells that I just completely lost it. I practically threw everybody to one side of the stairwells to clear a path. Because you could not move through them. It. Was. Insane. Sure you get this incredible, incredible high from being there. But I don't think everybody can keep that high for the rest of their lives.

We were at that hotel for several years—the Commodore, above Grand Central Station and right opposite a Howard Johnson's. We ran that Howard Johnson's out of coffee one year. There was a deli in Grand Central that everybody would go down to. They loved us; we bought them out of all their food stocks at these little local places. I can't remember which year it was, but Dave Simon, who was the youngest member of the committee and about 6'5", was wearing a barbarian costume that year. He was with somebody else in costume, and they went over to the Howard Johnson's. Dave sat down, his sword on the counter and shouted, "Innkeeper, bring me a Coke." Ah, it was so much fun.

By 1972, there were already quite a lot of *Star Trek* fans. By the time the *Trek* conventions started—the early ones, the ones from 1972 to 1976—they were all run by fans for fans. 1976 was our last one. We were totally burned out. The con was just too huge. Yes, huge and wobbly and expensive to run. It had sort of taken over our lives. Also at that point, some companies came in, started running the media cons professionally. Looking back now, I can't imagine how we did it. We were a bunch of amateurs running something approximately the size of a political convention. But we had ingenuity, we made do. Women are very good at making do with what we're given.

In addition to media cons, I went to Lunacon. In 1977 I went to WorldCon down in Florida, which was amazing. That particular WorldCon was called SunCon, but it was so badly organized it wound up being called StunCon. The great Robert Heinlein was still alive at that time; he was at the Georgette Heyer dance doing one of those quadrilley things. And I danced with him briefly, which made me feel like falling through the floor in awe, you know? Like, squee! Heinlein ran the blood drive at SunCon, where you could attend a meet and greet and a book signing with Heinlein if you had given blood at the convention that day, and could prove it. I think they ended up with about 400 gallons of blood!

I was also at a couple of New York media cons—Mor'Eastly Con and Mos'Eastly Con, out near LaGuardia airport. The first one, in 1980, was when my *Star Trek* fan novel *One Way Mirror* premiered. The funniest thing I remember from that year (remember, Star Wars had come out in 1977, and *The Empire Strikes Back* had just premiered) was sitting in the media viewing room behind a bunch of people when the show on screen was *I, Claudius*. So many of the fans who hadn't seen it were talking excitedly about the Roman Senate and a lot of them seemed to feel that *Star Wars* had been ripped off by *I, Claudius*. Which had been released in 1976, and was based on a book that came out in 1934. Rather like those people who read the Francis Crawford books by Dorothy Dunnett and then read the Lord Peter Wimsey series by Dorothy Sayers and think Dorothy Sayers ripped off Dorothy Dunnett, when in fact, Dorothy Dunnett was plowing a well-worn furrow, and Dorothy Sayers's first Peter Wimsey books came out about the time Dunnett was born.

To avoid this sort of confusion, always check the copyright page!

I found that reading a lot—and if fans don't read a lot that isn't fanfic, they should—really helps with writing fanfic. (But then, I was lucky, my family came from three generations of readers and we had books of all kinds from all time periods.) I was writing stories very early on (mostly in my notebooks when I was supposed to be paying attention to the times table), but then, when I was sixteen, *Star Trek* came along. It was the first thing that really zapped me, made me want to write about it. My first story was, as they are, kind of embarrassing, but once I was in heavy contact with the New York folks it jumpstarted my writing—Devra Langsam in particular opened the door to fandom and writing fanfic, and I happily walked in and stayed there under Elf Hill for 20 years.

I've got two favorites of my own fanfiction: *One Way Mirror* (a "Mirror, Mirror" story—sort of) and "It's Only Forever" (a *Labyrinth* story). A lot of my fanfic is now available at AO3. But for many of my early stories, as with so much early fanfic, there is no digital text. It's eventually going to go up online, but it all has to be retyped into a digital format. We did not have computers when they were originally written. We were lucky if we could use an electric typewriter instead of a manual one!

Fanfic didn't just mean writing, though. We had to get creative with getting the writing out to readers. I was pretty damn handy with a mimeograph. There was a Gestetner that had originally belonged to the House of Representatives (so it was used to printing bizarre wordage). Devra Langsam bought it secondhand, and she had it for 10 or 15 years before it finally gave out. I helped put together the fanzines, collate, and run the Gestetner.

A passionate Trekkie, I didn't think anything could be as good as my love affair with *Star Trek*—but then *Star Wars* came out. I adored that movie, but I don't recall feeling any urge to write anything about it. And then, in May of 1980, the second movie came out. I went with a friend to wait at the Loews Astor Plaza at, I think, 5:30 in the morning. And we were the last people to get in under the overhangs on the buildings, which was a good thing because it started pouring rain.

For some reason, *The Empire Strikes Back* just grabbed me. (Possibly it was the presence of Billy Dee Williams as Lando Calrissian, whom I wished to take home; Lando is my favorite *SWars* character.) I came out of the theatre after *Empire* just flying. I mean, it was one of those super highs that made me want to write lots of *Star Wars* stuff immediately! And so, among other *SWars* fanfic, I wrote a series with Anne Elizabeth Zeek called *Circle of Fire*, that unfortunately never got finished, but was sure fun while it lasted.

I'd pretty much written out my *Star Trek* fanfic after I wrote *One Way Mirror*. I'd started doing a lot of take-offs from *The Empire Strikes Back*— called the Vendetta Universe—and we would come up with all sorts of storylines. We never wrote any of them down... or if we did, it was more like notes, you know, I have pages and pages of notes about all the different variations of it. And we would run one storyline until we'd run it out.

Fanfic would sound insane to any outsider. But with our fanfic we created people and we built worlds. Fanfic wasn't just about "pairings", or about shipping. I've heard our writing called fan "lit" versus fan 'fic', which can be a good distinction. Out of information we gleaned from the show or the movie, fan writers built worlds that were complete. And no two worlds were alike; we made the show our own.

Fanfic led me into professional writing; I sort of accidentally wound up writing history novels set in ancient Israel. At that time, I was working at a place where my boss would go out all afternoon doing various boss things, while I was sitting off in a corner with a Wang word processor. About 15 minutes after lunch, my office work was done. (Unlike the previous secretary, I could alphabetize stacks of papers that I had to collate.) I didn't really have anything much to do in the afternoons.

So I sort of accidentally wound up writing a historical novel about King David. As one does. Now, I had just watched a two-part King David series—the one they did back in 1976. I was a fan of actresses Susan Hampshire and Jane Seymour. Seymour played Bathsheba and Hampshire played Michal. And Keith Michell was magnificent as the adult David. Anyway, I'd watched that and something rather intrigued me about it—possibly because I liked the two female leads so much.

So one dull afternoon I typed the first line or two of what was going to become my novel *Queenmaker*. Since I had nothing else to do in the afternoons, I decided to see just how far I could take this book using nothing as source material but a map of Israel and the Bible. Of course, I actually ended up doing a lot of research because I love doing research. I discovered really quickly that, as one writer about David said, the best you can say for David is his enemies had a habit of dropping dead very conveniently. And it was fun to tell it from Michal's point of view—she was his first wife—and see what it looked like from that direction as opposed to from David's point of view, which is pretty much what you get in the Bible. Once that was finished in 1991, I started submitting it with an agent who adored it. By 1995, my agent had to give up. We had a stack of the most glowing rejection letters you ever saw: "Everybody in the office loves this, but we don't know how to market it."

Then my agent died, and I didn't have an agent for a while. I can't remember what I was doing, exactly, but in 1997 *The Red Tent* came out, and all of a sudden publishers are scrambling around looking for more books about biblical women. Of course, if you start from scratch, it's going to take you at least a year to produce a book—but I had *Queenmaker* all done and ready to go. So Eluki took *Queenmaker* to her agent and they took it on. *Queenmaker* was bought by St. Martins—which, by the way, had tossed it out the door the first time they saw it, but this time considered it the new Jerusalem. I wound up with a two-book contract, and then another two-book contract, both under my professional pen name, India Edghill.

There tend to be two kinds of reviews with my books. Either: *This is so great. I've never read anything like it, it's so terrific,* or *How dare you take liberties with the Bible and talk trash about somebody like David who's beloved of God.* Yeah, well, God himself said that David didn't get to build the temple because he was a man of blood. Not to mention, after God's offered David a choice of being chased by his enemies for three weeks, or suffering the plague that his people are suffering for three days, or doing something else for three months, David picks the one that's least trouble to him, leaving his people to be plagued and all the other stuff.

What am I doing now? Well, I'm out of contract now, but, um, I'm working on a historical mystery set in ancient Babylon. We'll see how long it takes me to get that done.

From *Star Trek* and *Star Wars* fanfic to historical novels isn't actually that big a stretch. My fanfic was character-driven, and so are my historical novels. Many fan writers have become professional writers, many in the Romance field—again, a character-driven genre. And we learned how to write about that by writing our fanfic. You'd be surprised at how many best-selling authors started out writing fanfic!

The common fannish thread for me—from *Star Trek* to *Star Wars* to the historical fiction writer—is the characters. It's all about the characters. And as I've said before, I don't think I'm the only woman who was drawn into fandom because of character dynamics and my own desire to write about them.

Create people! Build strange new worlds! And make friends while doing it.

You don't even have to be a woman to write fanfic.

It's fun. Come and join us!

interview © Barbara Wenk

TISH WELLS
It's About the Words

"Dreams can come true if you overcome fear. Life's a smorgasbord.
Get out and taste it." —Tish Wells

In 2005, an exhibit of costumes from the *Star Wars* saga—then the prequels and the original trilogy—were going on display in Los Angeles. I was the webmaster, researcher, and a part-time reporter in for the Knight-Ridder newspapers chain in Washington D. C. I planned going out to California, on my own dime, to cover the exhibit.

I stood in a dim, mostly empty newsroom in the early evening, talking on the telephone to a press relations woman. She was from the Fashion Institute of Design and Merchandising in Los Angeles where the show was going to be held.

She finally asked, "And what time would you like to talk to George?"

I went into shock. Talk to George? Speak with film director George Lucas, the creator of *Star Wars*? I had always dreamed of meeting him, I was in awe of him. But I was just a librarian and a fan. Was I worthy of interviewing him?

Then, I thought that I would never again have the opportunity to make a decades-old dream come true. All I had to do was not to be afraid. I replied, "Whenever Mr. Lucas wants to speak with me, I'll be available. Any time he wants."

I'M A writer. Through thirty years of working with journalists, writing articles, writing fan fiction—alone and with others—it always goes back to the words.

I was never formally trained as a W*R*I*T*E*R. I exited college as a professional illustrator and graphic artist. When that didn't happen, after graduate studies, I aimed for a life as a law librarian. Then the newspaper world called. I became a webmaster, because I was the only one in the office who knew how to use those computer tools. I became a photographer because we needed pictures for our stories. I became a journalist because I saw snobbery in coverage of media fans, and decided fans deserved respect. Fandom became my beat.

Let's start with a basic definition. What is fandom? The definition has changed over generations. What's now termed "Fandom" or "Geek" and "Nerd" culture, refers to the abundantly marketed world of movies, cartoons, comics, books, toys, down to R2-D2-shaped fish tanks and LED-adorned lightsaber chopsticks.

I've been lucky enough to be able to weave fandom in with my professional journalism life and fan fiction writing. Looking back at some of the idiot things I did, I am still ashamed of them because they were poor decisions—or conversely, proud of them because I took a risk.

When I started in it, fandom was literary. That means books.

When I was very young my family lived in Hong Kong, then a British Crown Colony. Those coveted books belonged to my older brothers who read science fiction. The omnivorous reader that was their younger sister stole their books, putting them back carefully before the boys returned from school. Otherwise, they might be put out of reach.

I may not have understood what I was reading, but I knew it was very entertaining. My father gave me my first fantasy novel, *The Weirdstone of Brisingamen* by Alan Garner. My first science fiction book was either *Against the Fall of Night* by Arthur C. Clark, or *The Beast Master* by Andre Norton. Years later, I discovered Norton was a woman—Anne Norton, who wrote under a man's name. Writing science fiction at the time was very much a man's world.

I plundered the local American Club library. I read Hugh Walters, a British writer of juvenile space fiction, America's Lester del Ray, L. Sprague de Camp, Ray Bradbury, and Robert Heinlein.

Looking back, I never considered that being a girl could preclude having adventures. Most of the lead characters in these books were boys or men and they had adventures, so I assumed I would as well. I didn't realize the differences between boys and girls.

Outside, the world was moving swiftly. The Cultural Revolution in China spilled over into Hong Kong. I remember having a Molotov cocktail lobbed at our car as we drove away from a protest. The thick stone walls of the embassies were crowned with spikes of broken glass to protect the diplomatic corp. Typhoons (hurricanes in the U. S.) swept over the island, bringing landslides. The bus that took me to elementary school drove by wood barricades printed with "DANGEROUS" in yellow paint. That's where I learned to spell the word.

I walked with other children during the Chinese Lantern Festival, carrying my large goldfish. I remember going to Japanese ghost movies since my brothers had no compunction about letting their little sister have nightmares. All these memories went into the soup that would come out in due time as fiction.

Then, on April 26th, 1966, there was a new BBC program on our small black-and-white television. It was about an old man who time traveled along with his daughter in a big blue police box. It was called *Doctor Who*. It became a must-see weekly favorite for this 7-year-old. That is probably my first brush with "media fandom."

I know I was starting to write stories around then. I have a black-and-white photograph of me in a swimsuit at the local country club, intently writing who knows what.

After four years, we returned to the U. S. and elementary school. I spent those years in constant confusion as to how to navigate the murky waters of cliques where I was excluded for reasons never given. "Why didn't anyone like me?" was a question that still haunts me years after the time was long gone. In 2002, the book *Queen Bees and Wannabes* helped explain the social dynamic of schools, but unfortunately, the emotional scars still remain to this day. The best part of my time in American elementary and middle schools was spent escaping to the local library.

After, when we were transferred to Japan, I brought my hard-built social walls and developing imagination to a less restrictive world. Being a teenager, I was also moody, sulky, and reluctant to share problems with anyone.

I had read my way into more sophisticated science fiction, such as Roger Zelazny's *Amber* books, drawing my versions of each character. I read Tolkien and anything fantasy. I still have an oversize drawing I made of a coiled scaled dragon like Smaug out of *The Hobbit*.

In the outside world, the Vietnam War raged. Richard Nixon was elected, then re-elected, and Watergate started. In a safe city like Tokyo, I had two addictions to cater to: making small cheap plastic World War I model airplanes, and reading comic books.

The models led to an interest in World War I, World War II, and military history. This would become pivotal. It would get me a job that gave me great opportunities.

But fannishly, it was comic books. This was during what we now call the Bronze Age of Comics, 1970-1984. The intricate plotlines of the comics reflected an outside world with hippies, war, and drug addiction—all miles above my comprehension.

Despite my mother's best intentions, I still have many of those comics. I pulled them from the trash when she tossed them out one day, and hid them away. Little did I know that my interest in comics would pay off.

Decades later, there was a huge scandal at that high school in Japan. It turned out that a now-deceased male teacher had been preying on the young girls. I would have fitted the description of his interest, but I was more interested in passing geometry and reading about superheroes. Thank you, comic books, for saving me.

It was in Tokyo that I learned how to use every tool in the school library. Blame the Beatles. When I realized the librarians wouldn't give me articles, I taught myself how to find them. It gave me a huge advantage a couple of decades later when I became a newspaper researcher.

I returned to the U. S. for high school in 1973. One day, I walked into a Latin class, carrying Isaac Asimov's *Foundation*, and the girl next to me asked if I was reading it for class or because I wanted to. I replied, "For fun." We became close friends because she was also a reader of science fiction.

Our group revived the Future Mad Scientists of America, a moribund science fiction group at the school. Most of us were what we would now call "geeks." Back then we were the theater workers, costume makers, fiction writers, and artists. Two-thirds of the group were women. Out of this group came several college professors, a computer millionaire, businessmen, and at least one newspaper reporter. Me.

The Mad Scientists all read science fiction. We discussed Tolkien, Zelazny, and Anne McCaffrey in glorious detail. Costumes were made by hand. The Society for Creative Anachronism was a discussion at every party. We even put on our own Medieval "event" on a friend's farm where the sheep, and the girls, watched the guys bash each other with bamboo sticks. This was all years before Renaissance Fairs became trendy. I learned how to sew making history-based long court dresses.

We created a fanzine called *Tesseract*, laboriously typed on blue stencils and run off on mimeograph machines. It was a masterpiece of teenage writing. It had original science fiction, fantasy, and poetry. We used purple flocking on the cover of one issue, baking each copy in our mentor's oven so the fuzz attached. Another issue had a multi-colored silkscreen cover.

This was the time when the "fannish" world was starting to spread outside of the literary world. *Star Trek* had introduced the notion of "media conventions" where fans could meet, and talk the show. We got rooms at the Washington (D. C.) Hilton for the 1976 International *Star Trek* convention—girls in one, guys in the other—and had the first taste of the merchandising world otherwise known as the "dealers' room." The coveted we-want-it item was diffraction grating strips. Years later, I had a college friend who decorated his leather art portfolio with glittering stars made of it. I thought it was very snazzy. I envied that he could afford it.

I look back at those teen years and think of the terrible angst I carried through it. Adolescence is always a struggle. As usual, I didn't really understand the social rules, even in our small group. Now what is obvious is the rules were fluid, often made up on the spot, and everyone was confused.

As the oldest member of the club, I left first, going to art school— Pratt Institute, in New York City. That was when my past began to swirl into my future. One of the Mad Scientists group's mentors had an older sister who was an editor at Marvel Comics. In my spare time, for the next four years, I worked as a cleanup artist on the pages of the comic books I had avidly read years before.

I remember arguing with an artist about The *X-Men*'s Jean Grey/ Phoenix outfit, saying no woman could run in those high heels. (Anne Hathaway disproved this assentation in the 2012 movie *The Dark Knight Rises*. Oh, well.) I remember looking at penciled artwork submitted by prospective artists and realizing that they had used naked Playboy models for their "life" drawings. That's why each woman looked like she was standing on her toes. The artists had left out the high heels.

It was at Marvel that I got my first piece of professional job advice. On the first day, when I was desperate to not be thrown out of this magic place, a man behind me said, "Someone tell her she doesn't have to work so hard." I've always thought that was bad advice. For me, working hard is the only way to be successful.

Then, in 1977, in my second year of art school, out came a movie called *Star Wars*.

I knew it was coming, because I had picked up the novelization the November before. I'd read enough science fiction to be caught up in the story written by a man I'd never heard of—George Lucas. Years later, I discovered it had been ghostwritten by noted science fiction writer, Alan Dean Foster.

The movie instantly became my obsession, a deep hole that took until 1985 to scramble out of.

I was lucky enough to discover a new group of fans that let me tag along. Three of them became professional writers. The fourth let me share her fannish *Star Wars* universe, something that I'm sure she regretted at times.

Now a word on writing. I've read so many memoirs of professional writers, but I'm still amazed at their professed self-confidence in their writing ability from the start. In the early 1980s, I was a young writer coming out of a reader's background with no training in writing. I had gone to art school, not a place to nurture a writer. I felt as maladroit in writing as I did in the real world. I was also overly defensive to criticism since I hadn't taken "official" writing courses.

Years later, when I was in my 50s, I was amused to discover a letter from my first grade elementary school teacher to my mother saying that I was "too sensitive" to criticism. I was probably six.

By bouncing the stories off my editors, I gained more of an understanding of what was permissible, and what wasn't. Instead of asking questions and seeming "weird," I wrote them into my stories to elicit a response. As the stories grew more complicated and the characters richer, I outgrew the "question phase" and wrote them more independently. I figured out my solutions to real life through my writing.

From the start, I decided that I'd avoid the explicit sex and/or slash that dominated many stories by other fan writers. I concentrated on giving my characters difficult decisions that often led to life-changing choices. Treason. Bravery or simple courage in the face of hopelessness or despair. Hope coming out of tragedy. Death. Sex happened off stage.

Do I sound needy back then? You bet I was! I was desperate to belong to something. I've always thought that the first two or three years out of college are the most difficult for young people. Experts talk at length about the difficulties of middle school and adolescence. But when you first graduate from college, you are expected to be an adult, to know where you are going and what you are capable of in the real world. That's a flawed view. So many graduates flounder around, trying to understand a world where there aren't clear rules and goals.

I had graduated with the hope of *Star Wars* in my eyes. I went to California, got a state driver's license, but couldn't figure out how to make contact with Lucasfilm. I finally gave up on my dream and retreated home. At least there I could eat there at the family table.

The late 1970s and early 1980s were the time of a huge economic recession. That meant there weren't that many entry-level jobs. I worked in bookstores, in fast-food restaurants, and applied for every government job in Washington D. C. My art degree didn't open any doors.

Writing fan fiction became the solace to all the stress of failure (real or not), and I was learning the hard way. I wrote like mad. My editors were hard to satisfy. I earned my first set of writer's scars from my friends in the gladiatorial games of early *Star Wars* fan fic.

Years later, I realized one of the reasons I learned to write very tight and plot-driven stories. Back in those days, our group self-funded the printing of our fanzines. I might be a bookstore clerk, but I had pride and wanted to contribute my third in full. If I wrote long stories, the fanzine had more pages. That meant more expense so, by writing succinctly, I could afford my part of the printing costs without eating oatmeal every day for months.

We did two small fanzines, *The Nerfherder's Companion*, and then more ambitiously, *Contraband*. I used my art training to do unique airbrushed covers. My stories grew to have more in-depth characterizations and original storylines.

But a "sea change" was on the horizon. The term is defined by Merriam-Webster as "a transformation." The personal computer arrived. I learned to use one by writing fan fic for *Star Wars* on the first so-called laptop, an Osborne 1 with a 5" inch screen.

I pursued a graduate degree in Library Science. At that time, many smart women were often channeled into that field by assessment tests. Also, I looked at the want ads in the Washington Post. There were jobs in libraries. I wanted a job.

By 1984, the stresses of graduate school, combined with the changes in *Star Wars* fandom as it shrank after *The Return of the Jedi*, dropped me into a deep pit of insecurity and depression complete with minor paranoia. Then came the accidental death of a very close friend. I made a decision that saved my sanity. Of all the things I was facing, there was only one I could do something about. I walked away from my deep unhappiness with *Star Wars*, the entire fandom, and some of my closest friends.

I went out into the real world, got my first job in a law firm. It was a bad fit. Instead, I ended up with a temporary job that gave me my career. I was sent to Gannett Corporate, and six months later I went to their newspaper, *USA Today*; first as a temporary, then as an employee. I worked as a librarian there from 1985 to 1999.

Journalists live in the real world. They don't really understand fans, but they can report on them. The world I'd been involved with since the age of seven was still dismissed as "weird" and "unimportant." I decided that we needed to start covering this thing called "fandom." I had the need to explain it to a bigger, more suspicious world. Fandom was the hidden parallel world that walked alongside my newspaper articles on costuming (now called cosplay), science fiction or fantasy book reviews, and a long piece on Renaissance Fairs.

I straddled both worlds in my first news article on the 1989 World Science Fiction convention in Boston. It started by not letting my editor use the word "geek" in the opening paragraph because we fans don't "bite the heads off live chickens" (the dictionary definition). I remembered many women authors who chose to use initials to disguise their gender. After discussing that fact with a female editor, I chose to write professionally as Tish Wells.

I can hear you asking, "Why not try to go pro fiction?" Well, journalism is a very intense profession. I was the web editor, reporters' support, and writing articles. I didn't have time to go professional.

In 1999, I switched jobs from *USA Today* to the Knight-Ridder Bureau with the adjacent international newswire, KRT. Part of the reason was that the Bureau Chief I interviewed with was awed by my knowledge of the World War II campaign in North Africa. Why did I know about the latter? Researching the background for *The Rat Patrol*. To write in that fandom, you really had to know your military history. My fannish interest got me my new job.

All this time, I was still writing fan fic on the side. I moved on to shows like *The Equalizer, Airwolf, Max Headroom, The Wild Wild West,* and more. I found an editor who took on all the costs of publication, so I could tell longer and longer stories and not be forced to write tight to save money. The professional researching skills honed in the newspaper world helped create the backdrop for my fiction. Whenever I ran into a plot problem, I'd do more research, and the problem would vanish.

The 1960s war drama *The Rat Patrol* led to three novels and numerous short stories based in World War II. A *Kung Fu: The Legend Continues* novel led to in-depth research on South Africa and mercenaries. The Falkland Wars became the background to two novels for *Voyage to the Bottom of the Sea.*

I collaborated with two others on the six-issue, multi-fandom fanzine, *CrosSignals*, which ran against the then-fannish thinking that said a fanzine should be based around a single universe. Our fanzine had crossovers (now called "mash-up") stories between different shows or movies. It was a hit.

CrosSignals was quoted in college professor Henry Jenkins' *Textual Poachers* (1992). Unfortunately, he managed to misspell my last name, so I became invisible to the bigger world. In 2018, I mentioned this fact to him, and he said it was a pity that it was too late to change for an anniversary re-issue. I decided it was too late to remind him that he'd promised to correct it in future editions when we complained in 1992.

Then came the World Wide Web. The online fan fic world seemed to have a vast number of unexplained rules, a familiar situation for me. Internet discourse also seemed to be afflicted with the same negative aspects of past fandoms. It took another couple of decades for me to finally post some stories online.

"Fandom" had become mainstream. Marketers realized they could reach out and introduce you to more buying opportunities. The comic books of my youth became the multiple movies of the Marvel Cinematic Universe.

In 2001, I hesitantly let *Star Wars* back into my life. At a convention I met a group making a fan film, *Star Wars: Revelations*. For the next several years, I followed the filmmakers and their quest. Then, in 2005, I wrote a feature story. The avid fan attention promptly crashed the fan movie's computer servers.

I realized that, like years ago when I came back to the U. S. and found the tormentors of elementary school had moved on, the problems I faced in *Star Wars* fandom were gone as well. We'd all grown up. We'd moved on.

But nagging fannish issues remained. In a master index of *Star Wars* fanzines, I found all my early stories had been listed under someone's else's name. I asked the editors in 2000 to fix it, but never followed up to see if it was done. 9/11 happened, and mislabeled stories seemed a minor annoyance compared with that. Still, it bugs me, even as the Jenkins misspelling still does.

I ended up writing articles for the Knight-Ridder/Tribune newswire, about television programs like *Turn, Copper, The Musketeers*. I did many book reviews. I interviewed actors like Peter Capaldi of *Doctor Who*, Benedict Cumberbatch of *Sherlock*, and talked with Academy Award nominee Alfre Woodard about *Copper* as she hauled her suitcase across an airport. I went to several of the mega-Star Wars Celebration conventions and wrote about Ashley Eckstein—the voice of Ahsoka Tano in *Star Wars: The Clone Wars*, who had created a women-centered fan clothing line, Her Universe. I did it all on my time and funds. The Bureau, which covered Congress, wars, and politics, didn't consider popular culture as part of their definition.

I was fine with that. It gave me freedom to cover whatever I wanted.

The real world lent texture to the fan fic writing. I reconnected with a noted fan writer, Maggie Nowakowska, and started a very enjoyable collaboration that led to more short stories and novellas.

Over the decades, I wrote over eighty fan fic-related stories, fiction and nonfiction, novels, short stories and articles, not including the unfinished works. I still have nineteen drafts of one. Every now and again, it pops up with a new ending, asking me to write it.

Then, in 2015, the newspaper industry began to crumble. I was the first to be let go. I emerged blinking into the new world, shading my eyes from sunshine, and wondering what would happen next. Maybe write that professional *Star Wars* novel I'd always wanted to? I was invited to be in the *Star Wars* fan women documentary *Looking for Leia* as a journalist and writer. That felt good.

I can't imagine my life without fandom and the friends I made there. For better or worse, fandom and the imagination that it sparks is my true home. I can't imagine my life without it.

_____

*essay © **Tish Wells***

CAROLYN E. COOPER
Postcards from the Edge of a Long Time Ago
(In a Fan Culture Far Far Away)*

with apologies to Carrie Fisher

It's 1966. I'm babysitting my neighbor's four-year-old son until both of our mothers return from work. He wears a cape I made for him out of a dark blue tablecloth and a mask cut from construction paper. We are playing "Batman."

He is, obviously, Batman. He is always Batman. Tonight I am The Riddler. I do a pretty good Frank Gorshan Riddler impersonation for an 11-year-old. The campy TV series is adored by the two of us (and the rest of America). I create scenes for us to enact based on the latest episodes. In 40+ years, this will be called cosplay. Now, I am just his favorite babysitter. Both of us want to extend the pleasure we get from the TV experience. Unwittingly, we share exploring the characters and the world of "Batman."

I believe this is why I, and others, produce fan fiction (and fan art). We are touched in some way by someone else's characters and world and want to extend the contact. Conceivably, it's just an escape from our mundane lives. Or possibly it's to connect with our true inner selves. Or our inner child. Maybe it's just fun and a hit of endorphins. But in some way, we want to interact with those characters and that world. We want to dig deeper into ideas and emotions that are triggered. Like fans of anything, we want to share our interests, thoughts, and feelings with others, to be a part of something more significant and personally meaningful.

Even before there was a media fandom, I created fan fiction. I was the only child of a single, working mother at a time when women were supposed to emulate Donna Reed. My caregivers were mostly other extremely busy women *attempting* to emulate Donna Reed. I spent a *lot* of time alone reading and watching media. So I created my imaginary playmates and stories from that media.

IT'S 1979. Due to family loss and the "Rust Belt" financial crisis of the 1970s, my husband and I couldn't return to college until now. Shortly after enrolling in a small college in an isolated community, we

157

started a science fiction and fantasy (SF/F) club. From there, we discovered SF conventions, known then as SF cons. Traditional fan-run conventions usually had a writer Guest of Honor, an Artist Guest of Honor; a Dealers/Vendors/Hucksters Room; the Hospitality Suite, an Art Show, frequently a Costume Contest, possibly a Writer's Workshop; and many panel discussions on SF/F topics—mostly literary with a few panels on film and television. A few gamers would tuck up in someone's room or a tiny, unused meeting room. Dungeons & Dragons was just emerging, and a tip on where to find 20-sided die was a hot commodity.

Some conventions, like Aggiecon at Texas A & M, rented SF/F films to show. Other cons bullied or cajoled fans who had private collections to drag out their projectors and run episodes of old movies and television shows like *Twilight Zone, Outer Limits, Voyage to the Bottom of the Sea, Stingray, Doctor Who,* or *The Prisoner.*

(As a side note, the *MST3K*[14] concept of talking back to the film while watching bad SF movies was created at Armadillocon 1, when the original film programming failed to show and author Howard Waldrop's collection of truly awful 1950s & 60s SF films and television was substituted.)

AT A TRADITIONAL, fan-run convention in Houston, Texas, I enter a room scheduled to show original *Star Trek* episodes. At this time, there are no affordable VCRs or tapes. (The series ran continuously on independent TV channels *somewhere,* but there was no independent station running the series in my area at a time I could watch. And, of course, there were no DVRs or time-shifting. You watched a show when it was on or not at all.)

There are very few people in the room. One is a woman about my age reading a hand-bound magazine that has a Vulcan on the cover. Not being especially shy, I walk over, introduce myself, and ask what she's reading. The woman's name is Elaine Hauptman, a gracious, bright, delightful woman who takes no offense at this nosy stranger. Having no clue about how she's going to change my life, Elaine says she's reading "a media fanzine." She then tells me about Starbase Houston (the local *Trek* fan club), media fandom—and the world of media fanzines.

Wisely, as I was to learn later, Elaine has a policy of never loaning her zines. However, she invites me to come up and stay for a weekend and check out what she's collected.

---

[14] Mystery Science Theatre 3000 (ed.)

We sit in Elaine's TV room/library, as she recommends stories or entire zines. (I can't now recall all of the titles, but I know they included several *Warped Space, Southern Enclave,* and *Scuttlebutt* issues.) Then she hands me *Sahaj Collected* by Leslye Lilker.

Once I start it, I do not sleep. It is agony to stop reading and politely interact with Elaine for things like food. Elaine seems to understand, and we both spend most of the weekend curled up reading zines in silence, eating delivery pizza.

I return home with the address for zines to order, and for zines that will tell me about zines to order. I have very little spare money while working and going to college, but begin building my collection, starting with *Sahaj Collected.*

BEFORE THE Internet made publishing instantaneous and global, zine publishing and distribution were processes of anticipation and delayed gratification. For one thing, if you were a fan writer, you needed to have your story published in a zine. Sure, you *could* write your story, reproduce it either with carbon copies or mimeo (aka ditto), and snail-mail it to people, but that was slower and narrower in audience. Xerox machines (aka photocopiers) were uncommon and expensive. It's a time when writers use typewriters, and personal computers are a novelty.

MY FIRST stories are written on an Osborne Computer running Wordperfect on CP/M. The Osborne is the first portable computer, the size and shape of a portable sewing machine, weighing a mere 26-pounds (11. 79 kilograms). I lug mine to work where everyone marvels at the technology and my ability to do wordprocessing, build databases and create spreadsheets. The IBM personal computer and Microsoft DOS arrive eight months after the Osborne, and don't include any productivity software. Windows and Mac technology isn't even a concept—except at Xerox PARC in Palo Alto, California. ARPANET, the government precursor to the Internet, is used illicitly by SF/F fans at research universities to organize conventions on the giant University workstations. The amateur fan magazine, or fanzine, was the best way to share your fan fiction and artwork.

I'll skip the whole history of fanzines (that is what Google and Wikipedia are for, or check out my brief video presentation for the London Worldcon).[15]

---

[15] The presentation is here: https://carolynecooper. com/a-very-brief-history-of-fanzines/

But I will mention that traditional SF fandom zines rarely contained fiction, unless it was a parody, and were mostly informational or containing "Letters of Comment", called LoCs. Before online forums, mailing lists, and discussion boards, LoC zines were how fans discussed hot topics of interest. Mark Zuckerberg wasn't even a zygote. Flame wars did exist, but were fought over months and years—and just as bitter and pointless. Imagine a battle between two sloths—in t-shirts and faded jeans.

If you wanted to place your story in a zine, or buy a zine, or tell everyone else about the amazing "My Mother the Car" (an actual TV series) story in the latest *I Watch Too Much TV* zine, you had to subscribe to an informational zine. *Scuttlebutt* was the media fan Facebook of its time.

Scuttlebutt contained letters by fans (often objecting to a letter in a previous issue by another fan). It also had announcements of new zines looking for stories and art, available zines to buy, zines that had closed, or conventions where zines could be purchased in-person while connecting to other zine fans. Think *Writer's Digest* and *Writer's Market*, but for fans. What started as a simple 2-3.5 pages folded digest-sized, stapled, and mailed for the cost of a single 1st-class stamp (15 cents) quickly grew into a thick publication with tiny text.

In 1980, the editors of *Scuttlebutt* retired, and like a star going supernova gave birth to many others, most notably *Universal Translator* and *Datazine*. *Universal Translator* had LoCs, reviews, personals, etc., while Datazine was almost exclusively an adzine. Think the Craigslist of its day. Occasionally, there would be notices by fans of money lost on zines that never appeared or other issues in the community.

THE ZINE EDITING AND PUBLISHING PROCESS

As publisher/editor, you solicit submissions—with a deadline that is mostly a wish. As you receive the submissions, you either send a (hopefully) polite rejection or send editorial notes on changes you'd like to see—and hope the person doesn't take offense. Many writers do take offense and send you hate mail. If you request changes, you must monitor the calendar, send encouraging notes, and hope the revisions arrive in time to type, edit, and proof the final draft in the format needed for the layout.

Even if you create all the fiction and art yourself, you still have to create a final master to deliver to the printer by the deadline—leaving enough time for collating and binding. Unlike online fan fiction, you can't revise after you publish. (Unless, like Leslye Lilker, you rewrite your tale 30 years later and re-publish it in digital format.)

I HUNCH over a table attempting to carefully align a Letraset dry transfer letter for the title page of *From a Certain Point of View*, the first publication from Whine Press. I am slightly high from the fumes of the spray mount I'm using. My entire zine master must be completed in two days to meet my printer's deadline, or I won't have the zine ready for MediaWest*Con.

I have already made two trips that morning to Texas Art Supply for more dry transfer lettering sheets, X-ACTO® blades, more spray mount, another pack of layout stock, and artist's tape. I'm holding my breath as I carefully place and rub the letter from the plastic Letraset sheet onto my key lining sheet sitting on my tabletop lightbox.

I hear the scrambling noise of a slightly hysterical cat. I look to the floor. My mad tortoiseshell rescue cat, Bella Donna, spins, hops, and shakes her front paw before streaking away to the kitchen and streaking back to the same spot. She falls to the floor on her side, panting. I reach down and pull the small, sticky scrap of layout paper from her front paw and toss it in the trash can. It's the fourth or fifth time in the last two hours I've removed sticky tape or paper from her. She sits up, glares at me, and proceeds to groom as if nothing has happened—before going to sit again in the scrap pile.

THE ZINE production process was slightly different for each publisher. The publisher was usually the editor, one of the authors, and possibly an—or the only—artist. A lot depended upon the publisher's skills and tools, interests, and, most importantly, how much the publisher could afford to spend on production, in either money or time.

Most early publishers approached fan fiction to hone writing and editing skills for a professional writing career. They took a book production approach to design. And in many cases, the text was produced only on a typewriter, hopefully an electric. Others, often with a graphic design or art background, used a more magazine-style technique—often mixed media zines like *Warped Space*, which contained content based on a variety of shows and films.

I AM in love with someone I will never meet. No, not Mark Hamill. I will meet him with some *Star Wars* fans after a Broadway performance in *Harrigan & Hart*. I'm in love with Jan V. White, author of *Editing by Design,* and *Designing for Magazines.* My copies of White's books are stained and sprout Post-its® marking favorite passages. I will soon fall in love with David Goines, artist extraordinaire, creating intricate posters printed with up to 26 spot-colors on a Heidelberg press, recalling the iconic poster art of the Belle Epoque. And if that sounds like bizarre jargon to you, don't worry. It means you're normal.

I treat my zines as design and printing production experiments. Each zine had a design theme and a new production problem to solve. Eventually, I buy a small, offset tabletop A. B. Dick 810 printing press to set up in my breakfast nook.

I started a small informational and LoC zine on publishing zines called *Blue Pencil* (A special blue pencil was used in professional production because it is non-reproducible). To my surprise, much of my piece on zine design is now on the Fanlore.org website.[16]

I think I met a total of six other fan publishers who geeked out on the subject of print design. Most publishers, like Jenni Hennig, stuck with straightforward, clean design—and much more content, leading to the mega-zines with more than 300+ pages.

Initially, with a small distribution and limited funds—from publishers and readers—offset printing, let alone xerography (photocopying), was too expensive. In the earliest days, most zines are produced on mimeograph (also called ditto or duplicator) machines, which were relatively portable and accessible. (I remember the sharp, sweet smell—and contact high—of purple test papers fresh off the mimeo.) For mimeo reproduction, you have to type (or draw with a sharp, hard, point) the content directly onto a master, also known as a single-page stencil. You couldn't make corrections on a master except by cutting out the error, typing the correction on a new master, and then trying a tedious, finicky attempt to tape the correction in place—with fingers crossed that the tape would hold through the printing. When printing, the master is attached to a metal drum that picks up an alcohol-based processing fluid and prints it on a piece of paper as the drum spins. Each master could produce a few hundred copies before fading out.

However, as word spread, many early media zines began selling in the thousands, and several accumulated sales of 3-5,000. This matched sales for many new, mid-range hardcover authors at the time. Also, the market wanted more—more stories, more art, more production values. Larger print runs and production values led to

---

[16] https://fanlore.org/wiki/Walking_the_Tightrope:_Experiments_and_Risk_Taking _in_Zine_Design

production values. Larger print runs and production values led to more offset printing—and more complex production.To GO to press—that is, get your zine printed—required a clean master copy. If you wanted to mix artwork with text or use a different font, it had to be on the master. When desktop publishing software and laser printers became affordable, this was reasonably easy to do—once you worked your way through 500-page manuals, blue screens of death, and incompatible file formats and hardware. However, before desktop publishing, going to press required an entirely different set of skills.

In the beginning was the word—and the word was typewritten.

TEXT

Unless it was a graphic zine, like *Future Wings Flypast*, text was your primary content. So you usually started by producing your body text. Before word processors and personal computers, you used a typewriter. You probably had no choice for your font. Standard typewriters had one set of keys in one font, pica or elite, in one size. The IBM Selectric® introduced an interchangeable ball that allowed you to switch to a different font and font size, but the machines and the type balls were not cheap.

But no matter what kind of typewriter you used, you couldn't go back and un-type. If you made a mistake, you stopped, manually corrected with a typewriter erasure or Wite-Out® (invented by former member of The Monkees and record producer Mike Nesmith's mother. Seriously.). If you had a high-end typewriter, you might have an expensive correcting ribbon.

When dedicated word processors and personal computers with word processing software like WordPerfect came along, correcting and editing became much simpler and easier. But not necessarily faster, since it encouraged making frequent changes to the text and playing with the layout.

Word processors also required a way to print out the text.

Initially, the only affordable personal printers were dot-matrix: very fast, but producing text that was hard to read and butt-ugly. Several typewriter companies quickly came out with what were essentially typewriters that could interface with word processors and computers. Some offered interchangeable daisy wheels, giving a choice of 2-4 font options.

IT IS early on a Sunday morning. I have had less than three hours of sleep. My Smith-Corona Daisy Wheel printer has been running for 48 hours straight. It uses continuous-feed tractor paper like a dot-matrix printer, making a large, growing, neatly folded stack on the floor. Tearing off the perforated sides cleanly and separating the pages with a sharp snap will soon be a lost skill.

I cradle my coffee like a life jacket on the Titanic and look at the 5" screen on my Osborne computer. I smell a burning odor. I sniff my coffee. Not that. I set my coffee down and follow the smell to my printer. The pages are an increasingly illegible smudge. There's much cursing. I pause the printing and inspect the ribbon. The ribbon is fine. I look closer.

The plastic daisy wheel is overheating and melting.

SOME ZINE publishers who worked in corporate or institutional offices had access to systems with typeset capabilities, high-end printers, or laser printers. Leslye Lilker's *IDIC 6* was the first typeset zine. Zine-design envy caused me to buy a $6,000 QMS laser printer as soon as they were available. It cost the same as a brand new VW Beetle.

With laser printers came desktop publishing—which changed everything, and nothing. The basics stay the same: acquire content, edit content, design the layout, produce the master, duplicate, collate, bind, and distribute.

ARTWORK

For mimeograph-type printing, the artwork had to be drawn (or traced) directly on the master. For offset printing, and later xerographic reproduction, artwork could be added by cutting-and-pasting into the masters, either manually (before desktop publishing) or digitally (after desktop publishing).

Pre-desktop publishing, you, as editor, had to decide where your artwork would go. Zines with a lot of art submissions might create an art gallery section, especially if they had a lot of art unrelated to the rest of the content. Laying out the artwork on a single page is easiest. Actor-based character portraits (Kirk, Spock, Han, Luke, et al.) were popular with many artists because they could sell the originals at media art shows. During the height of zine publishing and the famous MediaWest*Con art auctions, portrait originals by artists like Karen River could go for several hundred to over a thousand US dollars.

Story illustrations were not only more time consuming to produce for the artist, but sold for less, making them less profitable. (This is why I have several beautiful pieces of pen-and-ink story illustrations.) Great illustrators like Wanda Lybarger were in high demand. Also, incorporating story illustrations into the layout required more work. As a lover of the great magazine illustrators of the Golden Age (roughly 1880-1930), I always wanted more story illustrations—and then cursed during the desperate dash to get the masters laid out in time.

TITLES, COLOPHONS, TITLE PAGE, AND THE OTHER BITS

Titles and distinctive sections like the title page often used different fonts. Before desktop publishing and laser printers, if you wanted to have a different font, you had to typeset them separately and place them into the master page. And it was expensive.

By the late 70s, electronic typesetters, precursors to the laser printer, were available. But typesetting service was expensive unless you happened to have access to one through work or connections. For most zine publishers, that left dry transfer lettering.

Dry transfer lettering consisted of sheets of plastic paper with the letters of the alphabet printed with special ink on one side. The letters are transferred to another surface, usually paper, by positioning the letter where you want it and rubbing firmly—but not too aggressively—with a hard-edge tool on the front of the sheet. If you didn't rub firm enough or long enough, or if your lettering sheet was old, you might only get part of the letter. It was slow, tedious work.

The two dominant dry transfer lettering companies were Letraset and Chartpak. Letraset licensed or developed professionally designed fonts while Chartpak often created knock-offs that were "close enough." Chartpak also offered some delightful dingbats and faddish fonts. I preferred Letraset not only for the better quality of font design, but they also tended to be better quality transfer sheets with fewer failures. Neither variety was cheap. Though each lettering package had several of the most commonly used letters, I frequently discovered after laying out several pages that I was just one letter short. Somewhere in my storage unit, I may still have a couple of ancient, dried-out sheets.

ZINE PRINTING

I am standing at one end of an A. B. Dick 860 offset one-color printer in the crowded print shop of Shoestring Press, owned by Mary Lowe and Katharine Scarritt. All mom-and-pop print shops are crowded. There are boxes of paper: many, many 70-pound boxes of paper. The room is filled with equipment, tools, rags, and cans: soda, press cleaning solvents, and printing ink, mostly black. But right now, there are cans of primary colors on the sizeable work table. My fingers are steadying four pieces of cardboard that divide the spot color inks in the ink tray. I have ink on my face, in my hair, along my arms. I straddle the printer's paper collection bin squealing delight as interior page after page of *From A Certain Point of View #1* spits out between my legs with rainbow borders. This is not an OSHA-approved activity.

Despite having worked sixteen hours straight, Mary is also excited. I don't *think* it's because we each ate a can of frosting washed down with Coke a short while ago. Our insane experiment worked! *From a Certain Point of View #1* will have interior color, scads of interior *spot* color.

OFFSET LITHOGRAPHIC printing presses require etching plates, mostly metal. The press then applies oil-based ink to the image areas and then presses the plate against the printing surface (usually paper) as it spins past. Even a small offset printing press is noisy and messy and cantankerous, requiring regular maintenance and cleaning with toxic solvents after every print run or color change. Each side of the surface printed requires at least one printing plate and one pass through the printer for each color used.

Most mom-and-pop print shops, like Shoestring Press, could only print one color of ink at a time. To print two colors required running the paper through the printer twice—with a thorough cleanup to remove all of the first ink before the second run. That's why the price jumps significantly for every additional color. You can have any color you want—but just one—and it should be black.

Even a single color required two print runs if you wanted to do double-sided printing. A print run is each time you are printing a different plate. So even if everything was going well—the printer wasn't acting up that day (a rare occasion) you could expect at least a 10% loss on a print run.

If you need to produce 500 good, usable sheets of paper, you had to budget and expect to print at least 550 sheets. To do double-sided printing, you would need at least 600 pieces of paper. Usually, you'd add a few hundred just to be on the safe side because recycling paper was easier and cheaper than doing another print run because you didn't have enough useable pages for the project.

It was worse if you wanted to add color. The more times through the press, the more likely you would have misfeeds, stuck sheets, break downs, and registration failures. To do two colors on each side, you planned on printing at least 1000-1,200 sheets to get 500 useable pages.

A spot color is a single, flat, pre-mixed color. The colors in a tube of artist's paint or a can of house paint is a spot color. Say you wanted to print an illustration of *Star Trek*'s Uhura in her red uniform. There would be two printing plates: one for all the black lines and one for the dress's red shape. Since you want the black outline to print over the red forms, you would print all the pages with the red ink first, then, clean the press thoroughly to remove all red ink, ink the press with black ink, load the second plate, and run the paper through again to print the black lines and shapes, in the exact right position. If everything registers—that is, lines up correctly—you do a happy dance. But it's tricky getting things to register since it requires consistent flow through the press.

If you are trimming the final publication down to size, you can use registration marks. Major publications use registration marks and trim. But for small presses using standard paper, correct registration comes strictly from the paper feeding correctly through the machine. Due to the many possible problems mentioned, you expect many misprints.

Spot color produces flat, solid color like a rubber stamp or brush. Think Art Nouveau posters or a logo. To create shading, or tones, the artist has to draw lines of varied thickness called hatching.

To make gradient shadows and images, like a photograph, you have to use halftones. Halftones are screens of tiny dots. Where the tone is darker, there are more tiny dots. Where the image is lighter, there are fewer tiny dots. That is a simplified explanation, of course. But halftones are what made it possible to print black-and-white photos starting in 1869. To print color photographs and images, you need to use halftone screens and the four-color process.

MOST OF the color printed today uses the four-color process, also called CMYK, for reasons that will become clear. The four-color process, in brief, requires scanning the multicolor image through light filters that convert the images into four separate halftone plates: Cyan (blue), Magenta (bright pinky red), Yellow, and Black. Then, you rotate each halftone screen, so it's at a slightly different angle from the others to create the printing plate. Usually, you print Yellow first, then Cyan, followed by Magenta, and finally, Black.

I desperately want four-color process for the front and back cover of my first zine, *From A Certain Point of View #1*. But commercial printers want $1,200 ($3,755 in 2020) for a *minimum* of 1,000 copies. Mary Lowe at Shoestring Press wants to try four-color process work, but she doesn't want to do my covers as her first experiment. She negotiates with her plate-making vendor to print my cover art on regular glossy paper for only $250 as a test of their work. The color is a little off from the original Dr. Martin's Radiant Watercolors, but I'm still thrilled.

The debate rages who should be spray mounted on the front cover, Luke or Han. The other would go on the back. I decide to alternate front cover options. It's a hit!

THE PRINTED pages do not come off the press collated. So all 500 (or more) copies must be collated before binding. Large print shops often owned a collating machine; however, it was an additional fee. As was binding. So many zine editors had to do their own collating and binding.

IT'S SPAGHETTI. It's almost always spaghetti. Spaghetti is cheap, easy, and fast: boil pasta, heat store-bought spaghetti sauce, put out a large container of Kraft "Parmesan cheese," paper plates, a roll of paper towels, and plastic utensils. Generous editors offered a vegetarian *or* meat sauce option. Pizza was more expensive. Not to mention the problem of meeting everyone's pizza preferences and dietary restrictions. It's usually BYOB (Bring Your Own Beverage). Alcohol is discouraged until collating is done.

Zine collating parties consisted of people who owed the editor a favor, were in a relationship with the editor, were blackmailed, or volunteered for the promise of dinner and, usually, a free copy of the zine. If you were a media fan in an area with several zine editors, you stopped answering your phone around late-March. Every editor was trying to make the MediaWest*Con deadline.

If you were a zine publisher who was running late, your friends and family were already booked. Now you commandeered the living room, dragged all of your videotapes out, and re-watched *everything* while assembling your freshly printed zine.

The collating was done in sets of 8-12 pages because that's as far as most people's arms could reach. The sets were then stacked cross-ways and then set aside for punching and binding.

"THIS SET's out of order."

Everyone stops eating and talking and stares at the speaker, listening like the people in E. F. Hutton commercials.

"It goes from page 12 to page 26."

There's a collective groan. People put down their plates and start going through the sets to see how badly the collating is screwed up. It's going to be a very long night.

INITIALLY, ZINES are stapled. Stapling is the fastest, easiest, cheapest solution; staple-and-tape was a studier, more costly option. Some zines were hole-punched and used report fasteners.

However, as zines became thicker, most media zines used spiral binding, also called comb or GBC binding. Spiral binding machines were affordable, portable (you could even bind on the drive to the convention and in the room each night), and used cost-effective plastic fasteners that came in sizes for even the most mega of zines. And you could quickly fix collating or printing errors without damaging the pages. Similar to Kleenex as a common term for facial tissues, GBC became a common term for spiral binders.

Spiral binders also allowed the zine to lie flat for easy reading while eating—and photocopying. Spiral binding proved a boon to zine piracy.

I AM ecstatic. I have finished collating and binding all of the zines for MediaWest*Con three days before I start the 24-hour drive. Usually it's touch-and-go. I survey my living room. It looks like the aftermath of a Category 5 tornado. Extraneous pages of different zines lay scattered about with GBC-hole punched confetti. GBC binders in assorted colors act as traps for bare feet. Misprinted pages lay tossed helter-skelter. Cups, plates, empty pizza boxes, and chopsticks are strewn across bookshelves, under furniture, and sticking to cushions. Videotapes are in teetering or collapsed stacks by the TV and video player. Cats are ambushing each other from underneath the debris.

I am trying to decide where to start the cleanup when there's a knock on my door. I open it to find my Domino's Pizza delivery guy.

"Oh, I forgot I ordered something today. Hang on while I get my wallet," I say.

He holds up his hand, "No, ma'am. You didn't order anything today. And we were kind of worried since you always order at least one pizza by now. I had to be in the neighborhood anyway, so I thought I'd stop by and make certain you were all right."

I'm so touched that he worried about me, I order a pizza. Afterward, I'm not sure if it's touching or alarming that Domino's Pizza checked on my health.

DISTRIBUTION AND THE FAN-RUN MEDIA CON

LoC and adzines ran notices that zines would be for sale at certain SF conventions. Zine vendors created concentrations of media fan writers, artists, and well, media fans. You would think mass gatherings of media fans would be great for SF conventions. Unfortunately, the Secret Masters of Fandom (SMoFs), who were almost exclusively male nerds, did not like all of these women invading their conventions, particularly to talk about actors and shows. Traditional SF conventions were about things the mostly male attendees wanted to talk about—which involved a great deal of mansplaining about weapons and technology and sex (human and alien), and almost nothing about relationships. Many conventions prohibited the sale and distribution of media fanzines and banned media fan art.

And even before Disney purchased everything, Hollywood entertainment corporations complained about copyright infringement.

Copyright infringement has been debated since the first pieces of fan fiction (Sherlock Holmes stories published between 1887-1902, depending upon how you recognize fan fiction). Lucasfilms initially tried to kill all *Star Wars* fan fiction, eventually adopting a "don't ask, don't tell" philosophy and choosing to make more money from selling merchandise rather than waste it on lawyers. All of this led to the creation of fan-run media conventions like MediaWest*Con.

MediaWest*Con, held each year over Memorial Weekend,[17] was *the* convention where most zines—and later fan music videos—premiered. The hotel was small. The convention size was limited, dealers' tables and art show space even more limited, and hotel rooms prized above all. It was a glimpse of the kind of effort San Diego Comic-Con fans would endure in the 21st Century. Only without online ordering and instant confirmation.

Dogs, however, were welcome.

I'M IN Dallas/Ft. Worth at Jenni Hennig's home. I've just finished loading several boxes of *Far Realms* into my already-full red Ford Escort. Jenni can't attend MediaWest*Con this year. IDICon has not yet created the orphan zine table (where zines can be shipped and sold by the convention staff for publishers), so Katharine Scarritt and I are taking her zines to sell from our tables.

It is my first MediaWest*Con. I have limited funds, which I'll spend mostly on zines and art. Food is optional. It's a little over four hours from Houston to Dallas. It's roughly another 24 hours to Lansing,

---

[17] And only disbanded in 2019 (ed.)

Michigan—depending upon weather, road conditions, and the number of stops needed for refueling both the car and the people. Katharine travels on cigarettes and Diet Coke; I go on Keebler Danish Wedding Cookies and classic Coke. We are driving straight through until we reach Lansing. Katharine stands behind my car and asks, "Are the tires supposed to splay out like that?"

IT's 1984. Apple introduces the Macintosh computer with an iconic Super Bowl ad. MTV is ubiquitous. Girls just want to have fun. And there are rumors about the new *Star Trek* movie in development.

Star Trek II: Wrath of Khan, which came out in 1982, ended with the death of Spock and his burial. How could they possibly do a *Star Trek* movie without Spock? Debate rages.

But that's not the only debate. As women become sexually liberated (in part because the 1970's economic crisis turned them into breadwinners) and Gay Liberation comes out of the closet, things are getting steamier—from Romance novels to male strippers to zines. Several zines have pushed past the erotica of Hurt/Comfort into openly same-sex relationships between characters. It's called "slash" because the partnerships are designated with a "/"character: K/S for Kirk & Spock, S/H for Starsky & Hutch, etc. Unfortunately, many places and many people are opposed to erotica in general and homo-sexuality in particular. And this includes many SF/F and media fans.

IDICON 1 is *the* first media convention to allow erotica and slash, both in zines and art, openly. It is a bit risky in deeply conservative and Christian Texas at the time. Frequent raids are made on bathhouses, adult book stores, and male stripper clubs. Every attendee at IDICon 1 must provide an age statement proving you are over 18. It's a contest. My entry is a white, ruffled, obviously 60s micro-mini dress with matching silver ballet flats and tiny silver purse. It comes with a note stating that I wore the ensemble to a party once—and no one laughed at me.

The hotel is older, slightly shabby with the dealers' room and art show in the single ballroom next to the hotel kitchen. Shortly after I arrive, the convention committee (aka concom) discovers that eight VCRs were stolen from the connecting convention office room. VCRs were expensive at that time, running ~$800 on average (or ~$2000 in 2020 dollars) and owned by the convention members, who are not rich. During the ensuing uproar, it's discovered that the doors to the ballroom cannot be locked due to fire codes.

It's Saturday evening. I hunker down in the IDICon combined dealer/art show room. I am the new Night Security Guard. I volunteered when the concom found no one wanted to miss the evening's entertainment of filking and skits. I can't sing, but I can easily shop for a lot of zines during that time. The hotel provides me with a folding cot. The concom provides me with some dinner. My husband, not in attendance, provides me with toiletries and a change of clothes for the next day.

I am reading a new zine when a woman in a rose-hued professional suit, lots of large gold jewelry, and big 1980s hair like Suzanne from *Designing Women* comes through the fire door and marches toward the hotel kitchen. She stops and stares at the art show. Her eyes grow wide.

The art is enormous, some a full panel's width, and nearly as long. Massive erotic, explicit drawings of naked Kirk and Spock entwined in various embraces and poses, surrounded by smaller pieces. The woman turns and glowers at me before continuing to the hotel kitchen. She stomps past me again on her way out. Moments later, she returns with another woman dressed similarly, and they walk as if going to the kitchen but slow to a near stop skimming the zines and the artwork. They enter the kitchen, but the door doesn't even close before they head back out through the fire door. On their suits are badges I can't quite read.

A short while later, one of the concom tells me I'm needed at the entertainment held in the bar. She'll watch the room for me. I arrive to discover I'm the winner of the age statement contest. My prize is a 2-foot tall piñata shaped like intertwined penises, one pink and one green, made by a woman who is exactly what she looks like: a suburban soccer mom. I blush profusely, say thank you, and start to scuttle back to the ballroom, trying to hide my prize with my body. As I head towards the door, a young man dressed as a policeman enters and says, "We've had complaints that there's pornography and indecency here." There's a gasp from the attendees, and several looks of alarm—right up until he starts the music and begins to strip by tossing his hat into the crowd. The crowd roars. I slip back to the ballroom with all the zines I need to read, er, guard.

Somewhere in the deepest hours of the morning, I can't read anymore. I push my cot in front of the fire door and fall asleep. My piñata sits conspicuously on a table.

On Sunday, I've just finished changing and folding up my blanket and cot when the hotel manager enters. He offers me a tray of coffee and asks if I slept alright. I assure him I did. He smiles a little nervously and says, "Good. Good."

A few minutes later, he returns, followed by a colossal police officer. This policeman is no stripper. He is an authentic Houston police officer. He is at least 6'2" with shoulders that make two of me. And this being Texas, I'd bet a lot that he was a defensive lineman in college. He looks serious.

As I sip my coffee, the manager slowly walks the officer down the rows of zines, through the art show, and back again, talking in a whisper until they return to me. The manager asks how the convention is going, and I say fine, except for the stolen VCRs.

Con Chairwoman, Cynthia Lockwood, sees the manager and police officer walking the art show through the con office's glass wall. The concom is a little on edge. Very recently, Houston police raided the brand new Chippendale's male strip club and arrested *everyone*. She enters the ballroom at full stride. She stops in front of the two men, pulls herself up to her full-but-limited height, puffs out her considerable bosom, clenches her fists, and looks up, up, up at the policeman. She is the mother bear ready to defend her cub; she's Alice Paul prepared to lead the hunger strike for the national suffrage amendment. She narrows her eyes and asks, "Is there a problem, officer?"

The policeman looks down on her and replies, "I have just one question." There's a pause. Everyone, including the manager, is holding their breath. The officer continues, "Do you think Spock's really dead?"

Cynthia blinks. She blinks again. She deflates and looks slightly puzzled as her brain tries to process the question. Then she smiles at the officer and says, "Well, you know, there are several different fan theories about that right now?"

As the two walk back towards the con office, the manager explains to me that the officer is here because of the theft report. But there was a complaint of pornography from some women attending a Christian women's retreat being held in the same hotel the day before. The penny drops. It was the woman with the big hair and loud suit. He confirms this.

The convention is winding down. Dealers are packing. People are hugging and exchanging addresses (snail mail) and phone numbers (landlines). Fans are making final dashes through the dealers' room, ignoring personal spending limits. I hear two women arranging with new Houston friends to ship a box of non-essentials to their homes. They don't have room for their clothes and the zines in their luggage. The clothes are being mailed.

I'm trying to figure out how I'm going to a) sneak the piñata into the car without showing it to my husband and b) how I'm going to dispose of it without offending the friend who made it. An out-of-state fan who is waiting to share an airport shuttle comes by and tells me I'm so lucky to have won the piñata. She loves it! I offer it to her. She can't believe I am just giving it to her. She hugs me. She runs back a moment later and hands me a zine and hugs me again. She walks off proudly, swinging it from its cord.

To this day, I sometimes wonder how she got it on the plane.

I still have the zine safely packed in my storage locker.

MEDIA FANZINES will go on to open minds, expand possibilities for people who thought they were alone (and different), and launch award-winning professional careers for SF/F writers and artists. But most importantly, they bring joy and forge lifelong friendships.

essay © Carolyn E. Cooper

JULIE BOZZA
Word-Smithing Down Under

*"Fannish friends are always the best and most long-lasting of friends,
because you connect via a shared passion. Many or even most of my
close friends today were made via fandom in one way or another,
persisting and perhaps evolving as our shared interests changed."*
—Julie Bozza

As a child in Canberra, Australia, I would spend hours listening to and thinking about music—especially soundtrack albums such as *The Jungle Book* (1967) and *Jesus Christ Superstar* (1973)—partly because, it occurs to me now, they told a story. Even though I proved to be a bit of a fannish butterfly, I'm also very loyal. I'm still in love with Baloo the sloth bear (and how he wriggles his hips), and decades later I was still attending every *JCS* production I could and writing fic inspired by it.

I could have always told you I would love to be an author, but I was always undermining myself due to a lack of confidence. All my early attempts were fannish: a happy ending for a novel that ended tragically; an exploration of a romantic relationship given too little screen time in a film; a story responding to David Bowie's song 'Heroes' (1977). My high school best friend and I were both in love with Tommy Shaw of the group Styx, and we'd each write romantic stories about how he'd fall in love with the other, and then exchange them. Sort of RPF Mary Sues once removed...

I studied creative writing in high school, and fancied myself writing a fantasy novel or two. One effort I began borrowed Princess Leia and Han Solo, and placed them in a faux medieval setting.

My biggest love was the Arthurian legends, and I promised myself that if I ever did manage to become 'An Author' I would write my own Arthurian novel. I was my own harshest critic, though, and easily discouraged. Meeting other writerly folk in college helped me keep trying, and maybe start failing less egregiously.

The way I discovered Fandom Itself was absolutely classic. I was spending a long weekend at my future in-laws' house, and we were all lazing about the lounge room with *Star Trek* (the original series, 1966-69) on the television. It was an episode in which Kirk, Spock,

175

and McCoy are trapped on a planet with only one other (male) being and no hope of rescue ever, and I idly pondered about Kirk and Spock... stuck together there for the rest of their lives with no one else around. "Would they...? Nah..." A moment later I was all, like, "Oh Yes They Would!!!" and promptly began scribbling out this great long melodramatic story in my journal. God knows what the in-laws thought about my distracted scrawling, but, in any event, they did let me marry their son.

My sister and I hadn't been close as kids, but we both enjoyed watching *Blake's 7* (*B7*, 1978-81) from when it was first screened here in Australia. We'd talk about each episode afterwards—to which I owe my very best friend and writerly chum now.

One day I confessed to her that I was secretly writing stories about how Kirk and Spock Were Really Lovers, and she confessed that she was doing much the same about Blake and Avon. Furthermore, she had discovered other people who not only did similar things but also congregated, and published fanzines, and other marvels.

Reader, we'd found our people.

My sister is Bryn Lantry, an awesome author and artist, who has remained a huge *B7* fan all her life. After she and I submitted some *B7* fan works to our newfound friends and zine publishers in the Blue Mountains, Bryn and I attended Eccentricon (July 1987) in Richmond, New South Wales—and I stumbled upon my first multimedia slash zine, *Magnetism* (#1, 1985). The die was cast.

In direct contrast to Bryn, I became a multimedia fan flitting here and there and everywhere. There have been some significant long-term fandoms in my life—*Buckaroo Banzai* (1984), *The Professionals* (1977-83), *Due South* (1994-99), BBC *Merlin* (2008-12), and *Merlin* RPF (2008-forever)—but while loyal I was also easily distracted, always falling in (but rarely out of) love.

I think I have always been fannish. To me, a fan is someone who enthusiastically engages with a text (TV show, film, album, book, and so on) and not only reads and re-reads the text, but devotes time and energy to thinking about it and imagining meanings and scenarios that are not already explicit in the text. An "active" fan might then be someone who creates something in response to that text (fic, art, cosplay, meta, and so on). For example, I would call myself a fan of the Marvel Cinematic Universe (2008-present), having loved and re-watched the films a number of times, but I've never written any fic or meta in response, so I don't consider myself an active fan.

Much as I'd love to be a visual artist, if I have a talent, it's with words. I recently uploaded a lot of my older fan fiction to *Archive of Our Own*. I can definitely assure you that, like everyone else, I had to start somewhere. Still, it was an interesting process to look through my creative fannish history, and I ended up sharing far more than I'd thought I would. There were a few sparks of possibility in some of the early stuff, and it's fascinating to be able to trace some themes and concerns that run right through the whole. On the embarrassing side, it's also clear that I had to work through some issues (such as personal boundaries), though I think that my fic and the honest feedback I received in response were an important part of that process, so three cheers for fandom in that regard!

While attending Eccentricon, I went to a panel run by our Blue Mountain friends, Susan Batho and Joanne Kerr (formerly Clarke & Keating Ink), on producing fanzines. I was intrigued! This wasn't Bryn's thing, and I didn't feel at all confident about attempting such an enterprise myself—but eventually *Buckaroo Banzai* seemed to demand this extra effort from me. It was a relatively small fandom, and frankly someone had to do it! The first issue of my zine *Samurai Errant: Cavalier Tales Quixotic and Profane* (I stole the subtitle from Bryn—sorry, mate!) was published in 1988. I discovered that publishing was also a vocation, though not so strong as my devotion to writing.

In those early days, we would run off the zine's pages on the Clarkes' offset printer in the shed out the back, and then collate them once dry the next day, and bind them with coil binders. This involved a weekend staying with our friends, along with any volunteers we could rope in, and a group effort for the collating and binding. Much fun was had! Then it was driving back home with boxes of zines, and mailing out the contributors' copies and pre-ordered issues. Eventually I bought myself a small photocopier, and printed my zines that way at home. While it wasn't as fun or as sociable, at least it was convenient, enabling me to print-on-demand some of the older issues.

In the 1980s and 90s in Australia, along with particular friends, I got into the habit of attending the National Science Fiction Media Convention each year. Australia being huge in size but modest in population meant that conventions really needed to provide a range of content, even if each con had a particular focus. But that suited this fannish gadabout nicely! And it was a great way of socialising and meeting up with old and new friends.

I was always primarily a slash fan, however, and those were the days when slash zines were still only barely tolerated—they were literally sold under the table at these conventions, and I felt there was a mostly unspoken requirement to remain discreet. It was quite a step when we were finally allowed to schedule a fan-based panel on slash.

The next zine I launched in 1991 was *Homosapien*, a multimedia slash anthology—which was so very me, until I felt the urge to expand with *Espresso*, a multimedia multi-relationships anthology. I was always heavily into slash, but after a while I didn't want to be confined by it either. More focused zines included: *Pure Maple Syrup*, a *Due South* slash anthology that dated back to the Fraser/Vecchio era; *Westering Boundaries*, a Western multi-relationships anthology; and *Horatio Hornblower & the Prix d'Amor*, a Hornblower slash anthology.

I had published my first *Blake's 7* fics under my own name, and I might well have continued to use it, but one of the fun things about *Buckaroo Banzai* fandom was that we all chose our own Blue Blaze Irregular names. Mine was "Stew," in honour of Stewart Copeland of The Police. Bryn had the best BBI name, I thought: "Faux Pas"! In later years my pseudonym evolved into something closer to home: 'Julien'. However, my real name was never a secret, given the practicalities (and trust issues) of dealing with payments and postage for the fanzines. The pseuds were more about having fun with nicknames.

Joining LiveJournal necessitated choosing something new for my account name—especially as by then I had branched out into pro fic under my own name, and I didn't want to create any confusion about which fic was what. I chose "Slashweaver," as a combination of the slash genre and the Dreamweaver HTML app. When I finally developed an overwhelming urge to publish *Merlin* RPF fic, I created a secret new identity with which to do so: "Mrs Leary". I know a lot of people still have issues with RPF today, and half of me does sympathise, but even ten or twelve years ago, RPF was barely tolerated and kept very much under the table. As you'll gather, though, I ended up coming out as Mrs L, so even that is an open secret now, too.

Beyond the formal conventions, I met up with fellow fans as and when we could. The *Buckaroo Banzai* fandom was particularly fun for this, with a group of us having dinner at a Mongolian restaurant in Melbourne in honour of Buckaroo's ancestry, or fans coming to Canberra to view the film in all its widescreen glory when screened for a couple of nights at the Electric Shadows cinema.

Otherwise, a lot of us relied on "snail mail" letters to stay in touch. Dealing with the physical aspects of creating and posting zines—with submissions and letters of comment being printed or handwritten—

might have made me even more reliant on the post, but my heart still jumps whenever I hear the magic sound of the postie's motorbike approaching. (These days, it's more likely to be a book or DVD from Amazon, which brings its own excitement.)

Sometimes when the fannish passion fades, friendships fade, too, but it can also lead to some pretty intense partnerships. This can be the most absolutely awesome thing in the world, but it's also fair to say that these violent delights can often have heartbreaking ends. I'm still in touch with some of the old *Buckaroo Banzai* Blue Blaze Irregulars, while my more recent fandom BBC *Merlin* has forged such a wide network of friendships that we refer to ourselves as #MerlinFamily.

When it was announced that official *Due South* novelisations were being planned, I tried my hand at writing up the Vecchio-centric episodes "The Deal" and "Juliet is Bleeding". Alas, of course the publisher intended to only use their in-house writers, so I ended up publishing these in one volume as a gen zine.

I took a break from fandom for various reasons, and quit publishing fanzines, when I moved from Australia to the UK in 2004. For a couple of years, I wrote a whole lot of RPF fic that Will Never See the Light of Day... Set in the National Rugby League community back in Australia, and often featuring Pete Murray songs, this exercise was probably at least in part about missing "home."

I eventually emerged from hibernation when inspired by *Die Hard* 4. 0 (2007) to write a few John McClane/Matt Farrell fics. Fandom had definitely moved onto the Internet by then. While I was still in Australia, I had taken part in discussion lists, and had created my first (clunky) website in honour of actor David Marciano (Ray Vecchio in *Due South*). But my main focus then had been on the physical zines— so it was a big step for me to post my *Die Hard* fic to LiveJournal. I slowly learned to love LiveJournal, and I created more websites. I opened an AO3 account in 2010, which, as mentioned above, I am using as an archive for my fan works, old and new. And while I do miss those days of printed zines, shaped by an editor or by chance, I haven't felt the urge to return to creating print copies of anything fannish... Well, never so strongly that I couldn't ignore it, anyway!

In 1992, at 29, and having just attended HongCon in Adelaide (at which, not coincidentally, the guest of honour was the inspirational Neil Gaiman), I had a "Eureka!" moment about a particular fan fic I wanted to write. I started scribbling on the plane home, and soon the one story became three, and then I realised I just wasn't done yet. It dawned on me that a particular character was driving all this, even though he'd started out as a minor character in the first fic—and furthermore I realised he was potentially a novel-sized idea.

Was this my opportunity to try writing a professional novel?

After much research and girding of loins, I made a start, and wrote it over the following couple of years. Once I had (metaphorically) written 'The End', I felt I could finally consider myself An Author. So, I continued on with other smaller projects, with novels as my main focus, though I also tried screenplays. The first novel won me a literary agent for a while, and one of my screenplays caught the interest of someone who was moving from cinematography to directing. Neither of these opportunities came to anything, but I learned a lot from them.

Eventually I started up a small publishing business of my own, echoing my zine publishing experiences just as my novel writing echoed my fic writing. Alas, this wasn't a huge success, as I didn't focus on particular genres but published anything that involved quality content that spoke to me. I did publish a few LGBTQ+ novels, but that wasn't even half of my output. And, as with my zine publishing, I had to close the press when I moved to the UK.

Serendipitously I connected (via a fan fic of mine!) with some people in Britain who were looking to start up a small press focussing initially on gay romance and fiction. I already had a couple of manuscripts that were beginning to gather dust, so I sent them off—and that was the start of a beautiful friendship. I began to focus more on writing professionally, but it was always in tandem with my fannish activities.

There are a couple of things I'm particularly grateful to fandom for in regard to my writing. One is that it's a great place to learn and grow as a writer. You can try things out, receive feedback, and polish your craft, with enthusiasm counting for more than perfection. The other thing I'm grateful for is that I've always enjoyed trying to adapt my writerly voice to the canonical 'verse for which I was writing fan fic. This has stood me in good stead (I hope!) for adapting my writerly voice to working in different genres (there's that fannish butterfly flitting about again,) and with a variety of point-of-view characters, in my pro fiction.

I am definitely still a fan, and enjoy books, television and films in fannish ways, though I haven't moved on to a new fandom since BBC *Merlin* (despite the temptations of *Wynonna Earp* (2016-present). Instead, I've been getting more and more nostalgic for all my old loves. This may be because (a) uploading my older fic to AO3 prompted (b) writing a short fan fic bringing the characters Buckaroo

Banzai and Rawhide into the 21st century, and (c) I've been working on a pro novel that originated in my fannish love for the film *Tombstone* (1993). As with my very first pro novel, this one began with a canon text, which prompted fan fic, which proved to not be enough for me and my Muse.

Fannishness has always been a part of my life, and no doubt always will be. In fandom, I found my people and made some excellent, enduring friendships. It helped me develop the skills and confidence to also venture into professional writing and publishing—though these have always been entwined, one way or another, with fan writing and publishing.

Did fandom enrich my life? Would I do it all again? Hell, yes to both! I wouldn't be who I am without it.

interview © Julie Bozza

JACKIE (BIELOWICZ) KRAMER
From Fanfic to Pro

"I do have a dream. When I die, my soul will show up in ENTERPRISE'S sick bay, sipping down some mint juleps with McCoy." —Jackie (Bielowicz) Kramer

I was born April 25th, 1945, at the U. S. Naval Station in Lakehurst, New Jersey where my dad worked with the blimps patrolling the Atlantic for Nazi subs. And, yes, that makes me older than Earth's Atomic Age. This is important because I grew up watching B-class movies about BEMs (Big-Eyed Monsters) that mutated from atomic power used unwisely. This led to SF, books and movies, which hooked me on SF/Fantasy TV.

While I sort of knew about fandom, I was that weird girl who read the weird books... and I was alone. I lived in the Bible Belt where almost ALL activities were school, Girl Scouts, and church. In fact, some Okies to this day aren't sure the moon landing wasn't filmed in Hollywood! I spent hours reading Robert Heinlein, Andre Norton, and Isaac Asimov, but my favorite series was Dragonriders of Pern by Anne McCaffrey. Even now I reread the entire series about every couple of years, wishing I had my own dragon to fly Thread.

I was never a "fan" of anything. Not Elvis Presley or the Beatles or James Dean. (Ask your grandma about the latter.) My family did NOT understand my love of *Star Trek* or SF. My dad always thought the reason Gerald Ford wasn't re-elected was because he named the first space shuttle *Enterprise*. My entry into fandom got a slow start due to the Marine Corps and marriage.

All that changed on September 8, 1966, with the absolute first episode of *Star Trek*. I had been on tenterhooks for weeks. Every time the trailer came on, I'd be glued to the TV. Finally, the day arrived. It was the last day of my vacation and I had been staying with my maternal Grandma Kramer. Fifteen minutes before the show started, my paternal Grandma Jones arrived to wish me farewell. Can you spell "freaked out"? Luckily, my Grandma K. lured my Grandma J. with tea and gossip, letting me alone with my upcoming new love. And once I saw it, I was in all the way.

I only got to see the FIRST episode, because the Sunday after that showing, I left to attend the Marine Corps boot camp at Parris Island, South Carolina. I had picked up one of those movie magazines to read on the plane. In it was my first *Star Trek* picture, the one with Spock, Rand, and Kirk. On an old prop plane that was clawing its way through a thunderstorm, I'm cutting out that picture, in a bouncing plane, using manicure scissors, by only the reading light over my seat. I immediately fell in love with that sexy Vulcan Spock. That's why even now, I'm a faithful Spock/Chapel fan. But viewing that picture got me through many a stressful night. And I still have that picture in my pocket folder.

When I reached my first duty station, I discovered a little Marine Corps tradition. That means on EVERY Marine station, Thursday night is "field" day. That means EVERYTHING is deep cleaned in preparation for Friday inspection. For me personally? That meant the TV room in my barracks on Thursday (or what I called Trek night) was off-limits! Did that slow me down? Noooo! I bought a small portable TV that fit in my wall locker. I'm proud to announce that by the time I left San Diego, I had weekly meetings where I watched *Star Trek* with 10-15 fellow fans. The size of the group depended on who had dates that night.

A couple of years into my enlistment, I was stationed at the Marine Corps Supply Depot in Barstow, California. We supplied all needed materials to Viet Nam. At the time, on the wall of my personal space in the women's barracks, I had hung a 3 X 4 ft poster of Spock. You know, the one where he is holding a model of the Enterprise. My commanding officer, a brand-new second lieutenant who had less time in service than I did in rank, took one look at my poster and had a hissy fit. She made me take the "weird" thing down and told me she didn't want to see it again. A couple of weeks later, the word came down from the base commander that posters were allowed in our personal space as long as there was only one and not racy. So, up went my poster, and every time my "looie" saw it, she clenched her teeth.

A month later, we had a "Base Commander's" inspection, which occurs once a year. So, I'm standing at attention next to my area, when here comes the commander and his entourage. He stops, looks at my poster and says, "Isn't that Dr. Spock from that TV show?" Okay, he said "doctor" rather than "mister". Who am I to correct my commanding officer? After my "Sir! Yes, sir!", he nodded and smiled. "Cool." He continued on his tour while I gave my "looie" the biggest smug smile I could.

I never went to Viet Nam. I was trained in radio repair, inputting supply codes for materials sent to Viet Nam. The only exciting thing that happened to me was when the U. S. S. *Pueblo* was captured by the North Koreans on 23 January, 1968. Because their communications officer didn't burn his codes, my lieutenant and I spent 20 hours a day changing all the codes on the base for the next four days!

As for my marriage, *Star Trek* did interfere with it. It wasn't like my ex-husband hadn't been warned. The first time he asked for a date, I told him anytime *except* when *Star Trek* was on. He not only agreed, but he always had me in front of TV in time for the show, even if was in a bar. After the wedding, he joined me when I got more active in fandom, but over the years, he picked up other interests that took him away from the family for long periods of time. That worked okay for me because it gave me time to learn to write, and boy, did I write!

One great thing the marriage contributed to fandom was two new members. My sons. Frank and David never knew me when I wasn't in fandom. Both were in their teens before they realized that other cars had radios. No matter where we went, there was a filk tape going, all of us singing as we went down the road. Frank was 18 months old when I hauled him place to place, posting flyers about the fan group I was starting with other fans. At age five, when his father let him pick out a birthday gift for me, all by himself, Frank chose a plastic Mr. Spock bank. David wasn't as deep in fandom as Frank. At age 3 ½, he ran into a moving car, fracturing his skull in two places. He had an extended period of recovery and, by that time, I was deep enough in fandom that my fan friends became extended family. Meetings, parties, conventions... no matter where he wandered, someone had eyes on him. Today, Frank is a *Doctor Who* fan, and David is into fantasy. No *Star Trek*, but geek enough to warm a fan-mother's heart.

Since *Star Trek* was my gateway to fandom, I did it all except art. After hooking up in a used bookstore with my oldest ST friend (in fandom, not age), Karen Fleming, I was introduced to FANZINES!! I have to admit, when I first started, I read *everything—Spockanalia, Babel, IDIC, Interphase*. I went from general to specialty zines like Spock/Chapel, Kirk/Spock, Klingon-centric, and character-specific. And I didn't restrict myself to the USA, but also zines published in England and Australia.

This habit led to writing my own fan fiction. I have had about 30 short stories published. Writing led to publishing my own fanzine, *Sol Plus*, with Karen and Mary Wallbank, another new ST friend I met from a 3:00 a. m. TV commercial I taped touting a new club we were starting, Starbase Tulsa. And what's the good of having a ST/SF group if you don't use your newly drafted slaves to start your own convention: OKon 1 in 1977 in Tulsa, Oklahoma. At the time, it was the largest science fiction con in the state, and we drew thousands of fans, dealers, and SF guest stars. We had always used Starbase Tulsa to introduce *Star Trek* fans to general SF. At this time there was a certain amount of conflict with long time SF fans and we wanted our younger members to learn about the rich heritage that the show shared with science fiction. While OKon was geared more towards SF, there was madness to our method. The stars from *Star Trek* wanted room/ board, travel expenses, AND a hefty fee. SF authors came for room/ board, travel expenses, a chance to sell and sign their books, and a bottle of their favorite booze, which they were glad to share. So, you see why the con was mostly SF, with *Star Trek* represented by panels, costumes, and merchandise. A win-win for everyone.

In my spare time, I collected memorabilia, fanzines, and filk tapes. I also attended conventions like Media*WestCon in Lansing, MI, Space Trek in St. Louis, as well as other cons (whose names escape me) in Kansas City, KS, and Dallas, TX. This where I found "family". First, my immediate group known as The Great Broads of the Galaxy (GBOG), then a wider group from Chicago, Denver, St. Louis, Iola, Kansas, and Houston. We all had attended the same conventions and really hit it off. When going to cons became too hit-and-miss, we started meeting at a church campground in Chouteau, OK, annually in November, and have been together for over 30 years. Of course, we named it "Kamp Khan." We shared many fandoms, sometimes the same ones or sometimes not. But the glue that keeps us bound is *Star Trek*, in all its forms.

The final thing I got into was filking. I learned to play the autoharp (sort of) and, after a couple of years of performing at cons with the GBOGs, Kamp, and at the GBOG monthly meetings, we wrote and recorded our own filk tape, *Cosmic Connections*.

I signed up for every letterzine around and exchanged letters with tons of my "best" friends. We shared the good, the bad, and the ugly. Yes, there was some ugly times; bickering about canon, the few people who received 'zines but never paid, and some friction from longtime SF fans who resented the attention *Star Trek* garnered from the public. But most of my fan life was something I would still be doing if I were younger, and got more than my Social Security check. When I became a single mother/nurse working twelve-hour shifts, a lot of my fan activities went by the wayside. But I'm glad to say, in retirement, some of the broken links are repairing. Friends re-friended, fanzines reread, and filks re-sung.

One of the greatest things fandom did for me was make me a published romance author. My first book was a Silhouette Desire *Baby Bonus*, which put me on the *USA Today* bestselling list. My next two books, *Broken Pledge* and *Coming To Terms*, and a time-travel novella, *The Bride-Seeker*, were published by one of the earliest epublishers, Hard Shell Word Factory. My fourth book, *Warrior's Heart*, was published by Five Star and won the HOLT Medallion for Contemporary Romance. The HOLT is the second most prestigious award in romance. My first book is available on all electronic platforms as *Christmas Bonus*, its original title. At present, I'm working at re-publishing all my titles electronically while completing my latest time-travel romance, *Tears of the Sun*.

Nowadays, when I speak to writers' groups, I proudly announce that writing for fanzines is where I learned to write. One thing other authors have asked me is if editors ever gave me trouble about starting my career in fan fiction. I have to say no. But then, when I sold my first book, the Internet didn't really exist, so editors didn't have a clue what fan fiction was! And since I've sold everything I've ever written, I'm guessing that most editors are more interested in the quality of your submission than where you learned to write.

One final story before I close. I'm a retired R. N. with 33 years experience in pediatrics. Any medical unit that specializes in kids does the same thing every Halloween: we dress up in costumes. Another thing that happens in ALL hospitals is that if one unit is short of nurses and another unit even or long on nurses, one of the second unit's nurses is "pulled" to staff the unit that is short. Can you see where this is going? Yep! One Halloween I dressed as blue-skinned Andorian and got pulled to an adult cardiac step-down unit. At first, I was a little embarrassed being the ONLY nurse in costume, but the patients loved it! They even gave the regular nurses a hard time for not dressing up! It had always astounded me how much *Star Trek* was embedded into the culture. And this was way back before *Star Wars* or superhero movies. Before being a *Star Trek* fan was cool!

Would I do the same again? Nope!

I would have entered active fandom a lot SOONER! I'd have written more stories, sung more songs, and gathered more friends.

interview © Jackie Kramer

KATHY AGEL
Fulfillment and Acceptance

"In the beginning, my fannish interaction was conducted via letter and letterzine, plus the occasional phone call. Considering the price of long-distance calls back then, writing a letter was much cheaper!"
—Kathy Agel

Born in Bayonne, New Jersey, just southwest of NYC, and now living in the fannish wasteland of north-central Florida, I'm proud of my hometown's heritage as the birthplace of politician Barney Frank, actors Sandra Dee, Brian Keith, and Frank Langella, as well as Joe Borowski, the Chicago Cubs pitcher who gave up New York Yankee Derek Jeter's one and only career grand slam.

Media fandom has been a significant part of my life—even before I knew that such a thing existed. For over five decades, I've written stories and free verse and, in the early days, the occasional filk. For seventeen years, I edited and published multi-fandom and single-fandom fanzines, both gen (Criterion Press) and slash (Straight Up Press)—over 175 of them from 1989 to 2006. I also ran Eclecticon, a no-guest media convention, from 1994 until 2006.

As a preteen in the 1960s, there were two shows that completely drew me in—*Voyage to the Bottom of the Sea* (four seasons, 1964-1968, ABC-TV) and *The Rat Patrol* (two seasons, 1966-1968, ABC-TV). Having them both canceled on the same spring day in 1968 broke my not-quite-13-year-old heart. These shows so captured my imagination that I'm deeply involved in both fandoms to this day. They're the two tent poles of the fannish universe I've created, *The Nexus Cycle*, which also includes *JAG, NCIS, M*A*S*H, The Cape* (the syndicated series about space shuttle astronauts, not the superhero series), *Stargate SG-1, Magnum PI*, and *Emergency!*

In a way, my parents are both to blame for my love of *Voyage*. I'm an only child, and I spent a lot of time with them. My mother and I went to the movies just about every week—she's the one who took me to see the *Voyage to the Bottom of the Sea* feature film in the local theater at the tender age of six. My father and I watched *Voyage* together every week while it was in first-run, and we watched *The Rat Patrol* together each week, as well. My mother was always a bit bemused about how active I was in fandom—she thought I should be writing professionally, but never tried to get me to stop writing fanfic.

When I was a preteen, I wrote horrid stories about both *Voyage* and *The Rat Patrol* and I'm thrilled that, years ago, they became worm fodder in a landfill somewhere in New Jersey. (Though I'm pretty sure the worms had heartburn when they were done.) These two shows remain closest to my heart, with *Stargate SG-1* and *JAG* pretty close behind. There was *Star Trek*, of course, which I watched from the first episode, but as much as I love it, I never really became as involved in the fandom. I never had the urge to write fanfic for any of the *Trek* series, though I edited and published several *Trek* fanzines.

The fandom which got me involved as an adult was Classic *Star Wars*. I loved *Star Wars* right from the start, but didn't get involved in the fandom until I bought an issue of *Starlog Magazine* in the spring of 1982. That particular issue featured a directory of various fannish groups and fan publications. I found *Universal Translator* and *Jundland Wastes* (a *Star Wars* letterzine published by the late Pat Nussman), and made my way into the greater world of media fandom from there. I was a hardcore Han and Leia shipper long before the term 'shipper' even existed (and still am). I wrote the *Starbird's Children* series for several years; those stories were published in various *Star Wars* fanzines as well as in multi-fandom zines in the early to mid-80s.

In 1987 I moved into writing *Voyage to the Bottom of the Sea* fanfic (inspired by two dreams I had about Lieutenant Commander Chip Morton, the executive officer of the submarine Seaview), and am still happily writing it. The first fanzine I edited and published was a *Voyage* zine, *Below the Surface*. It eventually ran to ten issues and three Special Editions (the novels *Grenada* and *Operation Corporate*, both written by LC Wells, and *False Faces*, one of my own *Nexus Cycle* novels).

I was employed by the City of Bayonne when I became involved in fandom, a job I'd keep for 32 years, from 1977 until I retired in 2009. Buying a computer for home and fannish use in 1987 (which allowed me to start producing fanzines a year later) influenced my job. The skills I learned on my own using my home computer carried over to use at work, which was woefully under-computerized as late as 1995. My professional life as an administrative assistant benefited from the layout skills I'd developed doing fanzines, and the database and spreadsheet skills I developed while running Eclecticon.

In the beginning, my fannish interaction was conducted via letter and letterzine, plus the occasional phone call. Considering the price of long-distance calls back then, writing a letter was much cheaper! In the pre-online days, I had a lot of fannish pen-pals, but then they all moved online. This saved a good deal in postage costs, since a lot of them were in the United Kingdom. Later, I joined GEnie, then, when I finally got full Internet access in the mid-90s, I joined fannish mailing lists (listservs at first, then lists hosted on eGroups, Yahoogroups, and similar services). Concurrent with Yahoogroups, I was active on LiveJournal, and I also ran mailing lists for *Rat Patrol* and *JAG* from the mid-90s until Yahoogroups went away. I'm presently active on Facebook and, to a lesser extent in terms of fannish activity, Twitter, Pinterest, and Instagram—though the latter three don't lend themselves to fannish interaction nearly as well as Facebook does.

There were no local fans in my hometown, but I often got together with fan friends from other parts of New Jersey and from NYC and Pennsylvania, with whom I'd corresponded or had met at cons and online. We had small get-togethers at my home, where we watched episodes; then we'd eat at a local Italian restaurant, or I'd cook on the grill. We went out to movies, or went over to NYC to hit Jerry Ohlinger's Movie Materials Store, or to go to the occasional Creation Con.

I wasn't involved in fandom when my husband and I met in the mid-70s, or when we married in 1980, but as my involvement started after we were married for two years, Bob's been along for the entire ride. While he's never been what any of us would call a Fan (capital intentional), he grew up watching the same SF TV shows and B movies that I did, and can snap out a line of dialogue from Classic *Star Trek* with more accuracy than I can. He can also name almost any Classic *Trek* episode from the teaser, not always by title, but always by plotline.

After I started editing and publishing zines in the late 80s, Bob, that poor soul, had to put up with having our small living room turned into a print shop several times a year, and listened to the copier constantly running in my office in the weeks before the premiere of new zines. I finally got rid of the unreliable toner-devouring monster when I found an affordable and reliable print shop in South Jersey—but that necessitated a 90-minute drive down just to drop off masters (at least they delivered the finished copies for no charge). Then Bob got to listen to the *ker-shunk* of my manual GBC binder for several days as I produced finished zines. I killed two manual binders before I finally bought an electric model (also GBC). It made a different noise, but one that was just as annoying.

Conventions eventually became a large part of my life. I went to my first convention in 1975 or 1976—one of the *Star Trek* Committee cons in NYC. I could only go on Sunday because I was unable to get time off from my part-time job as a cashier in a supermarket on Saturday (and I shudder at how I would have been mocked if I'd asked a manager for the day off to go to a *Trek* con). That was it for me until I attended Lunacon in 1983, with another gap until my first MediaWest*Con in 1989. After that, I attended MediaWest every year through 2003. I also attended Mostly Eastly, Shore Leave, OktoberTrek, and Farpoint for a number of years, and Revelcon for two (getting stuck in Houston for two days after that con in 1993 when a blizzard hit the East Coast, shut down Newark Airport, and canceled my return flight to New Jersey really put me off flying in the early spring). I also attended the odd small media cons held in various hotels in Newark, N. J.

In 1993 I started talking to a few friends about starting a small no-guest media con in the NYC area (Newark, N. J., convenient to the airport, public transportation, and major highways). The idea was to schedule it six months away from MediaWest, as one last media con before the winter doldrums. We called it Eclecticon, to acknowledge the eclectic interests found in fandom. My mother helped out after she retired by going to the post office—"I'm going right past there anyway"—and picked up Eclecticon mail from my PO box. She also helped out in the con suite for several years.

The first Econ (as it came to be known) was held in November 1994, and continued until 2006. We had four tracks of programming running from nine in the morning until ten or eleven at night, two dealers' rooms, and a charity auction that benefited various pet rescues. In 2002 there were rescue Basset Hounds at the con and a programming slot for attendees to meet and interact with them. In 2003, a parrot rescue brought some of their rescues, and con attendees adopted two of them. We eventually reached 300 attendees, which is pretty good for a small regional con.

Bob never attended a single day of Eclecticon in the years I ran it. He did go along on shopping trips for supplies for the con suite: trips to Sam's and Costco to fill my Plymouth Voyager (named V'ger, which was bought with con attendance and con running in mind) with cases of soda and water; all sorts of snacks, and the supplies we needed to serve them;, and then dropping them at the con suite on Wednesday afternoon. When we got home, we filled my van with the con registration/charity auction materials, the microwave and coolers for the con suite, racks to hold the zines, and at least a dozen boxes of the fanzines I was premiering at the con, plus backstock. I couldn't have run Eclecticon for as long as I did without him.

I stopped running Eclecticon in 2006, not due to lack of fan interest, but due to burnout. I had to take a step back. I'd lost both parents within fifteen months (my mother passed away on Eclecticon weekend 2006), and my husband was having serious back problems, retiring from a job he'd held for nearly 40 years. On top of that, I had a new position at work that brought with it a lot more responsibilities. I thought an emotional reset would be beneficial. I kept reading and writing, though, and participated in mailing lists about my favorite shows, and kept in touch with friends. After I retired and we got settled in after our move to Florida, I was able to resume a higher level of online activity, which I've maintained, but I haven't been to a con since 2003.

I have so many good memories of fandom.

Finding fandom, ordering my first zines. The thrill of having my first stories accepted for publication. Opening the envelope that held my first trib copy. Doing my first zine: from accepting submissions, to working with authors, to running the pages on my first junky copier—it was such a rush taking that first copy of *Below the Surface Number 1* off my GBC binder. Going to my first MediaWest*Con (1989), meeting people I'd submitted stories to, whose stories I'd read, who I'd "spoken" with in the pages of letterzines, and being almost instantly accepted as part of the tribe. Finding the online system, GEnie, in late 1990 and becoming a denizen of the wider world of online fandom. Running Eclecticon, which was a lot of physical work in the days leading up to and during the con, but which was immensely rewarding as well; I loved it and I still miss it. Fighting hard to save shows like *Star Trek*, *The Magnificent Seven* and *Lucifer*.

Then there was the bad.

Not being able to save *Alien Nation* no matter how hard we fought. It was just too early for its time. The specter of plagiarism in *Voyage to the Bottom of the Sea* fandom. A prolific plagiarist who had been a BNF in a different fandom came into *Voyage* fandom, and started submitting stories to the various existing *Voyage* zines, as well as posting others to the numerous online archives that existed back then. Several fans on the biggest *Voyage* mailing list on Yahoogroups accused her of plagiarism—which caused a huge foofaraw online for a few weeks because one segment of *Voyage* fandom supported her, insisting the story was indeed hers and that an author of her stature would never commit plagiary. Another segment insisted that the piece had definitely been plagiarized, and provided the title of the original story and the name of the *Starsky and Hutch* zine in which it had been published. The plagiarist then changed her tune, saying that she had actually written the original story under a pen name. Her supporters vociferously backed that statement. That ended when the real author of the original story turned up on the mailing list and proved that it truly was her story. It turned out that the plagiarist, who has since passed away, had stolen stories in multiple fandoms, changed the character names, and passed them off as *Voyage* stories both in fanzines and online archives.

The "ship" wars in *Stargate SG-1*. And all because the characters Samantha Carter and Jack O'Neill, both military, admitted to having feelings for each other, which was against military regulations. What an uproar was caused by one Season Four episode, "Divide and Conquer"! Sam and Jack shippers were thrilled, but the slash fans were definitely not. Longtime friends ended up at each other's throats simply because the slash fans wanted Jack to enter a relationship, not with Sam, but with Daniel Jackson, a civilian member of the team. They stated that it would change the dynamics of the team if Jack became involved with Sam, but ignored the fact that the dynamics would change just as much (if not more) if he became involved with Daniel—which was as much against regulations as a relationship with Sam would be, due to the US military's regulations at that time against same-sex relationships.

And then there was the attempted takeover of *The Rat Patrol* fandom by one fan, a handful of friends, and hundreds of "sock puppet" accounts in the late 1990s to early 2000s. One fan created 600 fake accounts on various online services, joining the listserv that I ran as well as the various Yahoogroups mailing lists that existed at the time. One of the "socks" actually claimed to be one of the actors from the show. Several of them plagiarized historic accounts of WWII that had been published on the Internet, changing the names to those of *The Rat Patrol* characters, and publishing them as their own work in their own fanzines. The group did their best to take over, driving longtime fans away and abusing newer fans. They plagued the fandom for a couple of years, and it took a concerted and dedicated effort on the part of a number of people in two different fannish factions to drive them out.

Some of my fandoms unfortunately faded away. *JAG* fandom pretty much disappeared after the show was canceled in 2005. Previously, it had been an active and vibrant fandom—it supported very few fanzines, but there were multiple large online story archives and mailing lists (general *JAG* discussion lists, lists devoted to specific relationships, lists devoted to specific characters, and lists exclusively for fanfic), plus numerous multiple web pages dedicated to particular characters. Within a year after the show was canceled, many archives closed and the mailing lists saw greatly reduced traffic. Right now, *JAG* fandom exists mainly to keep the reruns on the air. *Emergency!* fandom suffered the same fate once the reruns disappeared from TV-Land, and the same thing happened to *Stargate SG-1* when the show was canceled, though to a slightly lesser extent. Some of the SG-1 fanfic migrated to AO3, but unfortunately not all. A lot of very good to great fanfic in all three fandoms simply… disappeared.

Today, well, I'm still reading fanfic in my favorite fandoms, still participating in numerous fannish discussion groups on Facebook, still writing and posting my Nexus Cycle stories. Now that fanzines are pretty much extinct, I post my stories to my own website (*www.con-traryrose.com*—named after a Thoroughbred racehorse who ran at the New York area racetracks in the early 1980s), as well as to AO3.

I watch a lot of TV, fannish and otherwise, but nothing has grabbed me enough to make me want to write in those fandoms, to participate in online forums, or to get in any deeper than just being a viewer or reading more than articles in the entertainment press. In those, I'm happy being a consumer instead of an active participant.

Fandom has brought me fulfillment as a writer and good friends. Editing fanzines helped me develop the ability to work with newer writers and to help them develop their own skills, as well as helping me improve my own writing. To me, media fandom has meant acceptance. In media fandom, unlike in real life, I wasn't weird or stupid for loving a TV show or movie; I wasn't mocked for wanting to read and write stories set in that universe, or to talk about the characters. Instead, I was a member of a large, welcoming community with common interests. In real life, people (mostly schoolmates, neighbors, and coworkers, at my part-time job as a supermarket cashier during high school and college) didn't accept my interests, although many cowork-ers in City Hall, most of whom were older, were very accepting; they wanted to read my stories, and I named several original characters after them. One even typed my story submissions for me in the days before I had a computer—she has since passed away, but she was a very good and very fast typist, and I'm still grateful. And, of course, my husband's acceptance has been more valuable than diamonds.

The longest of my fannish friendships is close to 40 years old; my real life relationships are a bit longer (the longest of those is close to 50). I'm still in contact with a few former coworkers, though a lot of them have passed away or they just aren't online. But I'm in contact with my oldest fannish friends, and I make new ones all the time.

Taken all together, I would do it all again in a New Jersey minute.

interview © Kathy Agel

JAN LINDNER
A Place to Grow

"The best reward of writing, back then as it probably still is, was someone saying, 'They should have filmed your story!'" —Jan Lindner

I'm in my late 60's and would rather not be referred to as an age. Born in November. Originally from a small town in northern Illinois, got into fandom when I lived in Chicago. I was too young to go to the first NY *Star Trek* con, but was out of the house and on my own when I got into active fandom. My sisters were both fannish, though for my youngest sister it was peripheral to her mundane life.

I'd define fandom as a group of people with an intense shared interest in something, often expressed in creative work. One *Trek* fan friend is also into dogs in a serious way—show, obedience—and we'd sometimes refer to it as her "dog fandom." At this point, the Internet has caused fandom to expand exponentially into almost every area of media and entertainment, so I suspect the broader and less specific the definition, the better.

When I first got involved, it was *Star Trek*. Sci-fi fandom was a separate universe, mostly guys who wanted to be Isaac Asimov and girls and women who were either geekish—"honorary guys"—or willing to put up with the sexism in order to be part of the world of ideas. If that sounds harsh, consider the career of "James Tiptree, Jr", whose award-winning writing was no longer salable once her identity was revealed.[18]

SF fandom had a churlish attitude toward *Trek* fandom: we weren't in it for the money, so what was the point? Few men were secure enough to get involved with *Trek* fandom, dominated as it was by women, and for many who did it was because they were already active in the business aspect of SF fandom—I refer to the Dorsai/Klingon Diplomatic Corps, which ran superb security at many cons and could interface with the mundanes—or they were filkers. There have been exceptions, of course, very neat guys, some of whom have gone into sci-fi professionally.

---

[18] http://sf-encyclopedia. com/entry/Tiptree_James_Jr

When I entered fandom, I'd say the definition of *Star Trek* fandom was... people who would have liked to live in that universe, and who wanted to keep that vision alive, from the 'save *Star Trek*' letter campaign to fanfic exploring people on the Big E who weren't one of the Big 3—Kirk, Spock, McCoy, and sometimes Scotty. It was more of a community then, because we were all interested in the same universe.

The way I expressed that fandom was writing, mostly. I'd wanted to be a writer all my life, from that point in childhood where I realized books were not created by godlike beings, but written by ordinary humans. I did a bit of cartooning and a few attempts at drawing, but I've always been better with words than art.

A lot of women who started out in fanfic are now writing professionally—Lorraine Bartlett, the youngest of our original fannish gang, is probably the most successful, with cozy mysteries that have made the NYT bestseller list. Getting our writing feet wet in a critical but appreciative community made a huge difference. (Has anyone ever researched the number of fan writers turned pro? I'd love to see the numbers.)

Gateway fandom in writing terms? *The Man from U. N. C. L. E.* There was a series of paperback novels (some written superbly, some pretty awful) and a pulp magazine with stories by hacks—but they didn't come out often enough, so I tried writing one of my own. I hoped to produce something that could be sold as one of the paperbacks, but I was only about 13 or 14 and my writing skills just weren't up to it—nor was my knowledge of the world. But it was a start.

I got into active fandom in 1975 with the fanzine *Pegasus,* under my then-married name of Jan Lindner Rigby. It's interesting; in 'fanlore' that I find on the Internet, it appears my ownership of the zine has vanished. Not so. I bought the mimeo and typed all the bloody stencils, as well as co-writing and editing other writers' stories in the first few issues. I divorced and left the Chicago area due to a stalkerish ex-husband, and when I wanted to return with an Issue 7—I'd been inspired by *The Return of the Jedi*—I was told I was no longer a part of the zine and had no right to bring out another issue. I could have, of course; I had never relinquished my claim as an editor – but I was so disgusted with my former colleagues that I left the fandom. I've got to say this: sibling rivalry and middle-child issues are a real pain to deal with when the "child" never outgrew them, and I hope anyone who knows about this situation will take views other than mine with a grain of salt. A large one.

Back in the 70's and 80's, fans communicated through the postal system, mostly, and a thousand curses on the creeps who are trying to destroy it. Also by telephone—but long distance was horribly expensive. (50¢ per minute!) Sometimes it was easier and a lot more fun to drive a couple of hundred miles if you could find someone to share gas. I went to only 2 major conventions—the big one in Chicago (wearing the lovely shirt that had [gah] "Trekkie" on the back—fabric paint is your friend) and Torontocon.

My first fannish con was SeKwestercon2, and I've been to all of the Michigan conventions (and the one T'Khutian Press con in New York) until about 2012. That was when I adopted a dog who didn't do well at a kennel and was too noisy for MediaWest*Con—and yes, my dog is that important to me. By that time many of my fannish friends had gafiated anyway, and I wasn't interested in any of the new fandoms. (Gafiate: Getting Away From It All—leaving fandom). I went to a Marcon and Timecon in Columbus, OH, when I lived there, but one was strictly sci-fi and the other was all *Doctor Who* (before Timecon became a money machine). Not my fandoms, I was there to help friends putting on the con.

Fannish controversies? I'm sure there were, but that was, what, 40+ years ago and most of them just weren't worth remembering. The silliest was probably the infamous pair of sisters who wanted to start a petition and force George Lucas to re-film the last episode or two of the original trilogy with Han as the Most Important Hero. Yes. They were apparently serious. I wasn't involved except in the sense of being greatly amused at the notion (not being a Han Solo devotee, I didn't mind seeing his jets cooled in carbonite). The other, I guess, would be The Great Gen vs Slash Issue, which is kind of amusing in hindsight when I see how many of us were LGBTQ+. It was a fannish split at least as big as the short lived one between the "*Trek* as the One True Fandom" versus the *Star Wars* upstarts, when those who saw *Star Trek* as the only fandom that deserved fanfiction tried to ostracize folks doing *SWars* fic. That squabble dissolved when other fandoms started producing zines and doing art; MediaWest more or less made it official when they changed T'Con (A reference to T'Khutian Press, which produced *Warped Space* and the East Lansing *Trek* convention) to a name that acknowledged fannish diversity. For a decade or two before the Internet, that con was an El Dorado of fanzines and art.

The slash issue was more deep-seated because it challenged more than fannish affiliations; it hit religious beliefs as well, and I made it clear that folks who claimed they appreciated diversity really meant they accepted diversity as long as it didn't challenge their personal dogma. Not being out as bisexual at the time—even to myself—I didn't see the likelihood of Kirk/Spock. And... I still don't. With some pairings, the potential just leaps out (I remember one very short Uhura/Chapel fic that seemed quite reasonable) but those two? No. Some friendships can become sexual, as I know from personal experience, but some would be wrecked by introducing sex, and I think K/S was one of them. I had several verbal wrangles over this and probably appeared homophobic, but that wasn't the point—the point was compatibility and I just didn't see it. A good writer can convince me to suspend my disbelief if I don't see a pair as lovers, at least for the duration of the story, but writing such a pairing is really Your Mileage May Vary.

Looking back, I never really got active into the Mary Sue fussing, apart from a review or two pointing out what I thought were really egregious excesses. My wife coined the term Mary Sue, and her "Secret of Star Hollow" in the zine *Menagerie* really illustrated the cliches. It's true that almost all writers start out with a Mary Sue—the girl (usually in or just past her teens) who is the youngest, smartest, most wonderful new Lieutenant in Starfleet: she's braver than Kirk, smart as Spock, more compassionate than McCoy, weirdly beautiful (exotic hair and eye color, half-Vulcan parentage) and everyone falls madly in love with her. She would usually either die heroically or marry the character of her author's choice. The downfall of a Sue is that she is so much the author's creation that she doesn't leave much room for the reader... and she is always the same. I didn't much like Sues and I avoided writing them, though that was pretty much all my sister wrote, which was why there was so much of it in *Pegasus*.

I didn't think most of the heroes would be much of a relationship prize; media hero characters tend to be canonically murder on the ladies. Either they love and leave 'em, or the poor thing winds up DOA to create a Tragic Past. No thank you! My female characters tended to be people outside the orbit of the Big 3, and one was snarkily critical of Captain Kirk's habit of blowing up computers and leaving a mess for the social-science folks to clean up. Now, to be fair... men have always written Sues, and nobody thinks twice. Wesley Crusher, Luke Skywalker, you name it. I think the reason Mary Sues stuck out so much in fanfic was that there were so damned *many* of her.

I never was a big Kirk fan. Spock was... fascinating, but Dr. McCoy was more my role model—not a romantic ideal, any more than Hawkeye Pierce would be. (I wonder where I'd be now if my math had been good enough to even try for medical school.) The teamwork, the interdependence and complementary abilities, was what attracted me most. As Leonard Nimoy remarked shortly before his death, it was a perfection like a garden, something that doesn't last—at least, not in real life.

I did try a romantic adventure in the *Alias Smith & Jones* universe—I'd have to hunt for the zine, or the title—but the heroine was paired with Hannibal Heyes and I never really was attracted to him. When I wrote, I was more likely to see myself as the male protagonist—not because I wanted to be male, but because, as Dorothy L Sayers remarked in one of the Lord Peter books, men get to do all the fun things. (Did I find some guys attractive? Sure. Dave Starsky. Illya Kuryakin. Quite a few others, really. But not KSMc.)

I've switched from fanfic to pro, had a few books published, and don't watch much TV at all. There are only so many storylines, and TV has become increasingly predictable and uninteresting. My fandoms these days are passive appreciation, more like my original Sherlock Holmes fandom—of books. Mysteries and created worlds, mostly: Elizabeth Peters' "Amelia Peabody" mysteries, Lois McMaster Bujold's "Barrayar" books, and of course Sir Terry Pratchett's *Discworld* series. I think some of this is due to being past the "fantasy romance" stage of my life and settled into a real life. When I became a licensed massage therapist in 1984, I had less time to follow any TV show and far more interesting things to do. I hit a dry spell in writing when my father died—I was in my '40s—and it was years before my interest revived. And when it did, I was ready to make the jump to pro writing.

Memories... Lots of both. The first—at the Chicago con—actually getting my hands on real fanzines I'd read about in David Gerrold's book. Finding that some of the most obviously amateur publications, good old mimeo and xerox (*Spockanalia*, *T-Negative*, *Masiform-D*, *Menagerie*, *Warped Space*) had some of the best writing, as well as some of the best editors, people like Joyce Yasner and Devra Langsam. Getting hold of *Spock Enslaved* and finding that it was... obviously somebody's kink, but not what I watched *Star Trek* for.

That's one invaluable lesson about fandom and fan writing: how to write a recognizable character. It was inevitable that some people would have the reaction to my own stories as I had to *Enslaved*, but in general, there was far less of the "flame war" mentality. Constructive criticism wasn't automatically taken as a personal attack. Reviews were more detailed—sometimes a whole page on one story, explaining what the reviewer liked or disliked, and why. There were a few review zines—mostly short lived—in which readers could agree with or rebut the reviewer's opinions. We didn't have the Internet, with instant feedback and the thrill of flame wars and flouncing off. There weren't that many of us, and we had to learn to get along with each other.

Writers were expected to either accept an edit, or simply take the story back and do their own zine. Somebody producing a fanzine—going to the expense and bother of typing it up—did have the right to say what they would or would not publish, and many early zines had real editors. (There were lousy editors, too; word got around pretty fast.) There was even a phrase, "Don't make him say that!" It wasn't easy being an editor, either; once I published a story that I knew would get low marks, because the writer was a friend and had done the best she could. Because fandom was also about friendship.

The best reward of writing, back then as it probably still is, was someone saying, "They should have filmed your story!"

Because that was part of the fun. I think many of us knew we could write something better than "Spock's Brain" or "The Way to Eden." And we proved it.

Joyce Yasner called fanzines "the greatest practical writers' workshop in existence." I can't argue with that. It was.

Bad memories…? Well, there was the interesting hijacking of *Pegasus'* home base. The local fan who offered to "help", do the mailing and handle the checks. *Pegasus* now shows online as being "published" in Tinley Park, though it was produced in Chicago and only mailed from Tinley Park for one issue. This also led to the "fun" of people writing to me, or contacting me at cons and asking why they never got their zines, even though their checks had been cashed and they had queried at the mailing address and heard nothing. Innocent mistakes, no doubt, "must have been lost in the mail," but still unpleasant and expensive to replace the missing zines. I didn't confront the person with this at the time; I wish now that I had.

Important lesson: DO NOT let anyone else handle the cash if you're the one paying the bills.

On the other hand, there was the incredible generosity of fellow fen: one of my earliest fannish memories is of Paula Block bringing me a doughnut after I'd been on gopher duty at Torontocon for dog knows how many hours due to a shortage of volunteers. Sadie Fallwell to the rescue; she was a lifesaver. Sadie was Paula Block's alter-ego character, and if there was ever an example of how that kind of character *should* be done, Po hit the target. Sadie was a continuing character who eventually formed a relationship with a main character, but she was almost an anti-Mary Sue: quirky, klutzy (fall-well was a joke about her habit of spraining her ankle). Paula B is a wonderful writer and her gentle spoofing of the Sue resulted in a lovely, fun-to-read series.

Another great memory is of Marion Hale taking me and another *Starsky & Hutch* fan on a week's tour of the amazing national parks in Utah and Arizona, as a shakedown cruise for a relative's newly bought secondhand motor home. (And handling, for them, the little glitches of a missing drain tube for the septic system, plus a leaky skylight over the upper berth. Duct-taping trash bags over a horizontal window in the middle of a desert thunderstorm was an event I'll never forget. Or, if I'm lucky, repeat.) Hello, Marion, wherever you are! Marian Kelly's generous hospitality in Los Angeles, Huntington Gardens, meeting the Pacific on a warm California evening... a great human being and I miss her.

Most of the best travel in my life has been visiting fans in places I'd never have seen otherwise.

There was a group of Chicago fen including Jackie Paciello and Paula Block—Paula taught an "enrichment" sci-fi course at (I think) Loyola when she was there, and several of us signed up in support. We still exchange cards with many of them, though my wife's the real correspondent. Since moving to Canada we only saw most of them at MediaWest, and with the pandemic mess we may not see anyone in person for a long time. I hope not forever. Two other Ohioans were Cincinnati denizens Pam Berry and Margie Nimiskern, a dynamic duo who shared many collating parties and more mundane adventures... including Baryshnikov at the Cincinnati Ballet; they had season tickets. Pam was my first Black friend and I'm sure my naïveté about race appalled her. I'd grown up in a mostly white, bedroom community blue-collar neighborhood with a Mexican family next door and *Star Trek* as my basic guideline on race relations, i. e., human beings are human beings. I genuinely believed in IDIC; still do. Pam taught me a lot, and her death a few years back was a blow—though in some ways I'm glad that she, like my dad (a WWII POW) isn't here to see the current political dungheap.

After I moved to Ohio, there were intermittent collating parties for my own "One-Shot" *S&H* zine (and it actually was a one-shot); many issues of Lorraine Bartlett's *Zebra Three, Scum and Villainy* edited by Laurie Haldeman and Amanda Ruffin, and other zines of my own and other fans. (I still had the mimeo...) Those events were mostly the Central Ohio and Cincinnati friends, plus some of the Michigan gang.

I had a wider group of postal-contact friends from *Trek, Star Wars, Starsky & Hutch, Kung-Fu, War of the Worlds, Man from U. N. C. L. E. , Alias Smith & Jones...* fannish travel was most of my recreational activity. I'm still peripherally in touch with some of them; some have left this dimension.

And of course there's Paula Smith. We met after I wrote a parody of her satire, "The Logical Conclusion". Fortunately, she found "Abrasions & Contusions" entertaining (mostly due to my sister's cartoons, I suspect) and we met sporadically at various media cons and collating parties. After about 20 years, she offered to edit (and then publish) a piece of fanfic of mine that nobody else seemed interested in, and something in our friendship changed quite a lot. We were handfasted in 2002 at MediaWest*Con, and married in Canada in 2004.

MediaWest, which was a central event of my life for decades, seems to have finished its natural lifespan. Forty-plus years... not too bad. The list of fans I-knew-when has shrunken; it's an odd feeling to see folks your own age and sometimes younger turn up in obituaries. But we certainly produced a body of work that will go on beyond our lifetimes. To misquote Terry Pratchett, "Fans aren't dead while their names are spoken."

Fandom was... I hate to use "tribe" because it's become such a cliché, but it was a community in which those who didn't fit in the mundane world found a place to grow. Somebody who wants to write science fiction isn't likely to find kindred spirits among folks in an office whose interests are more along the 'sports-family-Disneyland vacation' lines. I'm no fan of the "bloom where you're planted" notion. If you can't thrive where you're planted, you're not a goddamn petunia—find a place where you can bloom. Having friends to share house space with when I wanted to get out of Chicago gave me the opportunity to do that.

For about 20 years, my "public" life was office work, and I was pretty much in the fannish closet. But—it's odd how fandom can open doors—my fannish interest in *Kung-Fu* led me to a Chinese bookstore and acupressure, which led me to massage therapy, and a night school course that resulted in my becoming a Licensed Massage Therapist and opening my own practice. And then somebody on LiveJournal complained about how wretched so much of the gay romance she read was, and wished that some of the fanfic writers she knew would start writing pro. So I did.

Certainly I'd do it again. But of course there are many things I would do differently, including not wasting a couple of decades in a dead-end relationship with a manipulative neurotic. And that applies to more than one individual, though I think those two know who they are.

One regret, though, one big regret, is that I might have spent less time in fan activity and more in political action. I thought we were helping to summon a future more like *Star Trek*, but instead greed and stupidity seem to have recycled fascism. It makes me glad I chose not to have children.

Then again, even the *Trek* universe had its "eugenics war" before humanity finally grew the hell up. And what is "eugenics" but Hitler's pretty-pretty word for racism?

Maybe we'll make it. I hope so.

interview © Jan Lindner

CHRIS EDMUNDS
The British Are (Still) Coming

"Yes, I grew up watching Star Trek, but it was just a little too clean and utopian for me. I preferred the grit of Star Wars. Kind of like comparing Disney to Warner Brothers cartoons. Disney was too sweet. I preferred Bugs and Pepe Le Pew." —Chris Edmunds

My home town in Iowa had only about 600 people when I was growing up. It was a little tiny town where you're related to half the people there.

There was no place to buy a comic book, and only *little* boys read comic books. So in the library, the closest I could get was Greek mythology.

When I came to Omaha, I found out there was a science fiction group, and I got started playing D&D with them... which I was lousy at. Everybody kept having to come back and bring me back to life. So I quit playing, but I would just still go and socialize once a week.

I met most of my friends through fandom. I was in my early 20s before I even discovered fandom. We're talking maybe about '77, '78, somewhere in there.

At that time, it was all about books. It was all about the Heinlein books and Frank Herbert. There wasn't much media fandom at a Worldcon. *Star Wars* had just kinda got created.

Kids nowadays! You can go to a modern con, and they've never heard of Worldcon, the big granddaddy of them all.

I started attending small local conventions in the Omaha area. At that time, if other cons wanted to advertise, they sent flyers to cons in the area. I would pick up a bunch of flyers to find out where and when other cons where going on.

I got my start in British fandom with *Doctor Who*. Tom Baker was the Doctor—we're talking late '70s. I started watching that before I started going to cons, and hung out with a group of fans who would get together and talk about the show. We did pledge periods for the Nebraska and Iowa PBS stations that were showing the series. Then I branched out to *Blake's 7*. Since there was already a *B7* club, I joined that.

I went to Cherry Steffey and Nancy Kolar's very first con in 1983.

They had it at their house. You went to one bedroom and you could watch videos. You went to their living room, and you sat and talked about stuff. You ordered a pizza, and that was the con.

If you wanted to see *Blake's 7*, you had to get bootlegs from overseas, because it didn't air here. The video turned people different colors, since it was filmed by aiming a camera at a television screen. British TV is on a different "region", or system. You can't hook an American video tape deck to a British TV to copy shows. And if it had been a while since you watched them, the videotape would have deteriorated to the point where you couldn't see anything anymore.

You had to buy blank video tapes by the case, and it was about $300 for a case of ten video tapes. You scrounged for every minute you could get, every commercial you could cut. Then DVDs were invented, and you couldn't give away videotape.

There was a group in Chicago who could get the bootlegs. There was one time—I can't even remember what convention it was—we hauled 13 video decks to the con in our car. One person stayed in the hotel room at all times, and we patched all those players together and made 13 copies of everything we could possibly get over the weekend.

One girl who lived in Des Moines had put some videos to music. She edited footage out of episodes and added a contemporary song to them. They were great videos, so at the 1984 Scorpio convention in Chicago, where the *Blake's 7* actors Paul Darrow (Avon), Michael Keating (Vila Restal) and Brian Croucher (Travis) appeared, we tried to talk her into showing her videos to the actors. She was too embarrassed, so friends and I stepped up and showed them to Paul, Michael and Brian in our hotel room. We did tell them that these videos were not made by us.

The first featured the last episode of B7 (not a happy ending to the series since the majority of the characters died, though that is still disputed.) She edited in the song, "Send in the Clowns," done by Judy Collins.

Watching the actors react to the video was interesting. Darrow, Keating and Croucher really got into it. It seemed to bring back memories of filming that last episode. Two of them were seated on the beds in the room and, as the video went along, they inched closer to the TV and leaned forward.

Then they asked, "How do you watch such lousy copies?"

We told them, "Well, guys, if this is all we can get, this is what we watch."

Afterward, we showed them another video. One of their fellow

British actors, Nicholas Grace, had played the Sheriff of Nottingham in a BBC production of Robin Hood,[19] and there was a scene of him in a tub of water taking a bath. The girl had edited in "Rubber Duckie" by Ernie from *Sesame Street*. They had a good laugh at that one. The next day we went out and got the three of them rubber duckies to take back home.

After *Blake's 7*, I discovered the UK's *Sapphire and Steel*. Trying to find copies of *that* was fun. I finally got clear DVDs because the A&E network aired it and released the series on DVD. When I found those, I started crying because it's like, "My God, I'm actually going to *see* what happened to these characters."

Then, in 1984, Showtime started advertising *Robin of Sherwood* *(RoS)*. Wow. (This adaptation of Robin Hood was created by Richard "Kip" Carpenter, and starred Michael Praed, Mark Ryan, Judi Trott, and in the third season, Jason Connery.)

I used to collect all sorts of Robin Hoods. Bless Turner Classic Movies. They ran a Douglas Fairbanks Sr. version one time.

Nancy Miller and Barb Hill were the other two ladies who started the *RoSNAB* (*Robin of Sherwood*, North American Branch) club with me in late 1985, and we were sanctioned by the producers in January 1986. I'm still not sure how Barb got an address for the production company in London. We used to tape the *Robin of Sherwood* shows off cable, then take them to conventions and set up video watching marathons in our hotel room.

We did the newsletter on a typewriter at first, then we got a word processor and thought we were really uptown. This was before cell phones and computers. We were willing to cut and paste and then go to Office Depot or some place and get the copies made. Then we'd come home with reams of paper. Had many collating parties around a large table, everyone doing the rounds, picking up each sheet of paper in order. Even my parents helped out. My family gave me grief about getting into fandom, but they also helped me collate, fold, staple and mutilate our club newsletters. I don't think they really understood, but they put up with me.

We hand-addressed the newsletters and had to sort them by country for the Post Office. We charged a membership; I think it was... I don't remember. It was really cheap, basically enough to cover the postage.

For news to put in the newsletter, we had to wait for Esta Charkham (*Robin of Sherwood*'s casting director) to mail us some

---

[19] *Robin of Sherwood*, ITV , 1983 (ed.)

British newspaper clippings. We would either call the creator of the show or write letters on onion skin paper (overseas postage was expensive, so the lightweight paper cut down on weight and cost). We'd wait a week for them to get it and then, if they wrote back right away, it was another week before we got a reply.

Charkham also sent the blooper reels to us. We got the Jason Connery bloopers before the 3rd season episodes aired.

Boy, trying to watch the episodes afterwards... I mean, here we are watching the bloopers and asking, "Why is Jason (Robin) bouncing Clive (Little John) on a trampoline?" Then you find it's from "Time of the Wolf," and he's supposed to throw him, so he's bouncing on the trampoline to get enough momentum to look like he's throwing Clive. You watch this stuff, and then you go back and try to watch the episodes, and it's, "I can't watch this."

We also got negatives of publicity photos sent to us, with permission to sell those to keep *RoS*NAB the club going. But British photos aren't the same size as American ones—larger than 8x10's—and we had to find a special photo shop that could print these off-size pictures.

We also did some t-shirts, along with calendars, buttons, key fobs, etc. Right after I got the t-shirts printed, my basement flooded. A gross of t-shirts (144) got pretty gross. Had to find an open laundromat at midnight to get them washed and dried. That was fun. Not.

That Michael Praed episode when they killed off Robin... Oh my God, the phone calls we got that night!

The fans all thought we knew this was going to happen and we didn't tell them, and "How dare we keep this secret from them!" They were just beside themselves.

But we had no idea that this was going to happen. The production company did not tell us. Our phones lit up for about a week with pissed-off fans. I know nothing here, folks. You have to remember there was no Internet, then, long distance phones calls were horrendously expensive, there was nothing. You ended up waiting for a letter to go across the pond and back before you found out anything.

Terry Walsh, who was the head stunt coordinator on *RoS*, came by once. I had no idea he was here. He had done a movie, and in one stunt, he's being chased by dogs. They were supposed to bite his arm. He was padded all up and everything, but the dogs bit into the padding and into his elbow. He had to have surgery and couldn't work for a while.

So one night I got a phone call going, "Hi, I'm Terry Walsh. What's the weather like in Omaha?" We said, "It's really nice here," and he said, "Great! I'm in Florida, it's been raining here for three days. I'm coming up to visit."

We had parties that went for two nights.

There was a convention already here in town and we talked them into bringing over Richard (Kip) Carpenter. The hotel had these retaining walls in the parking lot, and there were trees on these little islands. Some fans got dressed up, and Kip was up there with them... well, he fell off the retaining wall. We're thinking, "Oh my god, we're going to send him back damaged."

We actually put on two conventions. We had Mark Ryan and Robert Addie one year. Ray (Winstone) and Pete (Llewellyn Williams) came another year... we had a grand time.

One thing about working at conventions: you don't get to spend any time with the guests. You spend your entire time at the dealer's table and only see the guests at night. In those five years. it seems like I was always at the dealer's table selling pictures or tee shirts and stuff. Running a *RoS* con wasn't any different. You are always making sure the guests are up, showered, have had breakfast, and are ready to go. We had to oversee and made sure everything was on schedule. "Are you awake and presentable in time for your first panel?"

Everyone says, "Oh, it would be so much fun to run a convention!" No, it's a lot of work and you really don't get to see the guys except at night. I never got to go to the panels where the guys sat and talked and stuff like that.

The great thing was, at that time the "boys" didn't charge for their time or for autographs and pictures. Their appearances were considered part of the advertising and publicity for the show. We only had to pay for airline tickets, room and board. The cons were also very informal; no handlers for the guests, and people could actually spend time with the guests and vice versa.

I have so many stories of enjoying the end of the con by meeting up in the bars. At one of the *Blake's 7* cons up in Chicago, the hotel had a round table set up in the bar. Mark Ryan and Michael Praed were there, and they were all playing pool somewhere. Kip Carpenter was at the bar with us at this round table, and we were getting plowed, telling off-color jokes and stuff. A friend of mine went over to the bar to get something, and Michael Keating (*B7*) was there.

Keating turned to her and said, "I hear you guys say you're going to drive back home to Omaha. Are you guys okay to do this?" She goes, "No, Michael, we're not going to do this. We're staying another night because we are way too plowed to get in a car."

He was going to come over and take the car keys.

We follow these actors because of what they give to us from their roles, so to have Mike Keating go, "Are you guys okay?" is like—you don't think of actors like that. Which is sad, because they're just people. You think all the love kinda goes one way, and that they just put up with us. But it's not the way it is.

In 1987, I went over to England a Greenwood convention, my only time outside of the USA. I saw the filming sites and met some of the actors from *RoS*. It was run by the British fan club. We were the first club, and they were second, which kind of surprised me that no one over there had started one first. Just about everybody was at Greenwood con, but as usual, unless they came into the dealers' room, I never saw them.

Barb and I stayed at Kip Carpenter's house for a couple of days ahead of time. Kip and his wife, Annie, were going to take us around England. Thoroughly got lost. We saw Stonehenge at midnight. I asked him, "This island isn't that big, how can you get lost?" They took us to all the odd places. It was great fun.

I have memories of flying back home at the end of the con, crying because I missed my friends so much.

Barb told me that once I was there, I would always feel a string trying to pull me back to England. She was right. I see pictures of the English countryside and I start tearing up. It's home to me, maybe because I have ancestors that came from there, and maybe not. Not really sure, but it's where I would like to be.

We only ran the club for five years. Chris Alexander took it over and has kept it going for thirty years. We decided to shut down because I was tired of being broke all the time, and wanted to go to school to make more money. I went to a school for computer programming. I found out they lied about their job placement capabilities. The school was so bad—the man who owned the school took the money and went to South America.

They sent me to one job interview. The man looked at me, said, "You're a woman," and walked away. This was in the early 1990s.

I spent ten years repaying the loan, working three jobs, thinking, "And I gave up *RoS* for this."

I want to go back to England so bad because there is a gentleman named Barnaby Eaton-Jones, a producer, who has the UK fandom going again. He got permission from Kip's estate to use the one script that was never produced. He got it done as an audio book as a fundraiser for The Sherwood Forest Trust and, I believe, also the British Red Cross. Quite a bit of money was raised for that.

Barnaby runs a con every other year where he brings in all *RoS* guests. I keep thinking, "Oh, God, I'd love to go to one of those because I have never met all of the actors. I've never met Jason, I've never actually met Michael. I've seen Michael across the room. I've seen Mark, because Mark's been over here all the time, and he's actually been to Omaha. I've met Clive." There's a lot of them I've never met. But I have such fun memories of when I went and stayed with Kip and Annie, everything—we got to go and see all the stuff. It's not going to be as good. But it would still be a heck of a lot of fun.

Six years ago, when Mark Ryan was doing *Black Sails* on STARZ, Nancy Miller and I would get a pizza and we'd yell at the show. It was about that time that a guy had started a con here in town. He was a big *Doctor Who* fan—but we talked him into branching it out into all British fandom. He called it Britishfest, and we talked him into having Mark come over as a guest. Mark agreed, and he talked Adrian Paul (of *Highlander*) into coming.

Well, one night a couple of weeks before the con, I just got a feeling I had to call Nancy. She goes, "I don't feel good. I've called for an ambulance." I said, "Fine. We will find you tomorrow. You take care of yourself." The next day we called the hospital. Nancy'd had a major stroke.

By the time a few of us got to see her that night, she had a tube down her throat, and she just had that far off stare. So, I got hold of Chris Alexander, and put word out to everybody. Mark Ryan and Jeremy Bullough sent Chris a couple of emails for Nancy, just short little messages. She forwarded them to me, I printed them out, and took them along, and we read them to Nancy. You could tell she understood. We left them with her sister.

A couple of days later they read them to her again, and then turned off all the equipment. So, the last things she heard was from the boys.

Then, here shows Mark up at the Britishfest convention. I am bawling my eyes out. He's trying to be Mr. Tough, but I know better. He was ready to bawl his eyes out, too.

I will love these guys forever.

I talked to Mark and Adrian at the con, and on Sunday, instead of each doing a separate panel, they did a panel together on sword fighting for movies. I knew the fans would get a big kick out of it. I had two old wooden katana swords. We had painted the blades up silver so you could use them on a costume... so I gave them to the guys. If they actually connected, it's just wood, nobody's going to get hurt.

For two hours we had two grown-up 3-year-old boys beating on each other with sticks and talking about camera angles. It looks good for the camera, but you're off by a foot. Here's the two of them who know the heck what they're doing. They had a grand time. The room was packed.

It ended up that each signed a sword blade. The guy who owned them went home and shellacked the heck out of them. He has them hanging on the wall in his house, and you can see both signatures.

I haven't been to a convention where I haven't worked for a long time. There was a con supposed to be held this year (2020) that Mark was invited to... and we're talking about getting all the *RoS* fans to come to that one con next year, just to get together again.

I am a costumer. I am old enough that I prefer that term to cosplayer, mostly because I can't act, which seems to be a major requirement to cosplay. I did a long skit once and I'm not really sure how I got through it. But I am not that creative. I can't think of things off the top of my head, but if I see a costume, I can make it. I just can't come up with the original design.

I know nowadays you're supposed to be comfortable with what you're wearing and you can wear anything you want to, and it's okay if you are that brave. I figure, at 64, you don't want to see me as Sailor Moon with my b—t hanging out.

I made a real simple Greek costume one time, and wore it at a con, and we have one young man in town that does a great Thor. He really rather looks like Chris Hemsworth. I don't usually ask to get my picture taken with people, but I asked him, "Would you be willing to put up with an old lady?" and he said, "Sure." He gets down on his knees, and I've got one hand on his ear, and I'm wagging my finger at him like Mom's scolding him.

A friend (RJ) and I have been putting up a repair table at conventions. I started going to cons to talk to people about costuming, and I would always bring my sewing machine because I just can't stand to sit idle. People were like, "Can you fix this for me?" I'm always joking that this way everyone in costume comes to me. I don't have to go track them down.

Some fan came up with the idea for the table. It was called CAPERS: Costume And Prop Emergency Repair Station. RJ brings glue and wire and that sort of stuff, and I bring my sewing machine. We fix things for people, we don't charge, and I bring candy. For the last few years, I've been cleaning out my duplicate patterns and all my high heels, so I took them to the con and gave them away.

My nephew's daughter, Shelby, is still geeking and she is 17. I made her Kaylee's dress from *Firefly*, the one with the nine rows of pink ruffles. Being a typical costumer, I finished the costume about a half an hour before Shelby was going to compete in it. Shelby was really little at the time—she was like 8 or something... RJ and I were sitting there watching the competition—it was right in front of our repair table. The actress who played Kaylee (Jewel Straite) was at the con. She wasn't one of the competition judges, so here comes Jewel running in from the back of the room—"She's wearing my dress! She's wearing my dress!" Poor Shelby had never seen *Firefly,* so she didn't know what was going on. But the actress gave Shelby an autograph, and she put it in her little pink purse. Then Shelby's brother and a buddy showed up, and the kids were running and flopping on their bellies, sliding across the floor, and I'm going, "Well, there went those hours of sewing!" She wore that dress to bed at night.

It always seems to make people happier to wear a superhero item, even thru the pandemic. My coworkers now realize that I'm a geek, and you couldn't say it very loud for a long time. Some of them have now come and said, "Can you make my daughter this costume?" Now I'm making facemasks out of leftover *Star Wars* fabric, Mickey Mouse fabric, DC Comics fabric and stuff. So, everybody's like, "I want Wonder Woman or Superman".

That's what I love about fandom. It's about family. Either your own or the new family you can create with other fans. It's all ages, and everyone can join in. Sometimes you just have to find your niche. Like, in *Star Wars,* you have the fans who love the Rebellion, and others who love the Empire. You just find your niche and slide right in.

There has always been in-fighting in every group, but that's usually just egos getting in the way of people having fun. My group is better than yours, I know more about this fandom than you do, etc. You find that in any group bigger than 2 people, even if it's a sports group. Just ignore them. You won't change them and if they really make you mad, just quit that group and find another that fits you better. There are plenty of fandoms and clubs out there in the world.

My closest friends I have made thru fandom. They have seen you at your best and worst and promise not to tell anyone. I still prefer to call and talk with people over sending texts, but after using Zoom a few times, that comes in a very close second.

A few of us are doing Zoom meetings with some of the old *RoS* gang, and they're telling me stories. I say, "I don't know this story, tell me about this one. Guys, I didn't get to go to panels." Even when I went to England for a convention, we hauled stuff to sell there, so I was at the dealer's table.

Great to talk about the Old Days with people who remember them in the same drunken haze. But I LOVED every minute. What a lot of fun.

I would do it all again in a heartbeat.

_____

interview © 2020 Chris Edmunds

KAREN MACLEOD
Mentors and Friends

Fandom is to blame for it all. And I'm glad.—Karen L. MacLeod

I was a fan of *Star Trek* for a long time before I met Jacqueline Lichtenberg through her 1975 book *Star Trek Lives!*, which she wrote with Sondra Marshak and Joan Winston. It introduced many fans to fan fiction and *Star Trek* fandom.

I was born with Cerebral Palsy in the early 1950s. I was a premature baby, and according to my grandmother's diary, they didn't think I was going to live. As a child, I walked with steel leg braces and under-arm wooden crutches. It's not a hidden secret, it's known. Anyone in fandom who has met me knows that you can't hide my disability.

I came to fandom through reading science fiction and *Star Trek*. I've read all kinds of things: Isaac Asimov and Robert Heinlein (I loved Heinlein, I still do to this day), Anne McCaffrey, Mercedes Lackey, Marion Zimmer Bradley. As a youngster I couldn't stand Nancy Drew, I didn't like The Hardy Boys. As a disabled child, you didn't have that many friends outside of your school. My books became friends. I'd go to my local library, and my mother would say, "Well, if you're not happy with what's in the children's section, let's go look in the adult section."

My family moved to New Jersey in 1971. My father was ill with cancer. The doctor said, "You must find a cleaner environment in which to live." At the time, southern New Jersey was not casinos and not really built up. My father had a Masonic Lodge Brother living there that he knew, and that's how we ended up in South Jersey. My parents bought a house outside of Atlantic City, in a nearby town. I spent thirty years in the area, from 1971 to 2001. I graduated high school in 1970 in New York City, started college in New York, but finished in New Jersey.

If you think back to 1978, we had no Internet, no cell phones or computers. I did most of the *Star Trek* fanzine, *Organian Questor*, in southern New Jersey. The other editor, Teresa Ornas, was in New York, so doing that one was difficult. I only produced a few issues, and because it was pre-Internet, I used typewriters, correction fluid and mimeograph. The mimeograph machine was in my parents' garage. In the winter, it was real fun because the garage wasn't heated.

When I met Jacqueline Lichtenberg at a couple of conventions, she apparently had heard of *Organian Questor*. She said, "I have a book here. I'll sign it for you if you buy the paperback, and if you don't like it, you can send it back to me." This was her original spiel to everybody she sold a book to. And she meant it. It was the first of the Sime Series, *House of Zeor*.

Jacqueline was saying, "If you like *Star Trek* and like *Star Trek Lives!* you will like *House of Zeor*." So, that's how I got into that fandom. If you read the Sime~Gen books, or the short stories in the anthology that we released a few years ago, you'll see the elements of Spock and Kirk in the relationships that are in these stories; but it's not Spock and Kirk, it's the characters that the fans or Jacqueline Lichtenberg or Jean Lorrah have written.

Jean Lorrah's early *Star Trek* works were the Sarek and Amanda stories: *Night of the Twin Moons*. Jean later crafted *The Vulcan Academy Murders*, and *Survivors*, released through Pocket Books.

In the 1970s, I went to what is now called Atlantic Cape Community College in Mays Landing, New Jersey. I also spent some time at Stockton State College (now University), also in the same area. When I moved from South Jersey, I was unable to find secretarial work, even though I had been a secretary for many years and had trained at a secretarial school. I began to work at manuscript editing to supplement my Social Security income, and with the help and training of Jacqueline, Jean, and Sharon Jarvis, I also started to edit new manuscripts, including ones that Jacqueline and Jean had created.

The elements of *Star Trek* that Gene Roddenberry espoused, we all still try to emulate, because *Star Trek* represents a universe where we're all trying to get along with each other. That kind of "Tailored Effect," Gene Roddenberry used to explain, also was crafted into the Sime Series of books that Jacqueline created. After I decided that I enjoyed Sime~Gen, Jacqueline found me at another convention, and said, "Would you like to do a Sime~Gen fanzine?" So, that's how *A Companion in Zeor* came to be, which was the second Sime~Gen universe fanzine. They had several, and additional smaller newsletters, done by other people.

A Companion in Zeor is still alive, online, though I haven't had submissions in a long time. My first *A Companion in Zeor* issue was released in June 1978. I've worked with Jacqueline and Jean since then, and roomed with them at conventions in the past—they're good people. We have taught other people how to edit, so if it gets to a point where I can't, or there is a lot of work, other people now know how to work with manuscripts. I've been taught that if you've been trained, you pass the knowledge on to somebody else; you teach another.

I've become a professional book editor because of their training, and through learning the editing craft with Sharon Jarvis, the acquisitions editor at Doubleday, who bought the Sime series in the 1970s. I've enjoyed working with and knowing them over the years. I think they've also enjoyed the relationship, because they haven't gotten rid of me yet.

A lot of what I professionally edit is either science fiction, fantasy, or romance. I worked with a few little minor publishers but most of them have folded. I have a few clients I edit for, before they submit to a publisher. I'm grateful to have the work, which all can be traced back to my fanzine editing days.

Fandom has brought us together. I don't regret doing it. My only regret is that my mother never understood before she died in 1980. When I was doing *A Companion in Zeor* in the garage, and when I started to edit manuscripts for Jacqueline and Jean, my mother commented, "What are you getting out of this? You're making them famous. What are you getting out of this?"

I said, "I enjoy it. It gives me something to do, and I want to do it." She said, "I don't see you gaining from it." She never approved my fannish work, and I don't really care. She passed before I became the editor I am now. My body of work was something she didn't live to see.

I like all different kinds of books: mysteries, science fiction, history. When I was reading books for pleasure, romance was low on the list, but romance is very popular. I'll edit whatever they hand me, as most editors will. I've edited gay fiction, which is interesting. Not exactly my cup of tea, but I just tell the authors that, if they tell me how the sex scenes operate, I'll leave that portion untouched. I'll do the grammar, the sentence structure, spelling, but the construction of the scene, that's their expertise.

My disabilities unfortunately are getting worse as I'm getting older, but that's pretty common in some people who have Cerebral Palsy. I'm not going to as many conventions as I used to, but I'm still there. I need a little more physical help these days. I attended many *Star Trek* and World Cons. Also Darkover Grand Council conventions, based in the science fiction books of Marion Zimmer Bradley. I've also been a speaker at the Darkover convention's successor, ChessieCon.

Conventions were smaller, then, much more accessible, and the people very welcoming. Even the "stars" treated me with kindness when I met them. It's all so different now. There are the steampunk people, the anime people, the re-creation people, and the filkers, all who might or might not cross over to other fandoms. Many distinctive, smaller groups. It's a different set of people than the conventions of the 1970s. They're great people, but their scope of what they follow is smaller. All kinds of fandoms come and go. I still enjoy fan activities, but I just don't go to as many conventions as I used to because my mobility isn't as good as it used to be.

For years, I had therapeutic horseback riding lessons. Horseback riding is something I thought would be more enjoyable than sitting on a therapist's table. The therapist's table has never been fun for me. My understanding was that the horse would do the work for you because he supposedly imitates the human walk, and I might enjoy doing it. My doctor in New Jersey said, "Let's try it." I rode for something like twelve years. I was walking on my feet until I was in my mid-50s, and most of that attributed to the horseback riding therapy.

At one point I did own my own horse. He was trained for therapeutic riding, but other people also got to use him. He assisted a mentally disabled young man to reach his dream goal of participating in the International Special Olympics, where he won a silver medal. I had my horse for about four years. He had a registered name, "Perfectly Timed", and a barn name. We called him "Frosty," because when we first got him, his mane was quite blond. He was a red chestnut from mane to tail once he had a diet change. He was a Quarter Horse gelding. Unfortunately, I had to sell him to a very nice local man in New Jersey when I ended up divorced. I couldn't very well take him to an apartment. I was a former New York City girl who had a Jersey-bred horse.

I'm always reading. I've recently purchased some of the newer *Star Trek* books, including the authorized hardbound biography of Gene Roddenberry, which I haven't read yet. I grabbed both volumes of *The Fifty-Year Mission: the Complete, Uncensored, Unauthorized Oral History of Star Trek* by Mark A. Altman and Edward Gross. Some of this is rather interesting.

I helped Kris M. Smith edit six large paperback books of telephone logs of her friendship with DeForest Kelley (Dr. Leonard McCoy of *Star Trek*) and Carolyn Kelley (*Kelley Phone Tag: The Rest of the Story.*) I was one of three or four people who volunteered to edit the manuscripts. I wanted to do it to add something to fandom. It brought back a lot of fannish memories, because editing was what brought me into fandom. It was an enjoyable project to work on.

You give back. You take, you give back. Let's blame fandom for all of it. It's important. It brought us all together. It's hard to express, but that's it in a nutshell. I wouldn't regret doing it again as long as I would be as young and foolish as I was back then. I learned from the experience. I value the friendships I've received from my fannish connections. There are people I'm still in touch with, people I've known for years. Most of the people on my Facebook friends list are connected through conventions, or my riding therapy, and fandom. I'm grateful for it. We're all still connected.

It goes back to all that beginning, when we were cutting our teeth on editing, writing stories, and enjoying the creation of television programs that we all followed. It doesn't matter if it's *Star Trek*, *Star Wars*, *Quantum Leap*, or some other fandom. They've all influenced us. I think it's made all of us better people.

It's about all of us.

interview © Karen MacLeod

JEAN DEWEY
Fannish Friendships Endure

"It was a couple of years after Star Trek premiered that my older brother talked me into reading some fantasy books in his collection... written by this little old British professor named J. R. R. Tolkien. And the rest—as they say—is history." —Jean Dewey

I'm a native of Omaha, Nebraska—although I was unintentionally born out in North Hollywood (don't ask!) in the latter half of 1954. I was one of five children with a M. D. father and stay-at-home mom—and yes, they all knew I was the family oddball. But I count myself fortunate to have had pretty liberal parents, as well as an older brother who was directly responsible for introducing me to science fiction in general, then Tolkien specifically.

My younger sibs basically thought I was just plain weird.

But my older brother let me read the books he had read. Then, when I was 12, the original *Star Trek* series debuted. To keep peace in my family, each of us had our own little black and white TV in our bedrooms so there was no fighting over who got to watch what. I was also one of the lucky kids whose parents didn't object to my watching such a "strange" TV show, and I fell in love.

It was a couple of years after *Star Trek* premiered that my older brother talked me into reading some fantasy books in his collection... written by this little old British professor named J. R. R. Tolkien. And the rest—as they say—is history.

Early on I wasn't much involved in fandom—other than the renowned letter-writing campaign.[20] But a group of people brought together by their common interest and enjoyment of something—that's fandom, to me. Back in the day, it was primarily musical artists (the Beatles, etc.) or a specific entertainment figure (Elvis, James Dean, Marilyn Monroe, etc.). These days, it's pretty much the same, with movies, books, and TV series—or livestream programs—added in.

By the time I was in my early 20s, *Star Trek* had been revived in syndication, and the first movie was in the planning stages. I had

---

[20] There was a massive letter-writing campaign (headed by our own Bjo Trimble!) to keep *Star Trek* on the air after it was originally cancelled in the 1960s. (ed.)

met other *Trek* fans in Omaha, who introduced me to a fanzine editor. After that we all became friends with a locally based *Trek* "letterzine" editor and ended up as production staff of what became *Interstat*. We met once a month to assemble—by hand, mind you—the latest edition of *Interstat* and get it ready to mail out to the subscribers. I contributed a few letters, then wrote a little fan fiction which did NOT get published—thankfully.

In those days, communication came primarily through letters. Or phone calls. *Trek* fandom in particular had a really good grapevine, so if something was happening word could spread pretty quickly. There were conventions held around the country, such as the World Science Fiction convention, but most of them were for the literary form of the genre. Fans wanted to share their love of the show & the actors in a similar fashion. So, *Trek* cons were born. Word spread through the grapevine and the various zines. Small, localized cons started to happen. Then the first "major" con was held in New York City, with some of the actors appearing.

I was fortunate enough to be able to attend the second-ever major Star Trek Convention held in the USA: Chicago's *Star Trek* Con, the first convention to feature the entire cast along with Mark Lenard (Sarek) and Tasha Martel (T'Pring). Bjo Trimble emceed the event. It was all overwhelming and I was a little shy, so I stuck with my friends. I kind of regret that looking back now.

A few years later both Contretemps and Omacon were born on the local scene. I joined the Omacon staff to run their costume contest (among other jobs). Thus, my costuming/cosplaying life began.

I've had two fandom stories published in zines, one a *Raiders of the Lost Ark* fanfic, published in a mixed-genre zine; the other a story based on a short-run TV western called *Wildside*, published in a western zine.

I've also had a picture that I took published in the old *Starlog* magazine, thanks to Bjo Trimble. She was a regular columnist for them and wanted to write about the 2nd Omacon, where she'd been fan GoH. A friend had competed as Winnowill from *Elfquest* in the costume contest and Bjo wanted a picture of her to include in the article. Bjo had my address, so wrote to see if I knew about a picture. Gee... I just happened to have one...

Of course, there were controversies. The *Star Trek/Star Wars* debate[21] continues to this day. I've stayed out of that one because

---

[21] When *Star Wars* first came on the scene, many *Trek* fans didn't like that it seemed to encroach on their spaces. (ed.)

I like both. Costuming controversies pop up occasionally; most of the time I don't engage, but every so often, especially when it comes to bullying, I will step in. But otherwise, I've pretty much ignored most of the controversies. There are a few fandoms I've drifted away from, most recently the newer *Trek* offerings. They just haven't interested me as much as the Original and Next Generation series. I leave the new stuff to the youngsters.

But I'm still involved! I'm currently into two fandoms quite heavily. *Lord of the Rings* is probably my biggest obsession—and has been for over 50 years now. Actually, make that an obsession for just about anything related to the works of J. R. R and Christopher Tolkien. I have a library of over 300 books by or about Tolkien father and son, including multiple editions of *Hobbit, Lord of the Rings, Silmarillion*—every time a new cover was debuted... And then there are the collectibles—darn you, Peter Jackson! Of late, I've been involved with several of the Facebook groups dedicated to the works of Tolkien, getting to listen to fascinating discussions by noted Tolkienian professors & specialists and help "teach" the younger movie-initiated fans about the books. I've also had the privilege of becoming a fairly regular visitor to the Tolkien Archives at Marquette University, due to the kindness of the curator in charge of the Archives, Mr. Bill Fliss. I have a research paper that's been brewing in my head since the early days, and am bound and determined to actually get it done, now that I'm able to do research in the Archives.

Then there's my newest addiction— the livestream Dungeons & Dragons (D&D) game called *Critical Role*. It is one of the most addictive shows out there, being not just a D&D game, but some of the best improv out there. The DM and players are all friends working in the voice-acting community out in LA. The cast themselves are some of the loveliest people you will ever meet, as well as some of the biggest nerds and geeks, and their influence has very definitely influenced the fandom. "Critters", as we're called, are astonishingly generous people, a mix of good souls and a few that I wouldn't mind kicking in the backside (like most fandoms, you get good and not so good bodies involved). When the show went live on YouTube as *Geek and Sundry*, the cast decided to see if they could do a little fund-raising and connected with the 826 L.A. program (dedicated to supporting students ages 6–18 with creative and expository writing skills, and run by the Los Angeles public schools). In five years now, they have raised over $100,000 for the L. A. program and also money for some of the other 826 programs in the U. S. through the fan artists. The cast will allow the fan artists to sell *Critical Role* prints with the under-standing that at least 10% of the total sales must be donated to either an 826 program or to a charity of the artist's choice. It has become a family with fans in all parts of the world (literally—the joys of the internet). It has gotten to the point where the cast, now running *Critical Role* on its own Twitch channel and as a business, has made the decision to start their own charitable foundation. With the charity only up and running for a couple of weeks, they raised nearly $75,000 that will be going to some of the youth cultural groups in the southwestern First Nations. (Update; make that $100,000—reaching the goal amount—in a little over a month.)

I could go on for days, but I know there's other things to talk about. Oh—before I forget—I'm co-founder and admin for two CR groups on Facebook: Heartland Critters, specifically created for Nebraska/Iowa fans and friends; and Critical Cosplay, a group with well over a thou-sand members, dedicated primarily as a place our cosplay community can go for help, or to share what they've been working on.

Fannish ties and friendships endure. Probably my oldest friendship goes back to the days of working on *Interstat* with Sylvia Kleeman Kostitin. We've been friends for at least 40 years now. Sylvia was the proofreader for *Interstat* and the person responsible for dragging me in. We had a group of friends at the time, who were all local and went to the local conventions, often travelling to farther cons as well. Chris Edmunds became a friend through both Omacon and Contretemps, then *Robin of Sherwood* (looks significantly at Jenni). I've made friends with a lot of people in many fandoms down through the years, and I've drifted in and out of contact with many of them. I've even discovered a friend in one of my *Lord of the Rings* groups who was part of the Klingon security detail at that first *Star Trek* con in Chicago so many years ago. Fandom is such a small world sometimes.

Though I might want to go back and give my younger self some advice, being involved in the various fandoms, knowing the friends I've made (and lost), I wouldn't want to do it any differently.

interview © Jean Dewey

ERICA FRANK
A Younger Elder's Perspective on Change

"What can save conventions is the same thing that built them in the first place: the fannish sense of connection, the belief that it's important to host a space where people can gather to find each other." —Erica Frank

I Found My People

My first in-person convention was BayCon 86, at the Red Lion Inn (now the Doubletree) in San Jose. The author Guests of Honor were Spider and Jeanne Robinson, whose works I'd read and enjoyed, but I didn't go for the GoH. I went because I was into *Elfquest*, and the local club was hosting a room party.

I was sixteen; I knew nobody but the two friends who brought me; I had a blast. I wanted to try everything. For the first time in my life, I could be geeky and invisible at the same time: I could wear green and black nail polish or read a book in public or quote from sci-fi movies— and still just be a face in the crowd. I had Found My People.

I told everyone who would listen that *This is my first convention!!* because I knew this was important, that I had found a community I wanted to be part of for the rest of my life. I knew I would attend many more conventions, and that they'd all be different and I would love all the ways they could happen.

I bought a day pass, and one again the next day, because the full weekend pass would've wiped out my spending money. I spent the third day avoiding the parts of the con that needed a badge. I put a fake name on my badge because I could—an original character I worked into stories in my head. And then I spent the weekend awkwardly saying "that's not my name" because I hadn't figured out how pseudonyms worked; I was just thrilled at the idea that I could use any name I wanted to label myself.

I signed up for a LARP that I barely understood. I played it, I suppose, but I still have no idea what genre it was or what happened in it. This was long before Mind's Eye Theater and other formally structured LARP games; I recall nothing of the game system or the

223

story. I just knew that I loved RPGs (role-playing games), and the idea of acting one out was fascinating.

I looked at the gaming room, in the far back hall away from all the main action. They were playing games I knew (Advanced Dungeons & Dragons, Champions) and games I didn't (which of course I don't remember), and I considered joining a game, but I had gamer friends at home, and the convention was for new things. Playing with a new group wasn't as interesting as doing activities I normally couldn't.

The panels fascinated me. So many topics I found interesting or important! So many more that weren't directly of interest, but obviously related—my friends, current and future, would care about these subjects. I went to one with the friends who'd brought me, something about comic book art. Afterward, we waited to say "Hi" to one of the panelists. At the time, I had no idea who Chris Claremont was (Something *X-Men* something?), but I got to see his expression transform between "Ugh, random teenage fangirls who probably want an autograph" to "Oh hey, FRIENDS I DON'T KNOW YET" when my friend said, "Clovis said to say hi."

I barely knew Clovis and was just a tagalong for that, but the event stuck with me: the lesson that pro authors and artists are people, and even when they enjoyed conventions, they could still be overwhelmed. Many years later, one of my great delights at conventions is approaching someone who doesn't know me, whose face has that look of "who is this woman and how can I get out of this encounter with as little drama as possible?" and giving them a quick, concise bit of info that makes them light up. "ConOps has your keys." "Tony's waiting for you in the WesterCon party room." "Here's the extension cord you sent for." Interruptions were always welcome when they were (1) good news and (2) brief.

In the dark back corner of a room party, three people sat on the floor and sang "Banned from Argo" from a shared photocopy of the lyrics, and I was hooked on filk for life. I still love the song, no matter how much it's hated by other people (and the author). Some of the dealers had filk books and tapes for sale—all too expensive for me. Instead, I bought a Buckaroo Banzai embroidered patch that got compliments for years. That was my first introduction to the transitory nature of sci-fi merch and memorabilia: it didn't occur to me, that first year (nor the next few), that any item I saw might not be available in the future.

The masquerade included a group entry called "Who Invited All These Tacky People Anyway?" that had about a dozen hilarious cliché costumes, including "Unpronounceable the Alien and His Robot Dog, Spot." I could recognize that most of them were in-jokes I didn't understand but wanted to. One I did know: the Dungeon Master, carrying a messy armload of books and papers and a 2-liter bottle of Coke. Someone from the audience yelled out "What kind of DM doesn't drink Mountain Dew?" The DM shot back, "A good one!" and everyone laughed.

Later, I went to the anime room and watched episodes of *Fist of the North Star* in Japanese, with two guys whispering paraphrased translations from the front of the room. ("My shirt has torn off—now you are all going to die!") The program packet had a "Japanese Animation" guide, which of course I couldn't read in the dark room. But it didn't matter, because anime had such different characters and storylines from what I was used to, that the plot synopsis guides didn't help. I saw something-*Gundam*, which I didn't understand, and *Vampire Hunter D*, which I mostly did. Nothing was in English. That anime room was my introduction to getting the pictures and sound from the film itself, but the meaning from somewhere else: a spoken translation, or captions, or a book.

It was many years before anime really clicked for me; I don't care for many of the common genres and tropes. But the convention movie room is still my favorite way to watch anime. I love being in a crowd that's half newbies and half experts who've seen the show a dozen times. Almost everything has subtitles now, so people aren't actively translating, but I love the whispered comments of, "They translated that wrong." And I love how half the audience will say, "Wait for it... wait for it..." just before the big fight scene.

Almost three decades later, at FanimeCon 2014, watching *Attack on Titan* with subtitles: the entire room sings "Yeager!" when it comes up in the theme song. And when <spoiler> is heading for Certain Death, and <spoiler> dives in to save him... one lone voice from the front of the room calls out, "I ship it like FedEx!"

That first con, however, I couldn't afford food in the hotel restaurant. I ate snacks in party rooms, and peanut butter sandwiches, and drank soda from cans in bathtubs full of bags of ice. I hadn't paid for a room, but the *Elfquest* club had an open policy: paying people got beds; everyone else got crash space on the floor. I slept on my coat—a barely-cosplay plain brown cloak—with a fellow I knew only as "Wolf." (And hey, "Wolf," if you ever see this: I have no regrets. It's been more than 30 years; I think I have enough perspective to recognize a predator, and you weren't. I was awkward but never unsure.) I tried to learn people's names, but badges could have their *Elfquest* name or some other fandom name or their D&D character or a nickname or, sometimes, their actual-legal-wallet name. I decided it didn't matter what anyone's "real" names were. I needed a label for them in my head, and something to call them in public, and that was all.

I wished I'd brought a costume. I wished I'd brought something to collect names and contact info. I wished I knew more about anime so I could enjoy the shows better. I wished I had enough money for real meals. Or filkbooks, which were probably a higher priority than food. I wished I could remember everything but knew I wouldn't. I wished it would last another week, or that there would be another convention next month.

I got none of those wishes... but got to work toward all of them later. I went to the next BayCon and, at a panel on "Convention History," Tom Whitmore said the best way to get the most out of conventions was to volunteer, so I did. I was a gopher for several years at several conventions, and eventually ran the Information Desk at BayCon.

MY PEOPLE ARE EVERYWHERE

I had almost ten years of conventions before I had children, and a few more where the kidlets were small enough to carry around. I went to several more BayCons, and then to TimeCon and SiliCon—the "Bay Area Triple Threats"—and several smaller conventions. For a long time, I thought of literary science fiction and fantasy conventions as "normal" conventions and other conventions as "fringe." This was because the first ones I attended were founded by people who believed that, so I unconsciously absorbed their ideas of "how fandom works."

BayCon (Memorial Day weekend), TimeCon (mid-summer), and SiliCon (Thanksgiving Day weekend) were all of similar scope, held in San Jose, attended by the same communities, often run by the same people in different roles. BayCon was about books; TimeCon had more media content like *Doctor Who* and *Star Trek*; SiliCon had more science programming. But they had a very similar "feel," and for a few years there, they seemed like one long convention divided into pieces several months apart. I know they worked to differentiate themselves, and there were tensions in the upper staff membership... but the visible ops and security people had a lot of overlap. And of course, the same broke students gophered at all of them.

That was before hotels really started cracking down on the number of people in a room. Gophers often got a free membership with 20-ish hours of work, plus crash space in the "gopher hole." I was young and flexible and didn't mind sleeping on hotel carpets. A few cons would refund gopher memberships after they finished the required number of hours, but in most cases, it was "pay to gopher; do your hours; get free membership next year." I was grateful for the free membership, but that was never the major expense for conventions. Travel and hotel costs were bigger. I could only afford to go to local conventions—usually not staying at the hotel—but I was lucky that the Bay Area has a lot of cons.

At my first DunDraCon (DDC XII, 1988, at the Oakland Hyatt), a gaming convention, I won an 8-player card game of Illuminati, discovered Warhammer miniatures, and bought 34-sided dice. (Originally designed as randomizers for the Danish lottery; there are no games that require 34-sided dice.) I met my future partner of seven years there and watched more anime I couldn't understand. At a drop-in table, I learned to play Talisman, which I still enjoy. At a later DunDraCon, I bought Magic: the Gathering (MtG)cards, and got lucky: one of my two packs of Arabian Nights boosters had the "Ali from Cairo" card, which was considered immensely powerful until it was banned from tournament play.

I did not play tournaments. I played for fun. Of course, so did the guys in the tournaments. Gaming conventions taught me that everyone defined "fun" a little differently.

At Origins Game Fair (San Jose, 1994), another gaming con, I bought first edition, hot-off-the-presses roleplaying games that later turned out to be terrible. I got my Black Lotus MtG card signed. I listened to the updates of the Starfleet Battles tournament that ran hours past expectations. ("The judges have decided that, every 5 turns, they're going to remove one hex from the edge of the board, until they have to interact.") I bought more weird dice: 7-siders, this time. No game uses for those, either. (Later, they became usable in Button Men.) I discovered that I will never have enough money or time to play all the terrific new games released every year. I also discovered that, no matter how rare or small a print run my favorite games had, someone else loved them too.

I went to BayFilk (Oakland, 1986) and bought tapes and songbooks and sang along with Frank Hayes as he sang "Never Set the Cat On Fire." I got to hear some of my favorite filksongs sung by the original authors, and others sung by amazing singers who don't write. I learned SCA rounds with hidden puns. I learned that participating in fandom can mean writing, or performing, or cheering in the crowd.

And I heard Cecilia Eng sing Mercedes Lackey's "Reflections," which felt like it was written directly to quiet-introvert-me. The song speaks of how a person devoted to enhancing others has no strength of her own; she will always be at the mercy of whoever she allows to give her shape and purpose. To be whole and complete—and to bring light into the world—she must find her own voice, her own passions, her own truths. I pondered that one for a very long time.

In the early 90s, I went to Wondercon in Oakland, a Comic-Con-esque Creation con. Stayed home while my boyfriend (the one I met at DunDraCon) went to anime and media conventions; he came home with a signed picture of Paul Darrow, who played Avon in *Blake's 7*. I went to filk cons without him. We both did staff at Northern California's Renaissance Pleasure Faire ("RenFaire"), which was like conventions in some ways but not others. We went together to World-con: ConFrancisco in 1993.

The hot science news of ConFrancisco was the recent launch of the McDonnell-Douglas DX-S, Delta Clipper Experimental spaceship, which was single-stage to orbit, "just as God and Heinlein intended." The convention weekend included my birthday; we were poor, but my boyfriend bought me some jewelry and other goodies we knew we wouldn't see again. I bought a lot of 2" buttons: "C Code; C Code Run; Run Code Run; Run Dammit Run" and "Is Your Religion BATF-Approved?" (following the Bureau of Alcohol, Tobacco, and Firearms siege in Waco that ended in July) and "Reading on the 'net is like drinking from a firehose. Posting on the 'net is like shouting at people on a roller coaster. Archiving the 'net is like washing toilet paper."

That was in 1993, and it's certainly not less true now. We had a computer running Windows 3.1 and I read Usenet groups. Even back then, there was more fannish content than I could keep up with.

And then "Eternal September" hit, and convention life changed forever.

Times, A-Changing, Etc.

Nothing changed immediately, of course. Eternal September is noted in retrospect. Early online communities had a rush of new people every fall as students got internet access at college, but in the mid-90s, AOL and cheap home computers changed that. Suddenly every month was "September" with a constant influx of people, eager to play with the new toy and oblivious to the existing community norms. Anyone who'd been around more than a few months became an expert in online communications.

My boyfriend and I still went to conventions, some together and some separately, and we got a better computer. We read gaming strategy tips on Usenet and movie fan pages on Geocities, and I got a Yahoo email account and joined a dozen groups and clubs. Then there was The Baby, and our life got too busy and money got too tight for all the conventions. We still went to a few; I bought my very first CD: *Crosstown Bus*, a filk album, at a BayCon. But we skipped most of them. I mostly stopped attending conventions—as many young women do—when the combination of "full-time low-paying job" and "children too big to carry" made cons a hardship instead of three days of fun and community connections.

So I did more online activity. I read Tolkien language discussions and looked for filk lyrics and joined Pagan email lists. I learned to argue my points on email lists, and learned to condense them in Yahoo clubs, which had a character limit. I learned to make friends who had no faces, no voices. I learned that some sites will let you block the people you don't want to see, and some almost force you to interact with them. I learned that you can't control how your words are perceived: both in the sense of "your emotions don't go with them" and "they may be viewing with a different font." I learned that every social site has an additional rule on top of whatever's in the official Terms of Service: "Don't piss off the moderators."

I had a blast there, too. Again, I had Found My People. Different people. More people. Thousands more "my people" than could ever attend a single convention; certainly more than I could ever interact with during a weekend. And there was still The Baby, who had become Kid the Elder because I had a new partner and a Kid the Younger; money continued to be tight, so conventions became a rarity.

Eventually, money got less tight, and KtE and KtY got old enough to leave with a relative for the weekend, and I went back to a few conventions... and got a shock.

All my old friends were there! I still knew everyone! I could pick up conversations that had been on hold for 8 or 10 years; we reminisced and swapped book recs and laughed about how the video game industry was destroying what role-playing games were meant to be. We shared email addresses and favorite online forums. All the tables in the dealer room had websites. The Saturday night post-Masquerade dance played all my favorite 80s songs. The room parties had themes I liked and the people wanted to chat about the shows I loved. The filk continued to be amazing: sci-fi songs and high fantasy songs and the occasional RenFaire song, sometimes with a new sci-fi verse or two. I learned the fannish version of *Old Time Religion,* and suggestive songs about books.

I had taken all that time "away" from conventions, and here they were, just waiting for me to return!

While I still couldn't afford many of them, I started with attending a few local conventions, and was delighted at how comfortable and welcoming they still were. So I scrounged up my pennies and went looking for the ones I'd never been to because they were far away.

Escapade is advertised as "a slash slumber party"; a place to hang out with friends who share your interests. I'd seen it make the rounds every year on LiveJournal, and finally decided to go. Escapade 2008 in Ventura was the first convention I'd attended entirely on my own, not with friends, not meeting anyone I'd ever met before, not going home at night. My friends were people I'd only known online. I roomed with three other Snape/Harry fans—we had a big "Snarry" meetup—and again, I loved the whole thing.

The panel structure at Escapade is entirely different from other cons. It's not "four experts in the field have a conversation mixed with a lecture." It's "two moderators manage a conversation that includes the whole room." It has songvids[22], which I'd never seen before. I'd heard of them, but I had dial-up at home. Videos just weren't worth the time to download. Escapade is small—membership caps at 150—and everyone knows everyone. New people are welcomed and cherished: "Hello, new friend who shares our taste in fanfic! What's your OTP?"

I looked around at these women (and two men, I think), mostly my age, mostly talking about shows I knew and loved, and knew I'd found the subfandom within my larger fandom interests, and one that would be my True Fandom Home even more than filk.(I love filk music. I don't love singing, and filk is a very participatory community.) I spent the weekend learning the language of slash meta-discussion, and meeting the people who would become my best friends for the next decade and more.

Who were, as I mentioned, mostly my age. Like most of the people at the other conventions I attended. Hmm.

I started to notice an undercurrent of worry at conventions: they weren't growing, except the big media "Expo" conventions like Comic-Con. They were shrinking. The literary cons and the niche interest

---

[22] "Songvids" are a kind of fannish storytelling, where the "vidder" edits together available video and sets it to music—ed.

cons, always on a tight budget, were scrambling to survive. Some conventions just stopped—BAScon, the Bay Area Slash convention in SF, closed, citing committee exhaustion but also mentioning that hotel space prices had gone up and it was harder to cover them. Other conventions closed or moved to smaller, less-expensive hotels in other cities.

BayCon was once the SF Bay Area's flagship literary science fiction convention, filling a ten-story San Jose hotel to bursting (there were two spillover hotels), and converting almost every corner of public space into convention space. That alcove by the swimming pool? Autograph space. The lobby near the 10th floor suites? Readings. Parking lot? Science demo space. It eventually moved from the Doubletree to a convention center; I didn't attend those years. But in 2019, BayCon was at the San Mateo Marriott, a hotel with just over half the meeting rooms and event attendee capacity of the Doubletree.

I still recognized everyone because most of the regulars never stopped attending... but nobody new was taking the places of the people who left. Conventions as I knew them were greying and dying.

I blame capitalism. But only partially.

Part of the blame goes to the conventions trying to keep alive a fannish culture that no longer relates to how people discover fandom, to how they find their interests and their friends.

When I went to BayCon, to TimeCon, to BayFilk, to DunDraCon, it was to find my people. I no longer need to travel to find my people anymore; they're on the other side of the computer screen. Fans don't even need to go places to meet face-to-face anymore, to hear their friends' voices, to share favorite songs and interesting news articles. They can do all that online.

Nobody needs a convention to see four published sci-fi authors have a conversation on the future of ebooks. We have forums for that. Nobody needs to spend $100 for a membership and $400 for a hotel room to attend a workshop on How To Make Costume Armor. We have *instructables.com* for that. Nobody needs a convention to find the other three people who love the Creeks and Crawdads RPG. If they're too ashamed to mention their fave where Google can see them, it's not going to be on their badge next to their real name.

Conventions were created so that fans could find each other, have conversations, share their interests. And fans don't need to meet in hotels to do that anymore.

That, however, is only part of the problem. (It's a big part, though.) Leisure costs have gone up, and wages have not. The minimum wage has been flat for years. Cheap communication and international shipping means that basic get-by expenses have gone down, but the service industry's prices keep going up—including hotels.

Except for this year. In 2020 and the year of COVID-19, hotel prices haven't gone up; they've vanished. As a result, many conventions have "gone virtual." Some are free; some are full price (those are rare); some have a nominal charge that probably covers the software costs and little else. Some are pre-programmed streaming content only; some have Zoom meetings and Discord servers. There are no standards. Everyone's feeling their way along. It's all very exciting, which is another way to say nobody knows what works and what doesn't. And this is going to be yet another blow to the viability of in-person conventions.

VIRTUALLY FANNISH

I attended CoNZealand 2020, the first virtual Worldcon. I paid $200 US for that, and while I wouldn't say I felt cheated, that's only because I knew I was paying for the education as much as the experience: I wanted to see what they'd do with it.

Panels, is the answer. Lots and LOTS of Zoom panels. Those were the high point of the convention, and its only real selling point.

CoNZealand also featured:

A Discord server plagued by technical problems—the login security software did not play nicely with Discord, and not everyone figured out how to get in. A "virtual dealer hall" in a 3D walk-around space, resource-expensive and disconnected from every other event on the site. An art show also disconnected from other spaces. Online movies with login access problems. Time zone problems. Award ceremony fiascos. (Yes, plural.) Souvenir book delays, misprints, and missing information.

The people who love panels probably enjoyed it. I did. Back-to-back panels with no need to walk across a hotel (or two), coupled with the ability to grab a drink or snack without disrupting anyone else? Terrific! All the panelists were visible and audible—no problems with someone getting drowned out by audience whispers, or not seeing clearly from the back of a crowded room. Audience questions and comments that were easily understood, because they were typed. No ability for audience members to grandstand or hold the conversation hostage.

They also had the standard drawbacks of Zoom meetings. Interpersonal "chit-chat" is difficult; there's no back-and-forth banter among panelists. It's all about taking turns to speak. No way to have back-and-forth with an audience member, either. No way for two panelists to look at the empty space left by someone who didn't show up and say, "Hey you there, in the audience—didn't you speak on this at the last Westercon? C'mon up and help us talk about this." No way to see panelists in full costume; definitely no way to see costumes in the audience.

These are all minor, but they are a set of differences that aren't being carefully considered by conventions going virtual.

The people who don't love panels, who don't go to conventions for the panels, may have felt lost. The Discord chat was lively for those who got used to the interface, but complex and confusing for anyone else. There was nothing else social, and most other virtual cons are following the same pattern: Zoom or other streaming video software for panels; Discord for chat, website with downloadable flyers and an online storefront for dealers.

Virtual conventions have no "wander the halls and look at displays," and maybe find another insomniac to chat with. No "get coffee and a bagel and sit in the lobby to wave hello at old friends." No "see someone else buy a book by your favorite author and strike up a conversation." No swimming pool, no hot tub, no group of 12 strangers walking three blocks to the pizza place and coming back as friends. No movie room with whispered translations, no wandering into ConOps and offering to get coffee for whoever's at the table, no table of Klingons inviting Ace Rimmer for a drink. (No watching Ace Rimmer out-drink a table of Klingons.) Virtual fannish meetings have a lot to offer—I have found so many amazing friends online—but they can't bring many of the experiences that made conventions special.

The future of conventions may be hybrids: part virtual, part in-person. Several conventions are trying to figure out how that works— what can you offer online that works in tandem with in-person events? Can the additional technical costs for software and maybe cameras, speakers, and so on, be offset by online membership costs? Should there be online-only events, such that in-person attendees will open their laptops in their rooms to attend? But what they're really trying to figure out is: Can online attendees save the convention? Will we get enough money from people who can't or won't pay for membership + travel + hotel, to cover the cost of the hotel for the people who will?

Nobody knows yet. This is all new territory. But we do know, from the cons that are growing, what draws people to attend even as costs have gone up, even as social activity is freely available online.

The conventions that are thriving are the ones that offer something that the internet doesn't. Celebrity meetings. Costumes—a place to show off what you've made; a place to see what other people are wearing. A dealer hall and art show full of items you can't buy on Amazon or Etsy. Those movie rooms I love so much. A dance party with music that appeals to college kids, not just fogies like me. Game playtests and LARPs of today's popular genres, whatever those are.

None of those are antithetical to literary science fiction conventions. None of them requires a party-extravaganza "feel" for the convention. All of them connect to features I loved about my very first BayCon.

"Celebrities" aren't limited to actors; authors and artists and editors are celebrities to sci-fi fans. "The guy who designed the space ships in that movie" is just as much a celebrity (and more likely to be a sci-fi geek) as the actor who played the captain. Costumes are hard to share online, and one of the few fannish activities that crosses fandom boundaries. Attendees don't have to see the movie or comic book or animated series that inspired the 7-ft tall robot with glowing neon edges to appreciate it. The key value of the dealer room has shifted from "mass-produced items your local stores don't carry"— because Amazon probably does have them—to "handcrafted fannish goods (and costumery) with no shipping costs." Movie rooms may be harder to pitch—everyone knows they were something we put up with before we all had access to movies on demand—but they could be advertised, instead of quietly put on the schedule for the people who already know what they are and why they're awesome. The post-masquerade dance can start with my beloved 80s one-hit wonders, and then shift to more recent songs; I won't be dancing until 2 a.m. anyway. The game room can feature game design events—Designers, beta test your game with strangers! Players, try games you can't buy!— and LARPs, which have a lot more structure and scope than they did in the late 80s. A convention doesn't need nonstop high-energy festivities to be full of activities that people want to attend in person.

What can save conventions is the same thing that built them in the first place: the fannish sense of connection, the belief that it's important to host a space where people can gather to find each other. The technological options for that have changed, and may change more in the future. Climate changes may mean fewer flights, less long-distance travel, more small localized gatherings. But fandom is creative and persistent in the face of adversity; we can find ways to bring the diversity we need to survive.

We just need to be willing to let go of "how it's always been done." It wasn't wrong to do things that way. It's not so much outdated, as superseded. We no longer need conventions to find friends, to make social connections. But they were always so much more than that: we made conventions to build communities, not just friendships.

Community-building is what we need to save them.

essay © Erica Frank

BJO TRIMBLE
A Pioneer for Star Trek

*"We had adventures, no matter what. And part of that is being ready
to look for and find adventures."*
— Bjo Trimble

I was born in Oklahoma in 1933 at the height of the Depression and the Dust Bowl. My family were farmers, dirt poor, what would come to be called the "Okies." The government was going around taking away cows, because if you were *of a certain level*, you weren't supposed to have more than one cow. It didn't matter how many kids you had who might need all that milk.

It was an interesting and extremely hazardous life for my family. I was just a baby when they left Oklahoma, all of us piled in a car, probably looked like the *Beverly Hillbillies*, except no rocking chair on the top. We came out to California.

My earliest memory is staying in one of those little motels. They weren't even motels in those days, they were motor courts in greater or lesser degrees of wonderful. I just remember one that had a large duck statue. It was supposed to be Donald Duck, but it didn't look like him. I was fascinated by this. We're out in the middle of the desert and there's a duck.

The family had pooled their money to come out here, and when we got to Blythe, a little desert town out near the border, my grandmother, who was described by a cousin as the meanest old woman she ever met, threw my mother and me out of the car because my mother's money had run out. They drove away.

Yeah, that's the kind of family I have.

My mother was a survivor. Within the hour she had a restaurant job, and had worked out sharing a cabin with one of the other waitresses. The first people I ever met were people who came into the restaurant. But our family connected up again after a while later.

I grew up lonely. Nobody in my family was interested enough in what I did. It didn't take me very long to figure out that most of the world had no logical beginning and no logical follow through, but just go with it.

Education was not important. My family worried (as much as they did for anything I did) because I "read too much."

My schooling was wherever we landed. My family were crop pickers by this time. I'd get handed a bag lunch and told, "Follow all those kids," figuring that that pack was going to school – I don't know what I would have done if they weren't! Schools were so crowded that nobody noticed a mousey little person in the back of the room. I wasn't even signed in. Less than six weeks later, I'd be gone anyway, so I didn't learn to make friends in school because of that. At this time, I was staying with my grandmother because my mother was working in town, and it was a distance away. I just got handed around to relatives. It was very common in those days.

My early education was old *National Geographic* magazines that I got for free at the thrift shop because they were too damaged to put up for sale.

This one lady in Blythe realized that I really, really, really wanted to learn and she had no other resources but to give me these magazines.

I didn't know what real "stars" were until I read an article in *National Geographic.*

I learned to read pretty much on my own. By the time we finally settled down, it was fourth or fifth grade, and they put me in the back of the room, and I quote the teacher, "Oh, we put the Okies in the back of the room because they're too damn dumb to learn anything." Each time I was moved to another school, I was in the back of the room again. The one thing in the back of the room was the Columbia Encyclopedia, or what was left of it, and I started reading it.

Years later, we were in a trailer camp where there was just about enough room to walk between the trailers. In the main office, there was a little short shelf of books. On it was *A Princess of Mars* by Edgar Rice Burroughs, and I read it, and thought, "How cool! Someone living on another planet. I never would have thought of that!" Shortly after that the lady next door to me—I was whining on about being kept in bed because I had flu—came over with a stack of *Astounding Science Fiction,* dumped it on my bed, and said, "Now shut up for a while!" and went back home. I started reading. The first story I read was "I, Robot," by Isaac Asimov. I had no idea of what a robot was, and I had to read the story three or four times to even understand what was going on.

The Okies started to make money during the War. The reason for that was because even though a lot of the people looked fairly sturdy, they'd been pretty well broken down. Crop picking was "stoop labor" in those days. You can only do that for so long before you can't straighten up again. So, all of these people were 4F for the military. They ended up with the jobs back home, the war jobs and things.

My mother was a Rosie the Riveter type of person, and went out with her little bandana around her head, made cookies for the USO and stuff like that. She loved to dance. It never occurred to me that I was a "latchkey child." Back in those days they didn't have a term for that.

My father had disappeared when I was about 18 months old. He didn't reappear in my life until I was thirteen in 1946. By that time, he had five kids. He paid my way back to Oklahoma to meet him. We got off on entirely the wrong foot because he was by that time, Church of the Nazarene of the extreme Southern type—speaking in tongues, dancing around the church and so on.

I said, "Okay, I'm done."

Things got off on the wrong side when the one boy in the family was snapping off a cap pistol in my face. We're driving along with the windows down because this is Oklahoma in the summer, and I said, "Don't do that." I told him about four times and I finally grabbed the gun, and threw it out the window.

My father stopped the car and said, "You'll have to go get that," and I said, "I'm not going to go get that." The boy hadn't paid any attention and fired it off again. "So, if he wants the gun, he can go get it."

That started everything off on an interesting key.

My mother had remarried but my stepfather was a really mean drunk. He was a really mean human being all the way around, so to this day I click my jaw out of place because he hit me so often. You grew up dealing with it. I guess I was about 9 or 10 years old, and I was cooking breakfast, Okie-style with about that much grease. He walked up and said, "That's for nothing, start something," and, wham! He hit me.

Without even thinking, I picked up that hot skillet and swung on him. My goal was to knock his head off but he threw up his arm, and I broke his arm in two places. There were eggs and bacon up the wall, and I said, "Someone else gets to clean that up." I just walked out of the house. I stayed out of the house for 48 hours, and they couldn't find me. That was because I was at the top of a big old oak tree within sight of the house.

Once he shot at me with a thirty-aught-six.[23] He missed me because

---

[23] .306 Springfield rifle (ed.)

I'd already jury-rigged the sights since he liked to go out and shoot deer out of season. He was that kind of person.

He was stepfather #1. I had nine others. Why my mother married so many times, I have no idea. In those days, you could go down to Tijuana and you could get married, no blood test, no nothing, and if you stayed the night, and came back the next day, they'd give you a divorce.

My mother sewed costumes for Warner Brothers studios for a long time. She did a lot of things. She was a deputy sheriff, drove the school bus and raised beautiful flowers. She owned her own florist shop. She was a very talented person, not terribly likeable as far as the rest of the family was concerned.

Everybody else loved her. If you had met her, you'd say, "I don't see what your problem is, she's just a wonderful woman." But you're not living with her.

Once I had discovered "Science Fiction" and realized what in the world all this was about, it was like opening giant double doors. I began looking for people who shared my interest. The lady next door moved about that time, so I couldn't go over and talk to her. In those days, science fiction was not allowed in most libraries because it wasn't considered "literature."

It didn't dawn on me to look at bookstores for magazines, because I was just a kid. I didn't know how publishing worked.

So, what I did, I told friends that I wanted more of these things. I got a lot of interesting stuff like astrological magazines. Finally, I asked one teacher, and the teacher said, "Why aren't you getting it from the library?" I told her, and she marched to the library and told them to at least stock Robert Heinlein and Isaac Asimov. So, we got a few books. That was when I was introduced to the Heinlein books as well.

In my family, you either married the first jerk who asked you or you did something with your life that would remove you from the family. I joined the U.S. Navy. I was in only for a year and a half. I'm a Southern California girl. I have never learned to walk in ice. Ice balls up under your feet. My feet went out from under me, I did a half-gainer to see if I could keep myself from falling down, but did anyway and did bad news to my ankle. They decided I wasn't valuable enough to keep. I was only working in special services, so they let me out.

Next I freelanced in graphic arts for several large printing companies in LA, back when real typesetting was done since I could do that, too. I finally ran across an article in a little newspaper that the

Los Angeles Science Fantasy Society[24] was celebrating its umpty-umph birthday, and they met at some place in Los Angeles, on Thursday nights starting at seven.

I went one night. In those days, girls did not admit to reading science fiction because if they did, they appeared too intellectual and guys wouldn't ask them to marry them, right? It's the old "guys don't make passes at girls who wear glasses."

I didn't care. I was the only girl in a room full of guys. They didn't know what to do with me! Here I am, sitting in my corner and thinking, "Who are these people?" but at that point, there was no looking back.

I seldom brought a book home because they had a tendency to disappear. My mother, having no use for them, threw them away. So, when I found LASFS, I, of course, found people with books.

I had the ability to do cartoons and artwork, and I could do covers for fanzines. There were one or two of the fanzines that would publish short-short stories, but mostly they were talk and discussions. It was Facebook before the Internet. Someone who could do cartoons and artwork was of great value to publishers of fanzines. I could do caricatures of people, so all of a sudden that made me quite popular, which was unusual because I had never been popular before. I got a B.A. in art. I am the second person in my family to ever go to college.

I went to World Science Fiction Conventions in those early years. My first convention was Chicon II in 1952. Other groups—comics fandom, gamers, etc.—didn't have the money or the knowledge to have conventions. They would often hold small conventions inside the SF cons.

One of the first people I met at that convention was Robert Bloch, who stayed in touch his whole life. Others include many SF fans such as Big Hearted Howard Devore, and authors such as Harlan Ellison who proposed to me, Isaac Asimov who kissed me in the elevator, and others.

Forry Ackerman[25] was a sweet but very strange man. He was not raised by wolves, which sometimes I felt I was, but his mother and his sister just let him do anything he wanted. Now fortunately that didn't mean turning wild like so many kids did; he went introspective and began collecting things. When he died, he had quite a collection that got spread around the United States, unfortunately. He was a longtime friend. He was an interesting resource.

---

[24] LASFS, established 1934 (ed.)

[25] Forest Ackerman, magazine editor and noted science fiction collector (ed.)

In 1960, I met John. When we first met, he was still in his Air Force uniform. We entertained ourselves at a large party by exchanging stupid officer stories, of which there are many. We've been married now 60 years.

Then came the 1966 World Science Fiction con, Tricon II. I had planned a futuristic fashion show, and was working on that when a member of the con committee comes up and says, "We didn't want this (the fashion show) in the first place, and now that it's scheduled, you have exactly one hour."

I said, "Get out of my face and go away" and he scuttled away.

Then, a little bit later, he comes back (you'd think they'd have the sense to send another), and he says, "You've got three more costumes in your fashion show."

I said, "I've got 20 now. Getting 20 amateurs across that stage in one hour... no, I can just barely get them on."

"Well, we promised."

"Well, just unpromised."

"Well, it's this big Hollywood producer."

"Really? Who?" My mother had worked in Hollywood for years.

"Well, he's Gene Roddenberry."

"I never heard of him, go away."

Shortly thereafter I hear this deep voice behind me saying, "Are you Bjo Trimble?"

I say, "Yes?" Now, I'm standing on a runway, just about a foot high, and I'm eye-to-eye with the voice's owner, and he says, "My name's Gene Roddenberry, and can I take you to coffee?"

"Absolutely! Break!" and we all went out to coffee.

Well, twenty minutes later, that silver-tongued devil had talked his way into my fashion show. One of the reasons was that he had hired a couple of local models, and they were seeing a weekend job go down the drain. So the models said, "We'll help," and I said, "Okay." So that's what happened.

By the way, we'd never heard of *Star Trek*. We had no idea. This was when Gene had the first three episodes to show at Tricon that evening. I thought, "Well, okay, we'll go see it."

So, we saw *Star Trek* and I thought, "Production values pretty good, plot is very good, and will it stay this way?" Well, people liked what they saw, and they certainly loved the costumes. What could we take from that?

What we could take from that is that Hollywood had done this to us a lot of times. Fandom had been promised a lot of mature, grown-up shows on tv. *Lost in Space* was supposed to be one. *Voyage to the Bottom of the* barrel... all of these, and they didn't turn out to be that. *Lost in Space* turned into a kiddy show.

When we walked away from the fashion show, Roddenberry turns to me and says, "Let's do lunch when we get back to Hollywood. Call my assistant."

Yeah, yeah, yeah, like I'd heard that a zillion times, right? So, John was going on a business trip to L.A., and I arranged for a weekend baby-sitter. I said, "I'm going to call this guy tomorrow." So, I called him, and his secretary—then they were secretaries, not personal assistants—answered. Gene's connecting door was never closed—I discovered that later—so, when she said, "Bjo Trimble?" Gene picked up the phone and said, "Where are you? Well, come over. We'll go to lunch."

So, John and I went over and Roddenberry was so tickled because he'd gotten all sorts of bad horrible reviews. "It'll never last longer than three episodes" and so on. He took every fan that came to the studio over to the set. Desilu discovered that he was doing this, and their legal department had a cow because you shouldn't be taking people on a live set when there are cables like this all the way across the floor.

We were some of the first people in, and we liked what we saw. We liked the people a whole lot. We met DeForest Kelley and he asked if we had pets, and we said we had, yes, and he whips out his wallet and shows up pictures of his pets, the turtle and the two dogs. He was a lovely man. So whenever we got a chance to come down to L.A. from Berkeley, we would go visit the studio.

One thing Gene did, was that he went to the science fiction writers and asked for ideas and help on *Star Trek*. They said, "For one thing, use science fiction writers for your scripts." Which, by the way, the studio was not happy with, and the network wasn't happy, and yet look at what kind of quality stuff we have. Fifty-some-odd years later, it still works on the screen.

In 1967, after two years, NBC threatened to cancel *Star Trek*. We started a letter-writing campaign "Save *Star Trek*!" that convinced the network to run it for a third season. In an interview with Dave Tilotta, I said, "I took strips of film to a convention, where they were cut into single cells, and handed out." The avid fans then swapped them. This showed Roddenberry that fans wanted merchandise, so he set up Lincoln Enterprises, which we put together and handled for a while. The company sold stickers, film clips, uniform patches, and scripts. Several months later, it was taken over by Majel Barrett. Later, the company name was changed to "*Star Trek* Enterprises", and is now known as Roddenberry Entertainment.[26] In their mission statement, they say they are passionate about "entertainment that sustains the legacy of our founder, Gene Roddenberry."

We stayed friends with Gene as much as you can stay friends with a Hollywood producer. When it looked like there was really going to be a second series,[27] people came from everywhere who had worked on the first one, and wanted to work on the second one. Usually, without question, they were hired, and I think this made all the difference in the world.

I worked on the *Star Trek Concordance,* which was published in 1969, and the later updates. In 1982, I published a book called *On the Good Ship Enterprise: My 15 years with Star Trek.*[28] I have been part of the Society for Creative Anachronism since 1967, and have been a guest, along with John, at many conventions over many years.

I was in *Star Trek: The Motion Picture* in 1979. Director Robert Wise kept saying, "You know, we always hear about 400 some people (on the Enterprise) but we never see them. So let's do them on a big rec deck." Gene could go to the Screen Actors Guild and say, "I need to go on the street for more actors," and they'd get a waiver for that. They hired just over half of the professionals, and then the rest of them were fans.

So, both John and I could have gone, but John's boss wouldn't let him go. I was an automatic "in", as were several other people, so there's a whole bunch of us in this mile-long dressing room. There's this woman sitting there and I'm assuming that everyone is a fan, and said, "Hello."

She says, "I have no interest in talking with *Star Trek* fans. My interest entirely in this whole farrago is Lennie. I'm here for Lenny."

"So, you've taken up someone's spot who would have really enjoyed the entire thing to be here for Lenny? That is not only extremely selfish of you, but incredibly stupid."

And she says, "How dare you!"

I say, "How dare *you*! You're the one who should be thrown out, and I'd happily do it." But they'd probably throw me out too.

It was loads of fun. We had to get up about four a.m. to check in to the gate at five, and we didn't end until 11:30 that night. We were

---

[26] *roddenberry.com*

[27] *Star Trek: The Next Generation* in the late 1980s (ed.)

[28] https://www.goodreads.com/book/show/2395420.On_the_Good_Ship_Enterprise

getting paid one set fee. Only the actors were getting time and a half. That whole day was just quite amazing. The outfits were ski pants material, so if you stood up, you looked fine, but if you sat down you sort of closed up like a clam. And they zipped down the back. David Gerrold said at one point, "I have to go potty. Can someone come along and unzip me in the back?" and about four girls volunteered and I said, "Oh, no, honey, wrong. Those boys could volunteer…"

The movie was not memorable. If you gave a list of the top ten science fiction movies, it will not appear. Wise had solid workmanship and he was a lovely man, but he was well past the science fiction genre, and it showed.

Why they've never taken some of the top *Star Trek* books that have been published and made movies out of those, I will never know. Some of them are very well written. Some of them are crap. You know Ted Sturgeon's rule: "90% of everything is drek, 10% is pure gold." I'm willing to accept that through much of life.

The general public will accept a good science fiction story. They proved that with *Star Wars*. I mean, the theater was never half-empty from the minute *Star Wars* started, and with *Star Trek* pretty much the same thing. Lucas and Spielberg have both been very careful, though waiting far too long with what they produce. *Star Trek* seems to want to settle on some famous name who's never done science fiction.

I wish they would stop trying to do what didn't really succeed the first time. I wish they'd stop letting Tarantino and J.J. Abrams write anything. What the hell do they know about *Star Trek*? You want to have somebody write about things? You have science fiction writers, and you have a lot of Hollywood people who know *Trek* a lot better than that.

Now John and I are both retired in Southern California where we currently paint rocks. Kindness rocks. You either leave it by somebody's porch, or hand it to them as you walk by, and it's been a way of not going stir-crazy during this pandemic. It's just little messages, just things, but people seem to enjoy them. You're not supposed to walk off with a rock. You can certainly pick it up and move it somewhere else but you're not supposed to walk off with it. You share it around.

But right after these fires, everyone put out fireman-related rocks and they were disappearing. Nobody could figure out what was happening so our daughter phoned the fire department and said, "You know there were a whole bunch of rocks…"

They said, "We took them and we have them in our little rock garden in back of the station. Weren't we supposed to take them?" And she said, "That's perfectly all right." She told the rest of the rock painters, and everyone was just so pleased.

I found a nice family in fandom, as opposed to my real family. There were many fannish controversies. Even without computers, there were trolls. Many fans quarreled with one another. I got mixed up in a few of them, but only when I saw an injustice done. I dropped out several times, due to lack of funds or personal problems—which included having a developmentally handicapped child—but never due to infighting.

For me, fandom never faded away. It may have dipped now and then, but it was—and is—still here.

interview © Bjo Trimble

Glossary of Terms

You have likely seen these terms used in their various forms throughout this book. All are correct, depending on what decade, area of the country, preference, etc.
This is also neither an exhaustive nor a complete source.
For more, we suggest looking up the websites:
fanlore.org or fanac.org

APA: Amateur Press Association, usually edited and put together, then passed out amongst contributors or members of a club

ALT: Alternate universe of original source

BritFans/Anglofans: fans of British-produced media

BNF: a Big Name Fan; someone who is well-known in fandom.

CANON: the original source material

CON: a convention. Which, naturally, leads to terms such as: ConCom (Con Committee), Con Suite, ConOps (Con Operations), etc.

CORFLU: correction fluid for mimeo, a method of reproduction

D&D: Dungeons & Dragons, one of the first fantasy games

DM: a Dungeon Master, (often from D&D), the one who guides the game

DITTO: dittography, a method of reproduction

EGOBOO: accolades, an ego boost for one's fanac

FANAC: fan activity

FANDOM: the group and activities, as a whole, of FANS

FANED (also **ZINE-ED**)**:** a fanzine editor

FANFIC/FANFICTION: (also **fan fiction, fan fic**): fiction written by fans

FANLIT: a literary type of fanfiction, often including a massive worldbuilding effort

FANNISH: all things pertaining to being a fan

FANON: when fannish lore becomes its own sort of canon

FAN: a person who is devoted to a particular subject or activity

FEN: a plural for 'FAN'

FIAWOL: Fandom Is A Way Of Life

FIJAGDH: Fandom Is Just A Goddam Hobby

FILKSONG: (also **FILK**) songs written by fans about fannish subjects, some to original music and some to already-written tunes.

FRINGE: (as in **fringe fandom; fringe fan**) A small or new group of fans, when compared to a dominant fandom

246

GAFIATE: Getting Away From It All; taking a break from or leaving fandom/fanac **GEN:** fanfiction for 'general' audiences; later known as fanfic that isn't 'slash'

GOH: Guest of Honor at a convention

IDIC: "Infinite Diversity in Infinite Combination", a tenet of acceptance revered by the Vulcan people in Star Trek

LARP: Live Action Role Playing (game, usually)

LISTSERVS: electronic mailing lists

LOC: Letter of Comment

LOCERS: those who write LoCs

LETTERCOL: a letter column, often in a letterzine

LETTERZINE: a fanzine consisting of essays and LoCs written by fans, gathered in a newsletter format, and usually published on a regular schedule

MCU: Marvel Cinematic Universe

MUGGLE(S): a non-magical or "normal" person (from the Harry Potter books). See also MUNDANE

MUNDANE(S): Non-fannish people who aren't "of the body" (And if you have to ask what that refers to, well, you might be a mundane.)

ONE-SHOT: a fanzine intended to have one issue only

OTP: One True Pairing

RPG: Roll -Playing Game

RPF: Real Person Fanworks/Fanfiction

SCI-FI/SF: science fiction

SF (also **sf**): science fiction

SFF: (also **SF/F**): science fiction & fantasy

SFX: special effects, usually in a movie

SHIPPER (also **'to SHIP'**): a relationship; a circumstance in which characters are paired in a relationship, usually romantic or sexual

SLASH: a term that began with a typo "/", and became fannish code for a gay relationship between (often male) characters "canonically" portrayed as straight.

SMoF: Secret Masters of Fandom, who are rumoured to Rule the Roost.

SOCK PUPPET: an online identity used as a deception

ST, Trek: shorthand for *Star Trek*, the TV show, the movies, the ST universe

SW: *Star Wars*, the movie, the *SW* universe

TRIB COPY: a contributor's copy, often of a fanzine

TYPER: a typewriter

AFTERWORD
Endings & Beginnings:
Notes From A Project

"Angry is good. Angry gets shit done."
—Mister Nancy, from the tv series, "American Gods"

This book you hold in your hands is the poetic result of a group of geeky elder women, dancing around the fires of our past dreamings.

It also represents a furious refusal to let our fannish "herstory" be forgotten. After all, so many of our sisters' stories have been lost.

So this book is *for* those sisters:

For those who literally couldn't "out" themselves or their fannish passions; those who were threatened with mental institutions; those who were ridiculed or beaten; those who dared to question the supposed norms of sexuality and religion and culture and, well, everything; those who had to take stolen moments to write words in the dark; those who could have lost everything that mattered to them just because they found a method of expression that wasn't "appropriate".

For those who scrawled "forbidden" thoughts and images, secreted in notebooks hidden 'neath the bed; for those who lost friends and family due to fannish connections; for those who gained and lost book sales; for those who still have scars from making—not buying—a complex costume from spit and sweat and, yes, sometimes baling wire; for those who crafted songs to peal against the sorrow and give such bliss; for those who took the foundational tools of an electronics revolution and made magic from them.

For those who have always looked to the stars, and followed them into meaningful careers through a mix of luck and skill and heart and perseverance.

For the sisters that I often wanted to smack upside the head, as well as the ones I laughed and played and created with... as well as the ones I'll never see again.

For those sisters who have left us too soon.

This book you hold in your hands also represents a journey. All books are that—and more—but this project in particular has been not

248

only one of discovery, but an oft heart-full and tiptoed walk across my own memories.

One memory in particular that kept coming back to me? Saying in the mid-1980s that the internet would be the death of fandom.

I was wrong... and I was right.

The internet, for all its wealth of information—and misinformation, it must be said—has some bloody great holes in it. Particularly when it comes to women's participation in society and culture.

Now, this is offensive to me on many levels. I was taught from a tender age that we need to pay attention to history—and we do. But there's a substantial problem with history: it's told by the conquerors. (That also was taught to me from a tender age, being a child of not only immigrant Scots-Irish, but indigenous Choctaw.)

Offensive "facts" usually require subversive acts. I'd hazard a guess that every woman who participated in this anthology—indeed, every woman in fandom before the Internet—clocks that on a cellular level.

How apropos, then, that the beginning of this project began a convention with a rather subversive name: Geek Girl Con. (If you haven't heard of this convention, check out my friend Jamala Henderson's excellent Foreword in the beginning of this book. Or look it up online. One of the internet's joys is the ability to use "google-fu" on just about *anything*.) Jamala coined the term "Geek Elders" when she proposed a panel for GeekGirlCon '14 entitled "Geek Elders Speak".

For this wonderful panel, she gathered and moderated an equally-wonderful group of geeky elder women—all of them fannish despite the prevailing claim that women aren't fans and never have been. Twirl on outta here, O Fanboy Spin: these women proved you wrong. In fact, the Geek Elders could have held court for several hours—and did, as people kept coming up afterwards and asking excited questions.

The panel was a roaring, packed-to-the-rafters success.

But what really blew me away? The audience. I'd heard all these stories—*lived* many of them—and thusly took them entirely for granted. Most of the audience, however—younger women *and* men— had no idea of our past realities, let alone our existence. They'd no concept of a SF/media/fannish history that wasn't ruled by old white guys. And the ones who did remember—themselves mostly elder geek women—figured they'd been forgotten.

(You aren't forgotten, fannish sisters, however the dominant narrative insists on skewing that way.)

So, it only makes sense that, when the gears started to turn and I decided to spearhead this book project, I witnessed participative excitement and many a joyful *Yes!*—but also a refusal to engage and, occasionally, grumpy dissention. Like any project, right?

Some of the women were still loath to "out" themselves, a truly understandable concern. Some dissenters claimed the "young'uns don't give a damn anyway"—and yes, some don't. (Some "old'uns" don't care, either.) The insistence on believing that one has invented the wheel is rampant in our society. Unfortunately, a common and patent refusal to admit that we all stand on the shoulders of amazing and inventive people belongs to every generation. To instead turn away means less risk... I get it. Any woman alive before the turn of the twenty-first century has experienced plenty of "Shut up, woman"— and believe you me, that phrase grows its own fangs when you add the adjective "old" to it.

It's also an undeniable fact that there are curious and welcoming people, *both* young and old, for whom the history—the HERstory—of fandom is an undiscovered territory all its own, with wonders to behold.

Of course, like all supposedly "undiscovered" territories, it follows that any newcomers haven't discovered anything at all... only found a culture unknown to *them*. One already present and well established, one rich with its own culture, people, rituals, and lore.

But how can we claim to be fans of a SF/F based ecosystem, and NOT... well... "seek *out* new life and new civilisations"?

How can we *not* look beyond the status quo? Have we become that damned lazy?

I get that change is hard. It becomes more tedious with the number of years one sees pass. And any history is chancy as hell, made by those who have the power and resources to manipulate it. But that doesn't negate the reality: in the part of my culture that *isn't* based upon a corrupt capitalist/supremacy mode, elder stories aren't just some "old fool babbling about the good old days".

These stories—even if flawed, even if occasionally hemmed with uncomfortable narratives—are the tiny, running steps that have led us to *this* moment in fandom.

And elder *women's* stories?

Well. A nation is only as strong as the hearts of its women. A nation that dismisses women? Will fail. Eventually.

So despite tending toward Grumpy Misanthropocene m'self, I looked at this project and realised this much:

These women needed to be HEARD.

These stories, and these storytellers, deserve better than being another forgotten anecdote of women's history. The dominant narrative needs be brought down with a different sort of truth, and three factors in particular deserved to be called out: the misinformation, the willful ignorance, and the overentitlement that assumes we are It and have nothing to learn from those who have come before.

Those three factors really kicked me in gear. They were conjured not only by the amazement of the audience at Geek Girl Con, but conjured purely by chance in several subsequent panels, at several subsequent conventions.

At one of these cons, on one of these panels, three men had been chosen to talk about fanlit.

cues Twilight Zone *music*

Consider that, if you will.

Three. MEN.

(See, neither men nor boys rule fannish spaces, despite many of them trying to convince us otherwise. And the boys *never* ruled the fanlit ecosystem of the latter half of the 20th century. The per capita of men was less than two per hundred women. And yes, I had to discover this fact myself, because as a youth I tended to hang more with boys than girls. I believed there were no fannish girls like me. And was I *wrong*.)

So, back to the con with three older white guys, on a panel, at a convention, pontificating on a subject they knew little about... nothing new there, right?

But, as fanlit was *this* Geek Elder's old stomping ground, I had to see this Marvellous Event for myself. So I sat in the back of the room. (We introverted types tend to prefer a ready exit in a crowded room. And the room was CROWDED.)

Talk about misinformation... The amount spewing from these so-called "fanfic experts" kept coming. It was appalling. I kept shifting in my chair and growling to myself, muttering to the Amazing Spouse— who was sitting next to me with a rather wicked grin... no question he knew what was coming. I'd worked up quite a snit by the time the floor was open for questions. Snit, hell. I was bloody *angry*. When called upon, I began (in my fiercest *Don't Teach Grandmama How To Suck Eggs, Boy* mode) to point out their misinformation in some detail.

Srsly. *What the hell are you lads even talking about?*

The best score that day was the number of arms raised after I took these Old Boys to account. Young women, many of whom came up to me after the panel to say how uneasy they'd been about standing up...

until an Old Woman, who'd run out of fucks to give, handed over some agency.

Helen Mirren is right about this much: it's a mistake to wait until you're over 60 to tell people to go tup themselves. Particularly if you're calling someone out on their total bullshit...

Ahem. *Misinformation.*

Skip ahead a few years: another con, where a popular—and woefully ignorant—young author seemed to believe herself to be the leading expert on fanfiction. Once again in the back of the room, I listened. Once again, I got more pissed off by the minute... and added Willful Ignorance to the equation of my growing discontent. I also ended up adding Overentitlement—particularly when Popular Author prodded a questioner to 'out' another, older fannish person. Surely, Popular Author claimed, she knew them. (With the implication that if she didn't know them, they weren't worth knowing, I suppose.)

Oh, honey. Bless your heart. You really think a mere handspan of years in fanfiction gives you the right? Without, I might add, having to give two thoughts toward the added baggage of it affecting your career and livelihood? And the fact that you can even mention fanfiction and your legacy publisher in the same breath? That's entirely due to the women who came before you and often lost their careers—while you stand on their shoulders in your clueless, hobnailed boots.

Yep. Still angry. Particularly since we had just lost several fannish elders and friends.

So another gear clicked into place.

And then came 2020.

lights sage and offers up Smoke to honour the half-million victims—at this writing—for which this newest personification of misinformation, willful ignorance, and overentitlement are responsible—along with his vile cronies and ignorant cultists.

The gears spun and the project roared into action—with the flying sparks kindling it into a hallowed bonfire. Mister Nancy (and day-um, but is he missed!) is even more right than Dame Helen when he says:

"Angry is good. Angry gets shit done."

So. This got done.

© *Jenni Hennig*
January, 2021

This Project...

Would have not have been possible without the early-on trust and generosity of our Kickstarter supporters.

Julie Bozza — Nightwing Whitehead — Karianne Kleve — UF
Michael Llaneza — Susan Fox — Thomas Bull — Joanna Zwickler Weston
Sarah — Margaret — Aysha Rehm — Holly Hamlyn-Harris
Joshua Crowe — Sharon M. Palmer — Jeanne DeVore — Corinne
Karen L. MacLeod — Carole Cummings — elaineb7 — CE Cooper
Beth Singer — Lorraine Anderson — Kellen Harkins — Valerie Bristor
Allyson M. W. Dyar — Erin McIntyre — Sandra — Mary Jane Morgan
Chris Longhurst — Keziah Meg Cannon — Lara N — Natasha Light
Winter Downs — Beca Servoss — Stacy Lynne Hotes-Aprato
Heather Cartner — Kristiana Josifiv — Dori — Michael N
Trish Heinrich — Maggie Nowakowska — Christopher Wells
Letitia Wells — Maggie — S Olive Sheehan — Susan Bailey
Jodie — Amy Richau — Amanda W — Missy Roode
Mary Jo Fox — Gabriela — Amy H. Sturgis — Sue Nowakowski
Melo — Marie Lewis — Doris — Anna Daniell — Anne Smith
Carla Smith — Meghan — Brynn — Art Boulton III
Caroline Couture — Lakshana C Sivananda — Kyle Gould
Talulah Sullivan — Lee A Dalzell — Janka Hobbs — Casey Kizior
Elizabeth Williams — Jules Stotter — Eleanor M. Farrell
Kara DJ — Justice Schiappa — Anne Prewitt — Deborah Laymon
Tracey King — Heather Currey — Aaron Jamieson — Mary G. Puppo
Rayhne Sinclair — Patricia Gonzales — Catherine — Cecilia Tan
W. Scott Meeks — Annalise Ophelian — Kim — Kris
Emma — Kelly J. Cooper — Deirdre

THANK YOU!

About the Editors

MAGGIE NOWAKOWSKA began reading SF in the 1st grade (*Space Cat Visits Venus*) and, with her first *Star Trek* story published in 1977, found a home in media zine fandom. Her *Star Wars* fan fiction appeared in the first *SW* zines, winning fan awards. Maggie has remained active in fannish discussions on the web and is currently supporting efforts to familiarize new fans, especially young women, with the long history of active women in fandom.She has spoken in podcast interviews, sat on many convention panels, and appears in the brilliant documentary *Looking for Leia*. Maggie lives in Seattle, with her wife, SF writer Susan R. Matthews, and a varying number of Pomeranian dogs. You can find her stories on Archive of Our Own.

———————————

JENNI HENNIG is a pro novelist who learned much of her craft (as did many) through fanlit and a lifetime of compulsive reading. Her fannish participation and productivity spans from 1970-2010, and includes way too many panels, an attic full of costumes, the editing of several fanzines (one fondly [?] termed "The Rebel Alliance Phone Book"), as well as many years of storytelling, entertaining, & running conventions.

CPSIA information can be obtained
at www.ICGtesting.com
Printed in the USA
LVHW080356080521
686830LV00007B/42